PHONICS
CONNECTIONS

Teacher's Resource Guide

Consultant
Sharon Vaughn, PhD
University of Texas

capstone
classroom
www.capstoneclassroom.com

Phonics Connections Teacher's Resource Guide is published by
Capstone Classroom, 1710 Roe Crest Drive,
North Mankato, Minnesota 56003
www.capstoneclassroom.com

ISBN: 978-1-62521-960-2

Credits

Sharon Vaughn, PhD, consultant; Jennifer Huston, Jennifer Loomis, Christine
Peterson, Karen Soll, and Hillary Wolfe, writers and editors; Cynthia Della-Rovere
and Charmaine Whitman, designers; Katy LaVigne, production specialist

Cover photos by Shutterstock: fotoVoyager (Homes (right)), Kobby Dagan
(Celebrating Cultures), Matthew Jacques (Homes (left)), Rita Kochmarjova,
(Animal Babies)

Table of Contents

Table of Contents (continued)

Preface

What do we know about successfully teaching students to read? We know students must be able to read the words and map the phonology to the orthography (e.g., phonics); and they must know what the words mean, including having adequate background knowledge to make the text understandable. While this may seem easy, for youngsters making the language-to-text connection, there can be many challenges. For example, students learn to blend and segment sounds orally so that they can readily apply this process to print. They learn to read words that follow the rules (e.g., *ran, sit, fun*) as well as words that do not follow the rules (e.g., *was, the, from*). *Phonics Connections* provides a framework for guiding teachers through the instructional process of promoting phonemic awareness and phonics—helping students apply what they learn to reading increasingly complex texts.

Critical to success in reading are the foundation skills of phonemic awareness and phonics, which provide students with the necessary keys to unlock the magical world of reading for enjoyment and learning. *Phonics Connections* provides a series of exercises and lessons aimed at improving students' success at learning to read through application of phonics rules. What makes *Phonics Connections* a useful program for teachers and students? *Phonics Connections* takes advantage of what we know from research and integrates it into a series of meaningful lessons designed to systematically improve students' reading. Instructional routines for teachers provide a template for explaining the skills that demonstrate what students should do. They also give the instructional group an opportunity to respond with feedback and the individual students an opportunity to practice with feedback. This sequence maximizes opportunities to ensure that each and every student will benefit from instruction. Guidelines for active engagement of students in lessons are an integral part of the instruction.

There are several critical features of *Phonics Connections* that make it an attractive program for teachers and an engaging program for students. The program not only teaches students phonemic awareness and phonics through active and engaging lessons, it also teaches students to read sight words that are not readily decodable (e.g., *people, was, you*). Recognizing that success in reading is related to language development, target lessons also address building oral language, including speaking and listening. Thus, the foundation skills for both language and literacy development are addressed. Additionally, the reading-writing connection is a focus in the lessons in which students learn to write in response to the reading practices and skills they are learning.

Essential to success in learning to read is the design of effective practices for assuring students participate and respond to text during and after reading. *Phonics Connections* provides books jammed with valuable information for building students' background knowledge. Why are these comprehension practices during and after reading so important with young readers? They teach students the important strategies for monitoring text understanding early so that the strategies can be continuously applied to increasingly complex texts as students become more mature readers. Teaching students to read successfully is not an easy task and requires valuable materials, such as *Phonics Connections,* to facilitate effective instruction.

Sharon Vaughn, PhD
University of Texas

Introduction

Scientific research shows that the two best predictors for success in reading are phonemic awareness and alphabetic knowledge. The *Phonics Connections* program is designed to provide students with explicit, systematic phonemic awareness and phonics instruction. These skills are introduced, taught, practiced, and applied with engaging photo-driven, content-specific, decodable books.

Features of *Phonics Connections*

60 student titles

✓ Strong text-photo match with children engaging in authentic activities
✓ Culturally and linguistically responsive situations emphasized
✓ Text features highlighted
✓ Alignment to science and social studies content standards

Photo-driven cover to initiate discussion and prediction

new moon

full moon

Sometimes the moon is full. It looks round like a circle. Other times it looks curved like part of a circle. On some nights you can't see the moon at all.

4

On a clear night you can see stars in the sky too. They give off light. Most stars are much bigger than Earth. They look small because they are very far away.

5

Consistent text placement

Essential Vocabulary

Phonics Words Introduced
daytime, do, full, look(s), moon, nighttime, to, too

Vocabulary Words
circle, clouds, daytime, different, Earth, moon, nighttime, sky, stars, sun, warms

Sight Words
a, all, also, are, at, away, because, big, but, can, could, did, do, fit, from, give, go, in, inside, it, its, know, like, look(s), make(s), many, more, most, much, of, off, on, other, see, some, than, the, they, time(s), too, up, very, what, you

Word list including decodable words, sight words, and content words

Scientifically Research-based Scope and Sequence

✓ Highest utility skills and sight words taught first
✓ Review and practice of previously taught skills
✓ Progression of skills that build on one another
    ✓ short vowels
    ✓ consonants
    ✓ *r*-blends, *s*-blends, *l*-blends
    ✓ digraphs
    ✓ long vowels
    ✓ soft *c*
    ✓ diphthongs
    ✓ variant vowels
    ✓ open syllables
    ✓ consonant + *–le*
    ✓ words with *–ed* and *–ing* endings
    ✓ prefixes *pre–* and *un–*
    ✓ suffixes *–er*, *–or*, and *–ly*
    ✓ compound words
    ✓ homophones

Matrix of Skills

Title	Content Area Focus	Phonics Focus
On the Job	Social Studies: Jobs	short *a*; consonants *f, m, t*
Hot or Not?	Science: Properties of Materials	short *o*; consonants *h, n, s*
At the Farm	Social Studies: Farm Life	short *o*; consonants *g, l, p*
Animal Babies	Social Studies: Animal Families	short *i*; consonants *c, d, w, y*
In the Past	Social Studies: Life in the Past	short *i*; consonants *b, k, q, r*
Animal Homes	Science: Animal Habitats	short *e*; consonants *j, v, x, z*
Finding Animals	Science: Camouflage	short *e*; *r*-blends
Fun at the Fair	Social Studies: Traditions	short *u*; *s*-blends
Weather	Science: Weather	short *u*; *l*-blends
At the Vet	Social Studies: Service Providers	short vowels; *s*-blends
At a Fire	Social Studies: Everyday Heroes	final *e* (*a_e, i_e, o_e, u_e*); *r*-blends
Amazing Magnets	Science: Magnets	final *e* (*i_e, o_e, u_e*); *l*-blends
The U.S. Flag	Social Studies: Symbols of America	final *e* (*a_e, e_e, i_e, o_e*); digraph *wh*
Homes	Social Studies: Communities	final *e* (*a_e, e_e, i_e, o_e, u_e*); digraph *th*
Safe at Play	Social Studies: Need for Rules	long *a* (*ai, ay*); digraph *sh*
Holidays	Social Studies: Holidays	long *a* (*ai, ay*); digraph *ch*
How Plants Grow	Science: Plant Life	final *e* (*e_e*); long *e* (*e, ea, ee*), plurals
Terrific Teeth	Science: Teeth	long *e* (*e, ea, ee*); *r*-, *l*-, and *s*-blends
Frogs	Science: Frog Life Cycle	long *o* (*o, oa, ow*); digraphs (*ch, sh, th, wh*)

Sight Words	Content-Area Words
a, am, do, help, I, play, what, who	farmer, firefighter, musician, teacher
are, hot, is, not, or, these, this, what	soft, wet
a, has, I, is, it, little, on, pretty, red, see, the, what	cat, cow, farm, frog, hen, hog, rabbit
a, and, big, but, can, fast, get, has, is, it, jump, not, read, what, will	animals, baby, bill
a, about, and, big, did, hot, is, it, make, not, on, see, take, the, we, went, what, will	horseshoe, quilt, wax
a, an, and, can, does, fly, has, he, him, his, in, it, its, on, one, red, well, who	bees, cliff, den, eagle, fox, hive, live(s), nest, pup
a, big, can, I, in, into, is, it, on, pretty, red, see, the, went, white, yes, you	bird, bug, crab, fish, grass, lizard, rabbit, shell, striped, tiger
a, and, around, at, big, blue, can, fast, first, for, get, go, has, is, is, jump, make, of, over, people, pull, red, run, see, she, some, stop, the, they, time, to, too, yellow, you	fair, proud, ribbon, year
and, back, big, can, drink, get, help(s), is, it, its, light, make(s), now, the, them, up, us, warm, water, what, with, yellow, you	clouds, hot, rain, sun, warm, weather, windy
a, and, are, black, can, get(s), give(s), had, has, help, in, is, it, keep(s), little, make, much, not, now, of, on, out, soon, stop, the, this, to, well, white, who, will, your	heal, healthy, paw, scale, shot, sick, well
a, and, can, from, go, he, help, is, look, no, on, out, the, their, they, to, up, use(s), water, who, will, with	engine, firefighters, heroes, ladder, smoke, water
a, and, are, be, big, can, it, is, made, not, of, on, or, up, the, they, too, use, what, will, you	iron, magnet, metal
also, an, and, blue, each, even, first, for, from, has, in, is, it, look, of, on, one, our, red, that, the, there, they, this, up, white	flagpole, free, July 4
a, an, and, are, at, big, can, for, in, is, it, has, have, help, her, his, like, live, look, many, of, on, people, play, ride, see, she, small, take, the, there, these, they, to, where, with, your	cabs, country, mules
a, all, and, are, be, but, can, do, far, get, go, how, in, like, look, may, not, of, or, out, play, ride, run, safe, take, the, these, they, to, walk, way, when, with, you, your	rules, stay safe, take your turn
a, about, and, can, clean, eat, first, good, help, hot, is, it, of, on, or, our, pick, say, thank, that, the, think, this, to, too, up, we, what, which, you	celebrate, holiday, thankful, Thanksgiving
a, and, are, as, be, but, can, do, each, eat, first, from, give, has, help, how, in, into, it, like, many, new, next, on, pretty, see, the, then, these, they, to, too, we, will	bloom, fruits, grow, soil
a, also, and, are, big, can, come, do, eat, help, her, how, in, into, long, look, made, many, need, open, our, out, see, she, the, them, these, they, this, to, us, use(s), very, we, what, which, why, you	bite(s), chew(s), eat, food, front, sharp, smile, teeth
a, about, an, and, as, back, can, comes, from, get, go, has, how, in, into, is, it, its, like, live, looks, not, now, on, out, tell, the, this, to, very, water, what, will, with	air, breathe, egg(s), frog, gills, grow(s), lungs, swim, tadpole(s), tail, water

Comprehensive Teacher's Resource Guide
✓Includes step-by-step lesson plans
✓Develops phonemic awareness and phonics
✓Builds oral language
✓Introduces sight words and content vocabulary
✓Promotes fluency
✓Connects to written language
✓Assessment
　✓Diagnostic—Two Phonics Surveys: the first covers the lessons on pages 24–95 and the other covers the lessons on pages 96–143; the surveys are designed to diagnose student's phonics proficiency at the beginning, middle, and end of the school year.
　✓Ongoing—Every lesson includes a *Check Comprehension* and a *Connect to Written Language* section to help assess skill attainment and progress.
✓School-to-Home Connections
　✓Parent letter written in English and Spanish
　✓Read-at-Home book

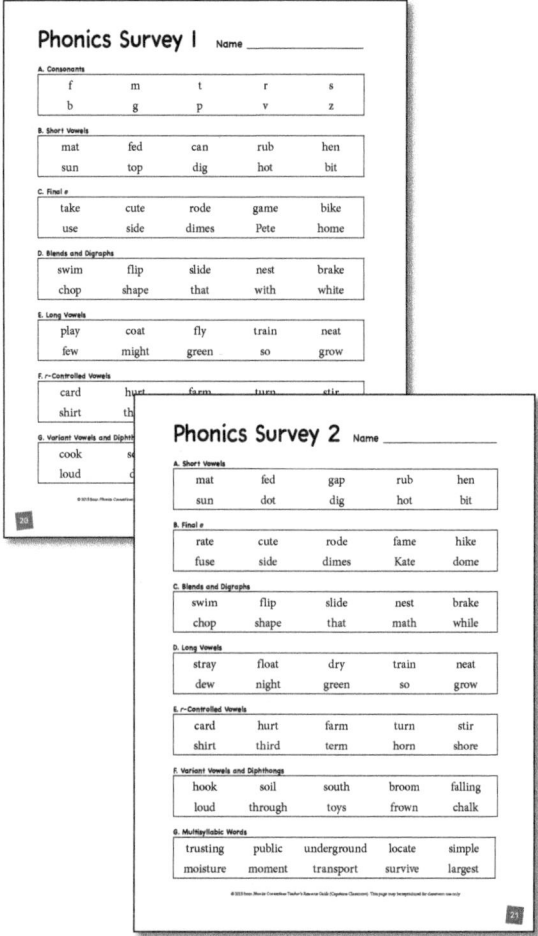

Phonics Surveys

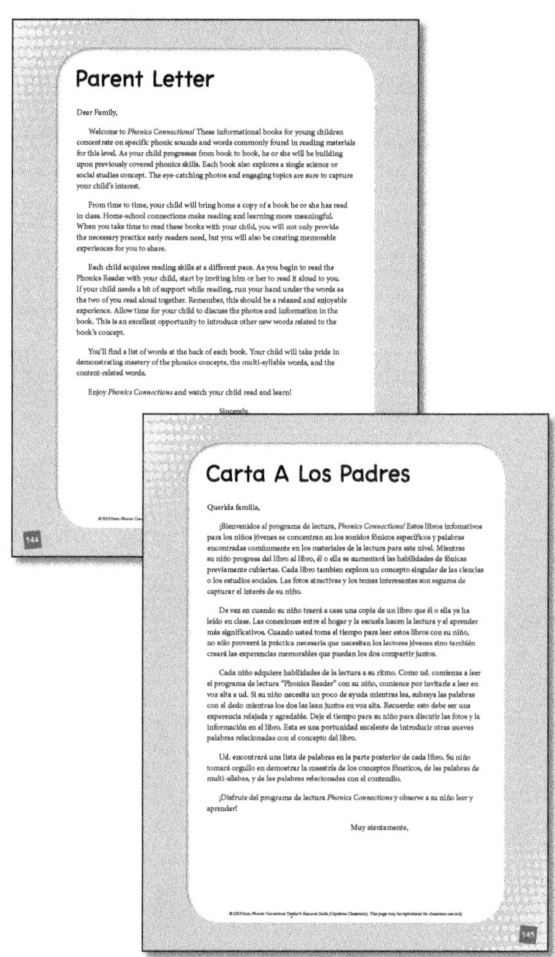

Parent Letters

Instructional Routines

Research shows that effective teachers rely on classroom routines. These routines help foster productive use of classroom time while creating a supportive environment conducive to learning. Routines are quite useful for ensuring that students are engaged in the learning tasks from the beginning to the end of the lesson. We expect students to read based upon previously taught phonics rules, previously taught sight words, and key content-specific vocabulary. The Instructional Routines provided on the following pages include step-by-step, research-based routines that will assist you as you use the *Phonics Connections* readers in your classroom.

BEFORE THE READING

Develop Phonemic Awareness and Phonics

Phonemic Awareness is the understanding that a word is made up of a series of discrete sounds. A related term is **phonological awareness**. This is an umbrella term that includes awareness of words within sentences, rhyming units within words, syllables within words, and phonemes within words (phonemic awareness). Phonemic awareness activities help students distinguish individual sounds, or phonemes, within words. This is a fundamental component of beginning reading instruction. Often, students have difficulty with phonics instruction because they have not developed the prerequisite phonemic awareness skills. This is why it is especially important to give students multiple opportunities to respond and to echo modeling by the teacher.

The two most critical phonemic awareness skills are **oral blending** and **oral segmentation**. Oral blending activities help students hear how sounds or word parts are put together to make words. For example, the teacher says a series of discrete sounds—/s/ /a/ /t/. The student blends, or strings together, these sounds to say the word—*sssaaat*. This skill is necessary before a student can decode a word in print. Therefore, oral blending exercises lead directly to decoding work.

Oral segmentation exercises help students separate a word into its component sounds or word parts. For example, the teacher says the word *sat*. The student is to say the word sound by sound—/s/ /a/ /t/, or count the number of sounds in the word (3). Oral segmentation exercises help prepare students for spelling words. To spell a word, a student must segment it sound by sound, then attach a letter or spelling to each sound.

Develop
Phonemic Awareness
and Phonics

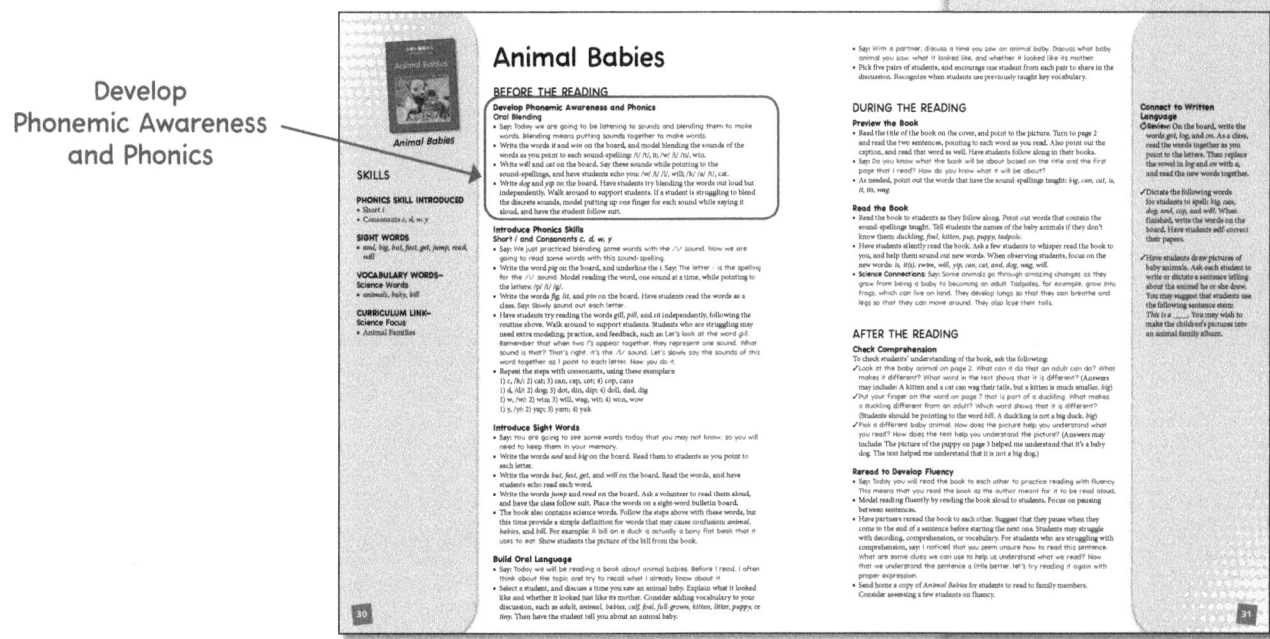

The following examples of phonemic awareness activities, including oral blending and segmentation exercises are found throughout the lessons.

RHYME Say the words *he, seed, seat, leaf, mean.* Have students say a word that rhymes with each word (*he, we*)

ORAL BLENDING Say the following word parts. Have students blend the parts together and say the whole word: m-e, h-ea-t, b-ea-n, t-r-ee, f-ee-t, r-ea-d, m-ea-t. (*mmeee, me*)

ORAL SEGMENTATION Say the following words: *say, see, weed, my, rake, tree.* Have students say each word, sound by sound. (/s/ /ā/, /s/ /ē/, /w/ /ē/ /d/, /m/ /ī/, /r/ /ā/ /k/, /tr/ /ē/)

PHONEMIC MANIPULATION (SUBSTITUTION) Say the following words: *dad, bell, beat, heel, hit.* Have students replace the first sound in each work with /s/. (*dad, sad*)

PHONEMIC MANIPULATION (DELETION) Say the following words: *hit, bill, sat, fan.* Have students say each word without its first sound. (*hit, it*)

Instructional Tips

- Carefully pronounce all the sounds. Avoid distorting sounds, such as adding an "uh" to a sound. (Say /b/ instead of /buh/.)
- When blending words that begin with continuous sounds (*f, l, m, n, r, s, v, z*), stretch the sounds and string them together as if you were "singing" the word. For example, say *ssssaaaat, ssat, sat.* If the word begins with a stop sound (*b, d, p*), say the first two letters quickly together, almost like a syllable. For example, say *baaaat, bat.* Don't attempt to stretch the /b/ sound.
- These activities should be quick-paced and fun. If students have difficulties, revisit the activities after the reading.
- Do not expect mastery of all activities by all students. The repetition in activities will allow them ample opportunities to practice these skills.

Introduce Phonics Skills

Phonics instruction teaches students sound-spelling relationships and how to use those relationships to read words. Systematic, explicit phonics instruction is beneficial for all students' early reading skills because it enables them to sound out words, thereby improving their word-recognition skills. As word recognition becomes easier, students become more fluent readers.

Routine

Use the following four-step routine to introduce sound-spellings.

1. Briefly explain the skill and the sound-spelling relationship. For example, tell students they will be segmenting sounds in words and listening for the long-vowel sound in silent final –*e* words, such as *gate*.

2. Model what students should do by writing 1–2 words on the board that include the targeted sound. Clearly state the sound, and point to the spelling as you model the word.

3. Introduce 1–2 new words, and have students demonstrate the skill together with feedback from you via choral or echo reading activities. Include kinesthetic activities (such as moving markers or clapping) and quick checks for understanding (such as using individual whiteboards or a thumbs-up) to gather formative assessments.

4. Encourage students to work on the skill independently using 1–2 words with targeted sounds. Offer support as needed, with additional modeling and scaffolds.

Introduce
Phonics Skills

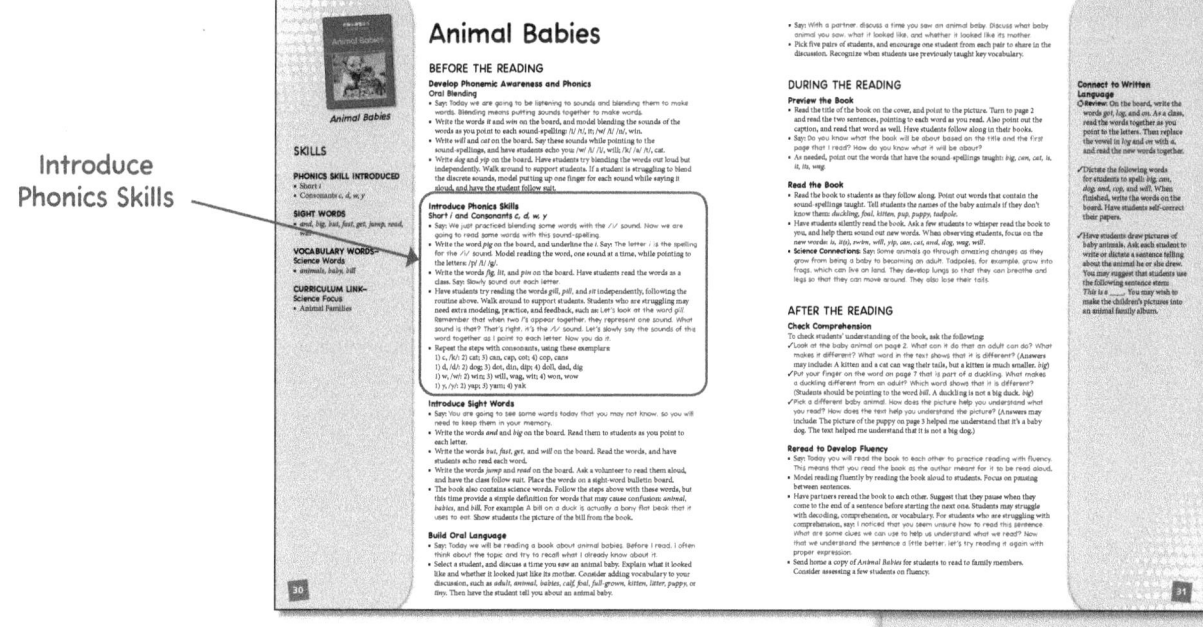

Introduce Sight Words

The sight words were drawn from the Dolch, Fry, and Zeno word lists. Some words are irregular, meaning they do not follow regular sound-spelling rules (e.g., *come*, *was*). Other words are used before their component sound-spellings have been introduced. For example, the word *them* would be considered a sight word if /th/ spelled *th*, /e/ spelled *e*, and /m/ spelled *m* hadn't been formally taught yet. Therefore, students do not have the skills to sound out the word. Other words chosen may simply be review. After students learn these sound-spellings, the word becomes decodable.

Routine

Use the following four-step routine to introduce sight words.

1. Write the words on the board. You may also wish to use letter cards and build the words in a pocket chart or on a word wall.

2. Model reading one word as you point to each letter.

3. Write a few more words on the board, read the words, and have students echo read each word.

4. Have a volunteer read another word from the board as the rest of the class follows suit.

Science and Social Studies Words

The science and social studies words are key concept words necessary for story content. These words are also linked to primary-level science and social studies curriculum standards.

Routine

Use the following two-step routine to introduce content-area words.

1. Write each word on the board, pronounce it, and provide a simple definition for words that may cause confusion. It is unnecessary to hold students accountable for the spelling of these words.

2. Point out pictures from the book that relate to the new terminology.

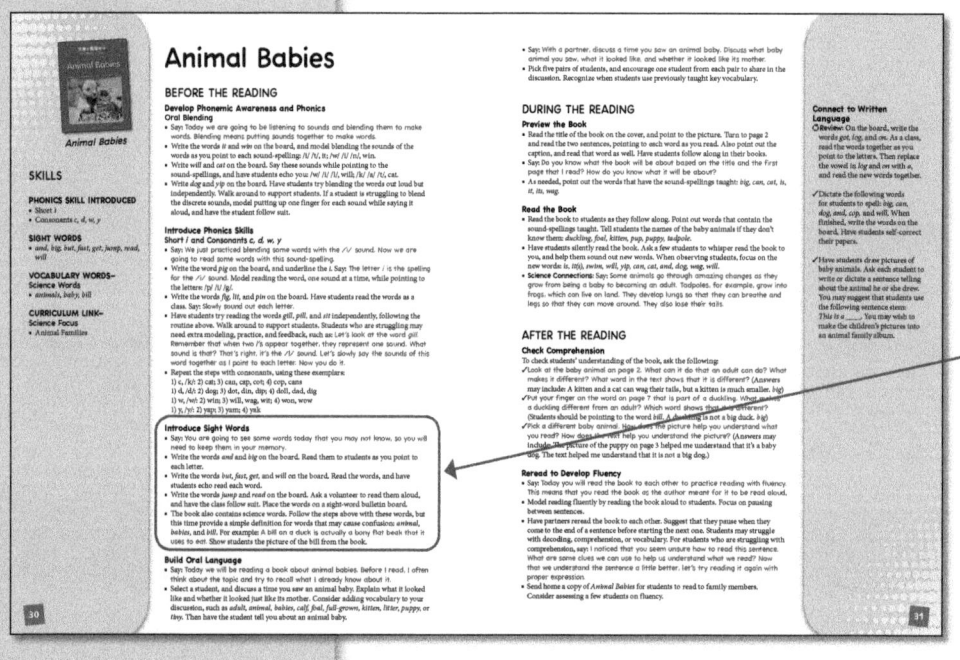

Introduce Sight Words and Content-area Words

Build Oral Language

Some students in the primary grades may have little prior knowledge of the science and social studies concepts covered in the books. Therefore, it is critical that you assess students' background knowledge prior to reading and fill in existing information gaps. One great tool for explaining new ideas and concepts will be the photographs used on the cover and throughout the book. Engaging students in conversations about these concepts will help students add words to their speaking and listening vocabularies—an important early reading goal.

> ## Routine
>
> **Use the following four-step routine to build students' oral language (speaking/listening) skills.**
>
> 1. Explain the topic of the book they will be reading, and model thinking aloud about any questions you may have or any connections you make.
>
> 2. Prompt a model discussion with a student. If you can, use the key content vocabulary in your discussion, and encourage students to use the vocabulary as well.
>
> 3. Have student pairs discuss the topic through interactive and collaborative conversations. Students may brainstorm, interview each other, and chart their ideas.
>
> 4. Select a few student pairs to share their ideas.

Build Oral Language

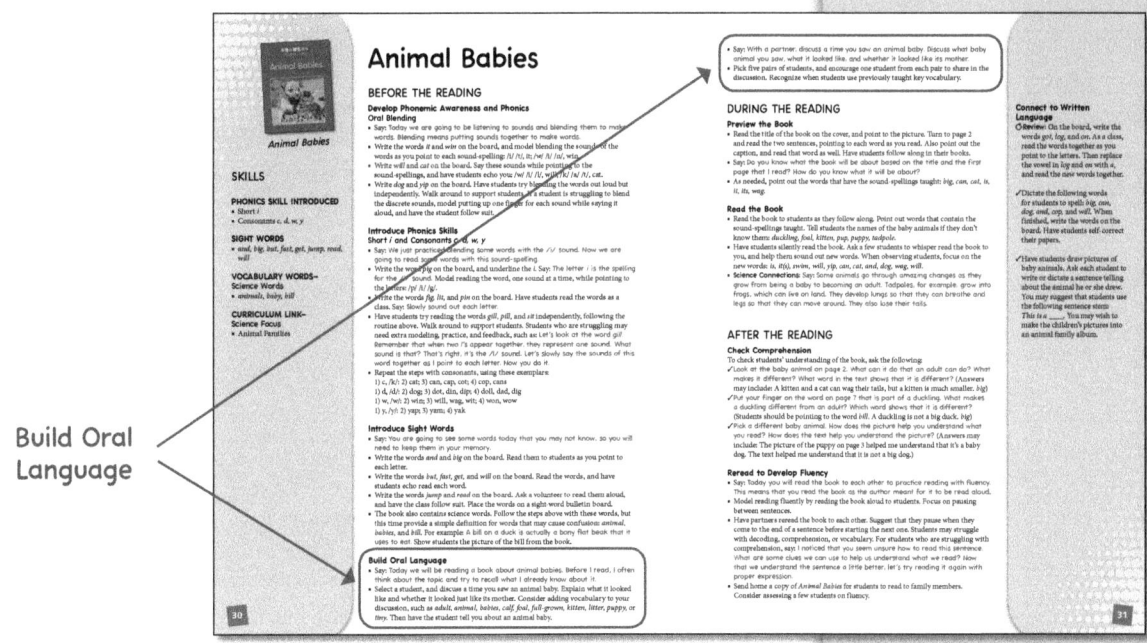

DURING THE READING

Preview the Book

Previewing the book is a critical before-reading routine. This allows you to introduce the book and further determine students' background information needs. In addition, it will help students make predictions about what they are going to read.

Routine

Use the following four-step routine to preview the book.

1. Display the book cover, read the title, and point to the picture. Read the first page of text to students. Have students follow along.

2. Prompt students to discuss what they know about the topic, or what they think the book will be about. Model through think-aloud how to ask questions of the text and set a purpose for reading.

3. Point out any text features that will be highlighted in the book, such as tables or diagrams. Explain what the feature is and how it is used by looking at an example from the book. Discuss the unique characteristics of the feature. Some examples of text features represented in the books include captions, chapter headings, charts, diagrams, graphs, an index, maps, photographs, table of contents, tables, and timelines.

4. Point out words in the book that have the target sound.

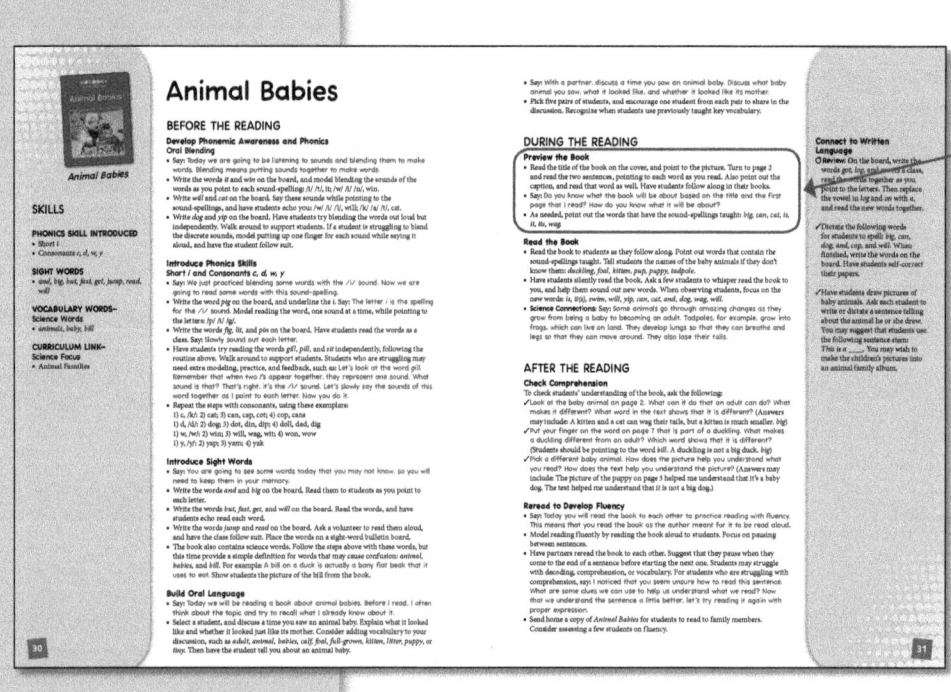

Preview the Book

Read the Book

Students need to read the book multiple times with varying levels of support in order to access all the levels of text complexity and reach deep meaning-making. During the first reading, offer students the highest level of support, including sounding out words, checking for comprehension, and summarizing the text. In subsequent readings, gradually release support until students can read the book independently with ease.

Routine

Use the following three-step routine to read the book.

1. Read the book aloud to students. Discuss words students may not know or words that contain the sound-spelling taught. Explain the text features as needed.

2. Have students silently read the book, but choose a few to read with you or to you. Focus on the new words.

3. Make a science or social studies connection using a think-aloud that connects to or builds background knowledge.

Read the Book

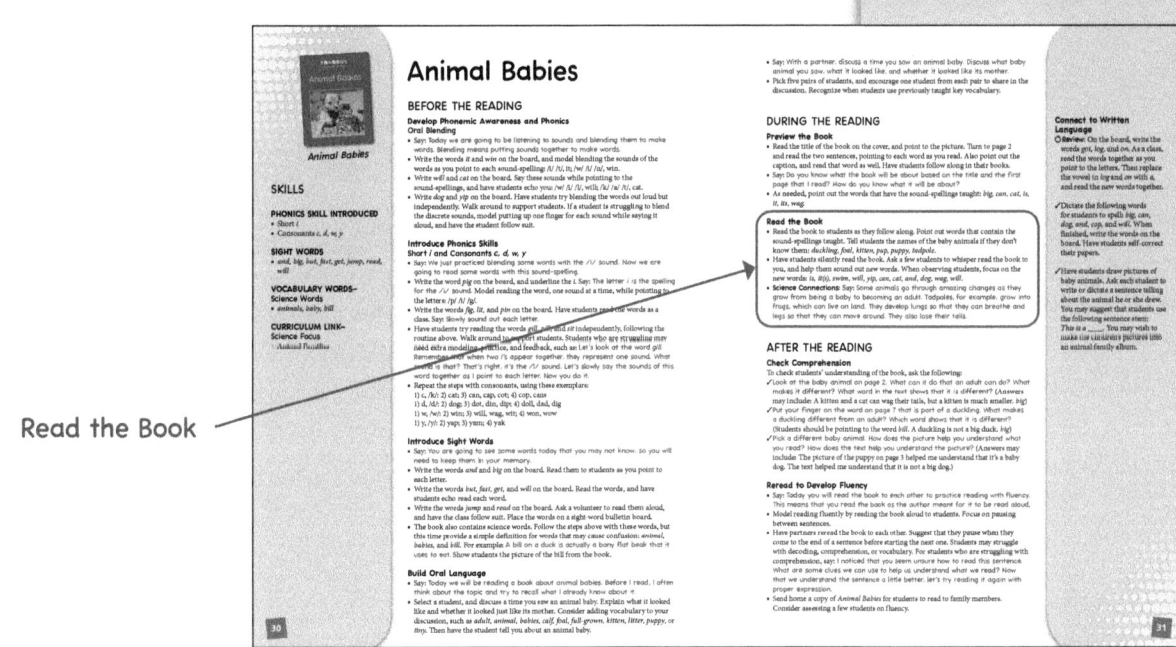

AFTER THE READING

Check Comprehension

After students read the story, ask questions to build close-reading skills and give them practice citing evidence from the text, which is an important skill for career and college readiness goals. The questions included in the lesson will help you check their general understanding, call attention to text features, highlight vocabulary, encourage students to draw inferences, and connect the text to the pictures and graphics.

Reread to Develop Fluency

Fluency is the ability to read smoothly, effortlessly, and readily with freedom from word-recognition errors. Fluency is the bridge between word recognition and comprehension. A fluent reader can decode all the words in the text and read with the proper intonation, expression, and phrasing. Fluency is one of the primary goals of reading these books. The books should be read first by you to model proper expression and pronunciation, then read by the students in pairs to encourage collaborative conversations and to promote speaking and listening skills. Have students reread the books enough times so that they can read them with ease.

Routine

Use the following four-step routine to build fluency.

1. Tell students that they will be reading the book aloud.

2. Model reading the book with prosody and expression. Call attention to a particular fluency skill, such as pausing for a comma or raising your voice for a question.

3. Have students reread the book at least two times, with partners and independently. Choose a few to practice a fluency skill, and offer support as needed for students who are struggling with decoding, vocabulary, or comprehension.

4. Send a copy of the book home for students to read to family members. Family members listening to their child successfully read stories is a powerful home-to-school connection. It validates what the student is learning in school and is proof of reading progress.

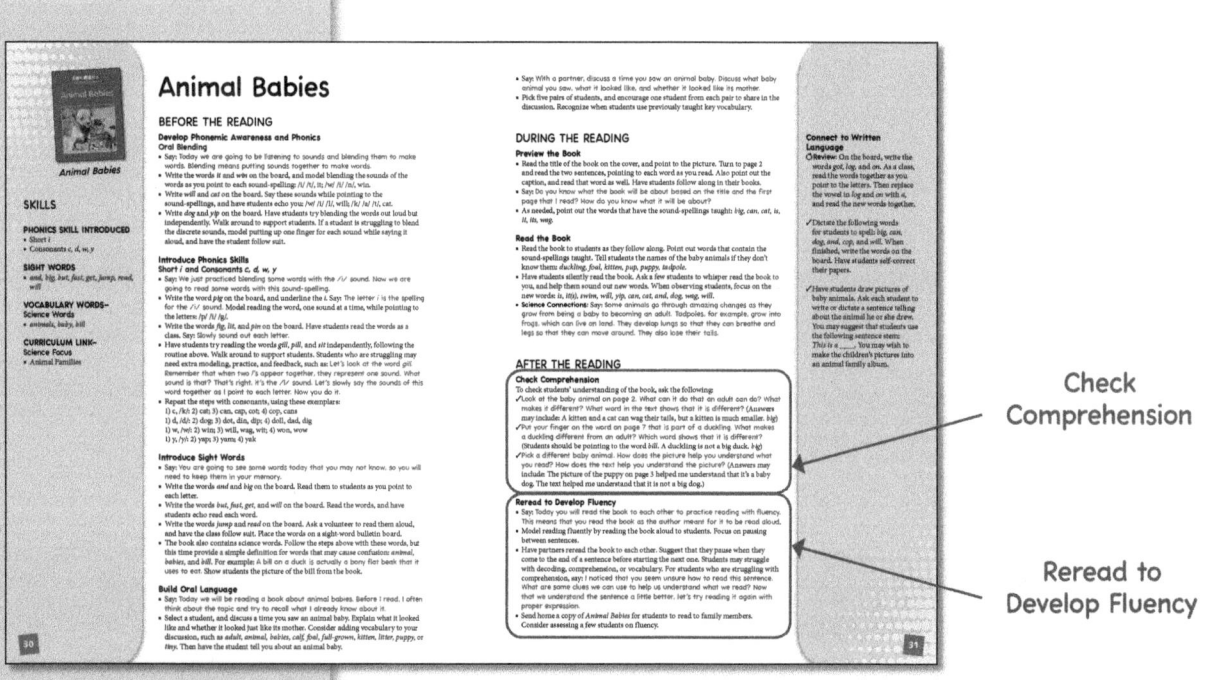

Check Comprehension

Reread to Develop Fluency

Connect to Written Language

The writing activities used throughout this program fall into one of two categories: Dictation and Writing.

Dictation is an ideal way for students to practice transferring their newly acquired phonics skills into writing and to review previously taught sight words to practice and maintain previous learning. You will guide students as they attempt to spell words with the new sound-spellings.

Routine

Use the following three-step routine to connect to written language.

1. Reteach words from the previous lesson, and reinforce the phonics skill that was previously introduced. Have students use the words in a writing activity to practice writing the words in an authentic context.

2. Dictate words that represent the new phonics skill introduced, and weave in previously taught sight words.

3. Write these words on the board, and have students self-correct their papers. Self-correction is a powerful learning tool.

Remember, students' spelling abilities generally lag behind their reading abilities. It may take some students a bit of time to transfer new phonics skills into writing. Doing dictation exercises and frequently modeling for them how to orally segment words while writing will be most beneficial. Therefore, when a student asks for the spelling of a word while writing, walk him or her through the steps of orally segmenting the word and attaching a spelling to each sound rather than just providing the student with the spelling.

The **writing** extensions allow students to connect to the book's content by focusing on the language conventions of the text. These activities are specific to each book and should be done independently or with little guidance. Conventions and word-study elements are the focus of this last activity.

Connect to Written Language

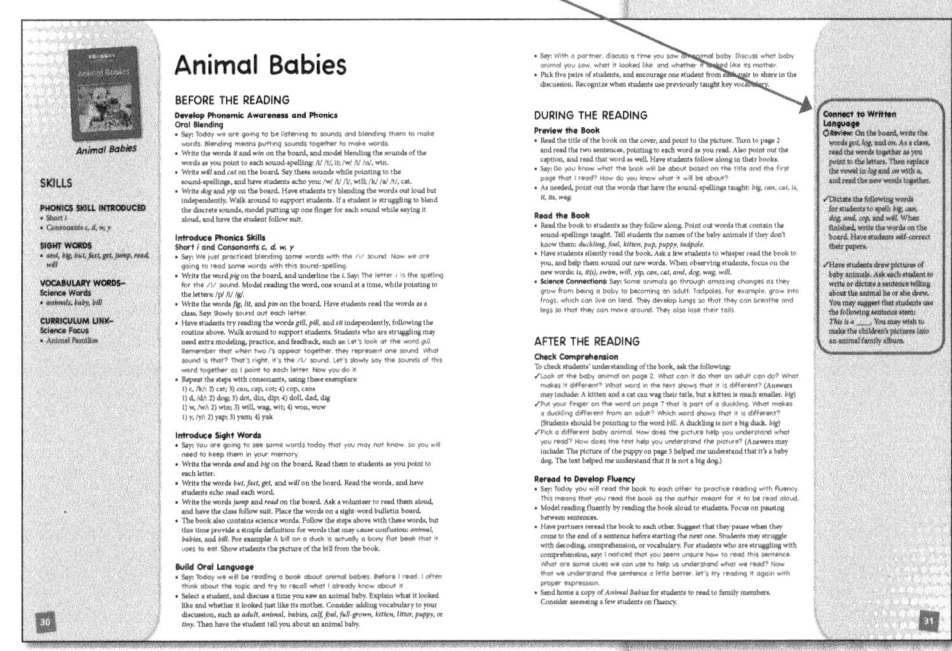

Classroom Management

The *Phonics Connections* readers are designed for whole-class, small-group, and independent use.

Whole Class/Small Group

Introduce each book using the lesson provided. If you have a limited number of books, have students read the books in small-group sessions with you guiding their reading. If whole-class sets are available, follow the plan provided. Once the books have been read multiple times, place them in your classroom library. You may wish to set up special social studies and science bins for the books. As an alternative, find other books (fiction and nonfiction) on the topics covered and include these collections in bins as text sets (e.g., a bin on plants might include stories about gardens or insects, a bin on community workers might include a trade book or song lyrics). Text sets help students make intertextual connections as they make meaning using a variety of diverse media and sources.

Independent Work

You may wish to simply add these books to your classroom library. If so, select one book each week to highlight. Display the book, introduce its content, and encourage students to read it throughout the week. Introducing the book during a science or social studies unit will encourage students to read it and emphasize the value you place on nonfiction, especially in content areas other than language arts. Provide time at the end of the week for students to share what they learned from the book.

Phonics Survey

The Phonics Survey is designed to diagnose each student's phonics proficiency. The result of the assessment can determine which books you provide students as well as which phonics skills you formally teach in small-group sessions. Consider administering the assessment at the beginning, middle, and end of the year to track each student's reading progress. There are two phonics surveys, one for the lessons on pages 24–95 and the other for the lessons on pages 96–143.

Preparing the Survey

You will need to make two copies of the survey for each student in your class. Make one for the student to read and one for you to record his or her errors.

Administering the Survey

1. Administer the survey to one student at a time.

2. In Section A of the first survey, have the student say the sound of each letter. In Sections B–G, have the student read each word. In the second survey, have the student say the words in Sections A–G.

3. As the student reads the words, circle each word read correctly. Write the student's response beside or near each word read incorrectly. This will help you analyze the errors.

4. The sections get progressively more complex. Therefore, if the student misses six or more words in any section, you might choose to stop administering the survey.

Scoring the Survey

1. Total the number of sounds and words the student reads correctly. Analyze the mispronounced words, looking for patterns that might give you information about the student's decoding strengths and weaknesses.

2. Focus instruction and reading practice on those phonics skill categories in which the student made three or more errors.

Phonics Survey 1   Name _____

A. Consonants

f	m	t	r	s
b	g	p	v	z

B. Short Vowels

mat	fed	can	rub	hen
sun	top	dig	hot	bit

C. Final *e*

take	cute	rode	game	bike
use	side	dimes	Pete	home

D. Blends and Digraphs

swim	flip	slide	nest	brake
chop	shape	that	with	white

E. Long Vowels

play	coat	fly	train	neat
few	might	green	so	grow

F. *r*-Controlled Vowels

card	hurt	farm	turn	stir
shirt	third	term	horn	for

G. Variant Vowels and Diphthongs

cook	soil	south	broom	falling
loud	do	toys	clown	chalk

Phonics Survey 2 Name _____

A. Short Vowels

mat	fed	gap	rub	hen
sun	dot	dig	hot	bit

B. Final *e*

rate	cute	rode	fame	hike
fuse	side	dimes	Kate	dome

C. Blends and Digraphs

swim	flip	slide	nest	brake
chop	shape	that	math	while

D. Long Vowels

stray	float	dry	train	neat
dew	night	green	so	grow

E. *r*-Controlled Vowels

card	hurt	farm	turn	stir
shirt	third	term	horn	shore

F. Variant Vowels and Diphthongs

hook	soil	south	broom	falling
loud	through	toys	frown	chalk

G. Multisyllabic Words

trusting	public	underground	locate	simple
moisture	moment	transport	survive	largest

Phonics Survey Score Sheet

Survey 1

Phonics Skill	Number of Words Missed	Error Analysis
A. Consonants		
B. Short Vowels		
C. Final *e*		
D. Blends and Digraphs		
E. Long Vowels		
F. *r*-Controlled Vowels		
G. Variant Vowels and Diphthongs		

Survey 2

Phonics Skill	Number of Words Missed	Error Analysis
A. Short Vowels		
B. Final *e*		
C. Blends and Digraphs		
D. Long Vowels		
E. *r*-Controlled Vowels		
F. Variant Vowels and Diphthongs		
G. Multisyllabic Words		

Notes

SKILLS

PHONICS SKILL INTRODUCED
- Short *a*
- Consonants *f, m, t*

SIGHT WORDS
- *a, am, do, help, play, what, who*

VOCABULARY WORDS–
Social Studies Words
- *farmer, firefighter, musician, teacher*

CURRICULUM LINK–
Social Studies Focus
- Jobs

On the Job

BEFORE THE READING

Develop Phonemic Awareness and Phonics
Oral Blending
- Say: Today we are going to be listening to sounds and blending them to make words. Blending means putting sounds together to make words.
- Write the words *at* and *cat* on the board, and model blending the sounds of the words as you point to each sound-spelling: /a/ /t/, at; /k/ /a/ /t/, cat.
- Write *mat* and *fan* on the board. Say these sounds while pointing to the sound-spellings, and have students echo you: /m/ /a/ /t/, mat; /f/ /a/ /n/, fan.
- Write *tan* and *map* on the board. Have students try blending the words out loud but independently. Walk around to support students. If a student is struggling to blend the discrete sounds, model clapping for each sound while saying it aloud, and have the student clap along with you.

Introduce Phonics Skills
Short *a* and Consonants *f, m, t*
- Explain that students are going to learn the spellings for the /a/, /f/, /m/, and /t/ sounds. Say: We just practiced blending some words with these sounds. Now we are going to read some words with these sound-spellings.
- Write the word *at* on the board, and underline the *a*. Say: The letter *a* is the spelling for the /a/ sound. The letter *t* is the spelling for the /t/ sound. Model reading the word, one sound at a time while pointing to the letters: /a/ /t/. Repeat by introducing the /f/ and /m/ sounds and spellings.
- Write the word *fat* on the board. Have students read the word as a class. Say: Slowly sound out each letter.
- Have students try reading the word *mat* independently, following the routine above. Walk around to support students. Students who are struggling may need extra modeling, practice, and feedback, such as: Let's look at the word *mat* on a piece of paper. Slowly sound out each part of the word. What sounds do you hear? Yes, the /m/ sound, the /a/ sound, and the /t/ sound. Let's slowly say the sounds of this word together as I point to each letter. Now you try it.

Introduce Sight Words
- Say: You are going to see some words today that you may not know, so you will need to keep them in your memory.
- Write the word *am* on the board. Model reading it as you point to each letter.
- Write the words *a, do* and *help* on the board. Read the words, and have students echo read each word.
- Write the words *play, what,* and *who* on the board. Ask a volunteer to read them aloud, and have the rest of the class follow suit. Place the words on a sight-word bulletin board.
- The book also contains social studies words. Follow the steps above with these words, but this time provide a simple definition for words that may cause confusion: *farmer, firefighter, musician,* and *teacher.* For example: A firefighter is someone who helps put out fires. We use the word *fighter* because it is hard work. Show students the picture of the firefighter from the book.

Build Oral Language
- Say: Today we will be reading a book about different kinds of work people do. Before I read, I often look at the cover and see what it makes me think about.
- Select a student, and point to the picture on the cover. Discuss what the woman in the picture is doing and what her work might be. Ask about other jobs that people might have. Consider adding vocabulary to your discussion, such as *help, grow, build, work, sell,* or *teach.* Open the book to the first page, and ask what this person's job is. Then have the student tell you about another kind of work that someone might do in the neighborhood.

- Say: Tell a partner about a job that someone in your family or neighborhood has. Discuss the kind of work he or she does and how it helps people. Explain whether the job requires any special tools or vehicles and if the work is done inside or outside.
- Pick five pairs of students, and encourage one student from each pair to share in the discussion. Recognize when students use previously taught key vocabulary.

DURING THE READING

Preview the Book
- Read the title of the book on the cover, and point to the picture. Turn to page 2 and read the sentences, pointing to each word as you read. Have students follow along in their books.
- Say: Do you know what the book will be about based on the title and the first page that I read? How do you know what it will be about?
- As needed, point out the words with the sound-spellings taught: *am, fire, firefighter.*

Read the Book
- Read the book to students as they follow along. Point out words that contain the sound-spellings taught. Explain to students the kinds of work taking place in the picture if they aren't sure: *help, grow, teach, play.*
- Have students silently read the book. Ask a few students to echo read the book to you, and help students sound out new words. When observing students, focus on the words that have the /a/, /f/, /m/, and /t/ sounds: *am, animals, farmer, fire, food, music, teach.*
- **Social Studies Connections:** Say: Some people work indoors, and some work outdoors. Some people use special equipment, like a stethoscope for a doctor or blueprints for an architect. On some jobs, people have to wear special clothes to keep them safe, like a hard hat or a breathing mask. Some people wear uniforms so we can recognize them, like a police officer.

AFTER THE READING

Check Comprehension
To check students' understanding of the book, ask the following:
- ✓Who helps sick animals get better? Who helps sick people get better? Are these jobs the same? What makes them different? (Answers may include: They are both doctors, but one is a doctor for animals and the other is a doctor for people.)
- ✓What words on pages 4 and 5 begin with the /a/ and /f/ sounds? Point to the words. (Students should point to *am, animals, farmer,* and *food.*)
- ✓Look at the picture on page 7. How does the picture help you understand what it means to play music? (Answers may include: The guitar helps me understand that a musician plays on an instrument.) How is the word *help* on page 4 demonstrated in the picture? (Answers may include: The vet is taking care of the calf, so he is helping the calf.)

Reread to Develop Fluency
- Say: Today you will read the book to each other to practice reading with fluency. This means that you read the book as the author meant for it to be read aloud.
- Model reading fluently by reading the book aloud to students. Focus on pausing between sentences.
- Have partners reread the book to each other. Show them a question mark. Tell students to make their voices go up at the end of a question. Students may struggle with decoding, comprehension, or vocabulary. For students who are struggling with comprehension, say: I noticed that you seem unsure about what the farmer is doing. What are some clues we can use from the picture to help us understand what the word *grow* means? The farmer is taking care of the crops and the soil and using a tractor to help plant seeds. That is all part of growing food.
- Send home a copy of *On the Job* for students to read to family members. Consider assessing a few students on fluency.

Connect to Written Language
- ✓Write the words *a, am, at,* and *I* on the board. As a class, read the words together as you point to the letters. Then add consonants to *am* and *at,* and read the new words together.

- ✓Dictate the following words for students to spell: *a, am, at, do, fat, mad,* and *tap.* When finished, write the words on the board. Have students self-correct their papers.

- ✓Tell students that some words are actually two words put together, like *firefighter.* Brainstorm a few other compound words (*bluebird, birdhouse, rowboat*). Have students fold a piece of paper in half. Ask them to choose one compound word and draw a picture of the first word on the left. On the right, draw a picture of the second word. Ask each student to write or dictate a sentence using the compound word he or she drew. You may suggest that students use the following sentence stem: *This is a _____.*

Hot or Not?

SKILLS

PHONICS SKILL INTRODUCED
- Short *o*
- Consonants *h, n, s*

SIGHT WORDS
- *are, is, it, what*

VOCABULARY WORDS–
Science Words
- *soft, wet*

CURRICULUM LINK–
Science Focus
- Properties of Materials

Hot or Not?

BEFORE THE READING

Develop Phonemic Awareness and Phonics
Oral Blending
- Say: Today we are going to be listening to sounds and blending them to make words. Blending means putting sounds together to make words.
- Write the words *on* and *off* on the board, and model blending the sounds of the words as you point to each sound-spelling: /o/ /n/, on; /o/ /f/, off.
- Write *hot* and *sock* on the board. Say these sounds while pointing to the sound-spellings, and have students echo you: /h/ /o/ /t/, hot; /s/ /o/ /k/, sock.
- Write *not* and *mom* on the board. Have students try blending the words out loud but independently. Walk around to support students. If a student is struggling to isolate the discrete sounds, model tapping one finger on your chin for each sound while saying it aloud, and have the student follow suit.

Introduce Phonics Skills
Short *o* and Consonants *h, n, s*
- Say: We just practiced blending some words with the /o/ sound. Now we are going to read some words with this sound-spelling.
- Write the word *Tom* on the board, and underline the *o*. Say: The letter *o* is the spelling for the /o/ sound. Model reading the word, one sound at a time, while pointing to the letters: /t/ /o/ /m/.
- On the board, write the words *mom, off,* and *on*. Have students read the words as a class. Say: Slowly sound out each letter.
- Have students try reading the word *tot* independently, following the routine above. Walk around to support students. Students who are struggling may need extra modeling, practice, and feedback, such as: Let's write the word *tot*. Remember to isolate the /o/ sound. Now say each sound separately, starting with /t/, /o/, /t/. Let's slowly say the sounds of this word together as I point to each letter. Now you do it.
- Repeat the steps with consonants, using these exemplars:
  1) h, /h/: 2) hot; 3) hat; 4) ham
  1) n, /n/: 2) not; 3) nap; 4) non
  1) s, /s/: 2) Sam; 3) son; 4) sat

Introduce Sight Words
- Say: You are going to see some words today that you may not know, so you will need to keep them in your memory.
- Write the word *is* on the board. Read it to students as you point to each letter.
- Write the words *it* and *what* on the board. Read the words, and have students echo read each word.
- Write the word *are* on the board. Ask a volunteer to read it aloud, and have the rest of the class follow suit. Place the words on a sight-word bulletin board.
- The book also contains science words. Follow the steps above with these words, but this time provide a simple definition for words that may cause confusion: *soft* and *wet*. For example: Soft can mean how something feels, like a feather or fur, or it can mean how something sounds, like a whisper. Show students the picture of the kitten from the book. Ask: Which meaning makes sense here?

Build Oral Language
- Say: Today we will be reading a book about opposites. Before I read, I often think about the topic and try to see what I may already know about it.
- Select a student and discuss that you are tall but he or she is short, or you are older and he or she is younger. Explain that opposites are two things that are very different, like night and day. Consider adding vocabulary to your discussion, such as *similar, different, same, texture, temperature, color,* or *opposite*. Then have the student point out something in the room and find an opposite, such as ceiling and floor.

- Say: With a partner, play a game where you try to find opposites. Explain how one thing is the opposite of the other.
- Pick five pairs of students, and encourage one student from each pair to share in the discussion. Recognize when students use previously taught key vocabulary.

DURING THE READING

Preview the Book
- Read the title of the book on the cover, and point to the picture. Point out the question mark in the title. Turn to pages 2 and 3 and read the sentences, pointing to each word as you read. Also point out the periods, and emphasize the stop in your voice. Have students follow along in their books.
- Say: Can you guess what this book will be about based on the title and the first pages that I read? How do you know what it will be about?
- As needed, point out the words that have the sound-spellings taught: *hot, not.*

Read the Book
- Read the book to students as they follow along. Point out words that contain the sound-spellings taught. Tell students the names of the qualities depicted if they don't know them: *cold, hard, rough, dry.*
- Have students silently read the book. Ask a few students to partner read one page at a time to each other. As needed, help students sound out new words. When observing students, focus on the new words: *are, hot, is, not, soft, what.*
- **Science Connections:** Say: Think about how it feels to stand in the sun. What does it feel like? What does it feel like when the sun is covered with clouds, or it's nighttime? How would you describe the difference? All around us there are things that are soft or hard, wet or dry, hot or cold, bright or dark. What are the differences you notice in these examples?

AFTER THE READING

Check Comprehension
To check students' understanding of the book, ask the following:
✓What was hot? Was there a picture that could be two things, like hot and dry? (Answers may include: The desert could be hot and dry, the boiling water was hot and wet.)
✓Look at the text on page 5. The question on page 5 is asking for the opposite of soft. How does the picture help you answer the question? (Answers may include: It is showing rocks which are different from the soft kitten.)
✓Look at the pictures on pages 6 and 7. What do these pictures show? Do these pictures show opposites? (Answers may include: The picture on page 6 is of something wet. The picture on page 7 is of something dry. Yes, these are opposites.)

Reread to Develop Fluency
- Say: Today you will read the book to each other to practice reading with fluency. This means that you read the book as the author meant for it to be read aloud.
- Model reading fluently by reading the book aloud to students. Remind students that sentences ending with a question mark are read differently from sentences ending with a period.
- Have partners reread the book to each other. Model stopping when you come to a period at the end of a sentence and bringing your voice up when you come to a question mark. Students may struggle with decoding, comprehension, or vocabulary. For students who are struggling with comprehension, say: I noticed that you seem unsure about the meaning of the word *soft*. What are some clues in the picture that can help us understand what the word means? Now that we understand the word a little better, let's try reading it again.
- Send home a copy of *Hot or Not?* for students to read to family members. Consider assessing a few students on fluency.

Connect to Written Language
⟳Review: Write the words *am, fat,* and *mad* on the board. As a class, read the words together as you point to the letters. Then replace the initial consonant in each word with the letter *s,* and read the new words together.

✓Dictate the following words for students to spell: *tot, hot, mat, not, are,* and *is.* When finished, write the words on the board. Have students self-correct their papers.

✓Have students fold a sheet of paper in fourths. In each square, help students write one of the following words: *cold, hot, soft, wet.* Have students draw a picture in each square to match the word.

At the Farm

SKILLS

PHONICS SKILL INTRODUCED
- Short *o*
- Consonants *g, l, p*

SIGHT WORDS
- *a, has, I, is, it, little, on, pretty, red, see, the, what*

VOCABULARY WORDS—
Social Studies Words
- *cat, cow, farm, frog, hen, hog, rabbit*

CURRICULUM LINK—
Social Studies Focus
- Farm Life

At the Farm

BEFORE THE READING

Develop Phonemic Awareness and Phonics
Oral Segmentation
- Say: Today we are going to segment words so that we can say them sound by sound. Segment means to pull words apart by their sounds.
- Write the words *top* and *got* on the board, and model segmenting the sounds of the words as you point to each sound-spelling: /t/ /o/ /p/, top; /g/ /o/ /t/, got.
- Write *hop* and *pot* on the board. Say these sounds while pointing to the sound-spellings, and have students echo you: /h/ /o/ /p/, hop; /p/ /o/ /t/, pot.
- Write *pop* and *spot* on the board. Have students try segmenting the words out loud but independently. Walk around to support students. If a student is struggling to segment the discrete sounds, model saying each sound as you move a chip onto a line or sound box. Have the student follow suit, slowing down his or her speech if necessary.

Introduce Phonics Skills
Short *o* and Consonants *g, l, p*
- Say: We just practiced segmenting some words with the /o/ sound. Now we are going to read some words with this sound-spelling.
- Write the word *top* on the board, and underline the *o*. Say: The letter *o* is the spelling for the /o/ sound. Model reading the word, one sound at a time, while pointing to the letters: /t/ /o/ /p/.
- Write the words *hot*, *spots*, and *plop* on the board. Have students read the words as a class. Say: Turn to a partner and say the words one sound at a time.
- Have students try reading the words *on*, *lot*, and *slot* independently, following the routine above. Walk around to support students. Students who are struggling may need extra modeling, practice, and feedback, such as: Let's look at the word *slot*. Remember to say each sound you see in the word. How many sounds are in this word? That's right, there are four sounds. Let's say the sounds of this word together as I point to each letter, starting with the /s/ sound, /s/ /l/ /o/ /t/.
- Repeat the steps with consonants, using these exemplars:
  1) g, /g/: 2) got; 3) hog, gap, golf; 4) gag, glop
  1) l, /l/: 2) log; 3) lot, loss; 4) lap, lag, lost
  1) p, /p/: 2) pop; 3) plop, pal; 4) pot, pan

Introduce Sight Words
- Say: You are going to see some words today that you may not know, so you will need to keep them in your memory.
- Write *a*, *has*, *I*, and *is* on the board. Read them to students as you point to each letter.
- Write *little*, *on*, *pretty*, and *red* on the board. Read the words, and have students echo read them.
- Write *see*, *the*, and *what* on the board. Ask a volunteer to read them aloud, and have the rest of the class follow suit. Place the words on a sight-word bulletin board.
- The book also contains social studies words. Follow the steps above with these words, but this time provide a simple definition for words that may cause confusion: *cat, cow, farm, frog, hen, hog, rabbit*. For example: A farm is where animals and food are grown. It is a big place with lots of room for all the animals and food.

Build Oral Language
- Say: Today we will be reading a book about farm life. Before I read, I like to ask myself what I already know or remember about the topic.
- Select a student and discuss what you know about farms. Explain that farms are places where food and animals grow and are taken care of by people. Consider adding vocabulary to your discussion, such as *animal, calf, crop, eggs, grow, hay, milk, pond*, or *wheat*. Then have the student tell you what he or she knows about farms.

- Say: With a partner, discuss something you think could grow on a farm. Discuss what it needs to grow.
- Pick five pairs of students, and encourage one student from each pair to share in the discussion. Recognize when students use previously taught key vocabulary.

DURING THE READING

Preview the Book
- Read the title of the book on the cover, and point to the picture. Turn to the first few pages, and point out the girls in the picture, calling attention to what the girls are holding. Have students follow along in their books.
- Say: Do you know what the book will be about based on the title and the first two pictures that we saw? Tell me how you know what it will be about.

Read the Book
- Read the book to students as they follow along. Point out words that contain the sound-spellings taught. Tell students the names of the describing words if they don't know them: *little, pink, pretty*.
- Have students silently read the book. Ask a few students to echo read the book with you, and help students sound out new words. When observing students, focus on the new words: *got, hog, hop, lot, on, plop, spots*.
- **Social Studies Connections:** Say: Animals are an important part of life on a farm. For example, cats catch mice, cows and goats give milk, and hens lay eggs. We depend on farms for the food we eat. In addition to eggs and milk, we also get fruits and vegetables from farms. In a way, foods such as bread even come from farms because bread is made from wheat, which grows on farms.

AFTER THE READING

Check Comprehension
To check students' understanding of the book, ask the following:
- ✓Look at the hen on page 2. What has it got? (Answers may include: The hen has eggs in its nest.) Why does a hen sit on its eggs in the nest? (Answers may include: to keep the eggs warm until the chicks hatch.)
- ✓Look at the picture on page 3. How does the picture help you understand the word *nap*? (Answers may include: The cat's eyes are closed because it is sleeping.)
- ✓Look at the picture on page 4. What does a cow do on a farm? (Answers may include: graze, or make milk.) The milk from cows can be used for lots of other foods. Can you think of other foods that come from milk? (Answers may include: butter, cheese, and ice cream.)

Reread to Develop Fluency
- Say: Today you will read the book to each other to practice reading with fluency. This means that you read the book as the author meant for it to be read aloud.
- Model reading fluently by reading the book aloud to students. Focus on using punctuation when you read.
- Have partners reread the book to each other. Model how to show strong feeling when reading a sentence with an exclamation point. Students may struggle with decoding, comprehension, or vocabulary. For students who are struggling with decoding, say: I noticed that it was hard to read the word *rabbit*. Remember to slowly sound out the letters of each word. When two *b*'s appear together, they make one sound. What sound do they make? Yes, the /b/ sound. Now let's try the word again, saying each sound as I point to it. You got it!
- Send home a copy of *At the Farm* for students to read to family members. Consider assessing a few students on fluency.

Connect to Written Language
↻Review: Write the words *hot, not,* and *soft* on the board. As a class, read the words together as you point to the letters. Encourage students to write a sentence with the words.

✓Dictate the following words for students to spell: *got, hog, log, mop, see,* and *what*. When finished, write the words on the board. Have students self-correct their papers.

✓Say: Some words are describing words. They explain what an object looks like or tell something about it. Look at the word *spots*. This word describes how the cow looks. Write on the board: *The shirt has stripes.* Let's read this sentence together. This means the shirt has a special design. The word *stripes* tells us this. Encourage students to point out describing words as they read the story.

Animal Babies

SKILLS

PHONICS SKILL INTRODUCED
- Short *i*
- Consonants *c, d, w, y*

SIGHT WORDS
- *and, big, but, fast, get, jump, read, will*

VOCABULARY WORDS–
Science Words
- *animals, baby, bill*

CURRICULUM LINK–
Science Focus
- Animal Families

Animal Babies

BEFORE THE READING

Develop Phonemic Awareness and Phonics
Oral Blending
- Say: Today we are going to be listening to sounds and blending them to make words. Blending means putting sounds together to make words.
- Write the words *it* and *win* on the board, and model blending the sounds of the words as you point to each sound-spelling: /i/ /t/, it; /w/ /i/ /n/, win.
- Write *will* and *cat* on the board. Say these sounds while pointing to the sound-spellings, and have students echo you: /w/ /i/ /l/, will; /k/ /a/ /t/, cat.
- Write *dog* and *yip* on the board. Have students try blending the words out loud but independently. Walk around to support students. If a student is struggling to blend the discrete sounds, model putting up one finger for each sound while saying it aloud, and have the student follow suit.

Introduce Phonics Skills
Short *i* and Consonants *c, d, w, y*
- Say: We just practiced blending some words with the /i/ sound. Now we are going to read some words with this sound-spelling.
- Write the word *pig* on the board, and underline the *i*. Say: The letter *i* is the spelling for the /i/ sound. Model reading the word, one sound at a time, while pointing to the letters: /p/ /i/ /g/.
- Write the words *fig, lit,* and *pin* on the board. Have students read the words as a class. Say: Slowly sound out each letter.
- Have students try reading the words *gill, pill,* and *sit* independently, following the routine above. Walk around to support students. Students who are struggling may need extra modeling, practice, and feedback, such as: Let's look at the word *gill.* Remember that when two *l*'s appear together, they represent one sound. What sound is that? That's right, it's the /l/ sound. Let's slowly say the sounds of this word together as I point to each letter. Now you do it.
- Repeat the steps with consonants, using these exemplars:
  1) c, /k/: 2) cat; 3) can, cap, cot; 4) cop, cans
  1) d, /d/: 2) dog; 3) dot, din, dip; 4) doll, dad, dig
  1) w, /w/: 2) win; 3) will, wag, wit; 4) won, wow
  1) y, /y/: 2) yap; 3) yam; 4) yak

Introduce Sight Words
- Say: You are going to see some words today that you may not know, so you will need to keep them in your memory.
- Write the words *and* and *big* on the board. Read them to students as you point to each letter.
- Write the words *but, fast, get,* and *will* on the board. Read the words, and have students echo read each word.
- Write the words *jump* and *read* on the board. Ask a volunteer to read them aloud, and have the class follow suit. Place the words on a sight-word bulletin board.
- The book also contains science words. Follow the steps above with these words, but this time provide a simple definition for words that may cause confusion: *animal, babies,* and *bill.* For example: A bill on a duck is actually a bony flat beak that it uses to eat. Show students the picture of the bill from the book.

Build Oral Language
- Say: Today we will be reading a book about animal babies. Before I read, I often think about the topic and try to recall what I already know about it.
- Select a student, and discuss a time you saw an animal baby. Explain what it looked like and whether it looked just like its mother. Consider adding vocabulary to your discussion, such as *adult, animal, babies, calf, foal, full-grown, kitten, litter, puppy,* or *tiny.* Then have the student tell you about an animal baby.

- Say: With a partner, discuss a time you saw an animal baby. Discuss what baby animal you saw, what it looked like, and whether it looked like its mother.
- Pick five pairs of students, and encourage one student from each pair to share in the discussion. Recognize when students use previously taught key vocabulary.

DURING THE READING

Preview the Book
- Read the title of the book on the cover, and point to the picture. Turn to page 2 and read the two sentences, pointing to each word as you read. Also point out the caption, and read that word as well. Have students follow along in their books.
- Say: Do you know what the book will be about based on the title and the first page that I read? How do you know what it will be about?
- As needed, point out the words that have the sound-spellings taught: *big, can, cat, is, it, its, wag.*

Read the Book
- Read the book to students as they follow along. Point out words that contain the sound-spellings taught. Tell students the names of the baby animals if they don't know them: *duckling, foal, kitten, pup, puppy, tadpole.*
- Have students silently read the book. Ask a few students to whisper read the book to you, and help them sound out new words. When observing students, focus on the new words: *is, it(s), swim, will, yip, can, cat, and, dog, wag, will.*
- Science Connections: Say: Some animals go through amazing changes as they grow from being a baby to becoming an adult. Tadpoles, for example, grow into frogs, which can live on land. They develop lungs so that they can breathe and legs so that they can move around. They also lose their tails.

AFTER THE READING

Check Comprehension
To check students' understanding of the book, ask the following:
✓ Look at the baby animal on page 2. What can it do that an adult can do? What makes it different? What word in the text shows that it is different? (Answers may include: A kitten and a cat can wag their tails, but a kitten is much smaller. *big*)
✓ Put your finger on the word on page 7 that is part of a duckling. What makes a duckling different from an adult? Which word shows that it is different? (Students should be pointing to the word *bill.* A duckling is not a big duck. *big*)
✓ Pick a different baby animal. How does the picture help you understand what you read? How does the text help you understand the picture? (Answers may include: The picture of the puppy on page 3 helped me understand that it's a baby dog. The text helped me understand that it is not a big dog.)

Reread to Develop Fluency
- Say: Today you will read the book to each other to practice reading with fluency. This means that you read the book as the author meant for it to be read aloud.
- Model reading fluently by reading the book aloud to students. Focus on pausing between sentences.
- Have partners reread the book to each other. Suggest that they pause when they come to the end of a sentence before starting the next one. Students may struggle with decoding, comprehension, or vocabulary. For students who are struggling with comprehension, say: I noticed that you seem unsure how to read this sentence. What are some clues we can use to help us understand what we read? Now that we understand the sentence a little better, let's try reading it again with proper expression.
- Send home a copy of *Animal Babies* for students to read to family members. Consider assessing a few students on fluency.

Connect to Written Language
↻ Review: On the board, write the words *got, log,* and *on.* As a class, read the words together as you point to the letters. Then replace the vowel in *log* and *on* with *a,* and read the new words together.

✓ Dictate the following words for students to spell: *big, can, dog, and, cop,* and *will.* When finished, write the words on the board. Have students self-correct their papers.

✓ Have students draw pictures of baby animals. Ask each student to write or dictate a sentence telling about the animal he or she drew. You may suggest that students use the following sentence stem: *This is a ____.* You may wish to make the children's pictures into an animal family album.

In the Past

SKILLS

PHONICS SKILL INTRODUCED
- Short *i*
- Consonants *b, k, q, r*

SIGHT WORDS
- *about, did, make, on, see, take, we, went*

VOCABULARY WORDS–
Social Studies Words
- *horseshoe, quilt, wax*

CURRICULUM LINK–
Social Studies Focus
- Life in the Past

In the Past

BEFORE THE READING

Develop Phonemic Awareness and Phonics
Oral Blending
- Say: Today we are going to be listening to sounds and blending them to make words. Blending means putting sounds together to make words.
- Write the words *big* and *if* on the board, and model blending the sounds of the words as you point to each sound-spelling: /b/ /i / /g/, big; /i/ /f/, if.
- Write *kid* and *lip* on the board. Say these sounds while pointing to the sound-spellings, and have students echo you: /k/ /i/ /d/, kid; /l/ /i/ /p/, lip.
- Write *clip* and *fit* on the board. Have students try blending the words out loud but independently. Walk around to support students. If a student is struggling to blend the discrete sounds, model tapping on the desk for each sound while saying it aloud.

Introduce Phonics Skills
Short *i* and Consonants *b, k, q, r*
- Say: We just practiced blending some words with the /i/ sound. Now we are going to read some words with this sound-spelling.
- Write the word *hit* on the board, and underline the *i*. Say: The letter *i* is the spelling for the /i/ sound. Model reading the word, one sound at a time, while pointing to the letters: /h/ /i/ /t/.
- Write the words *Tim, lit,* and *mitt* on the board. Have students read the words as a class, and ask if they hear any rhymes. Say: Slowly sound out each letter.
- Have students try reading the words *dip, mitts, pin,* and *will* independently, following the routine above. Walk around to support students. Students who are struggling may need extra modeling, practice, and feedback, such as: Let's look at the word *mitts*. The letter *s* appears at the end of the word. When that happens, it means "more than one." One mitt, two mitts. Let's slowly say the sounds of this word together as I point to each letter. Now you do it. Provide feedback as needed.
- Repeat the steps with consonants, using these exemplars:
  1) b, /b/: 2) bit; 3) bag, big, bin; 4) bat, bid
  1) k, /k/: 2) kit; 3) kick, Kim, kip; 4) kid, kiss
  1) q, /kw/: 2) quit; 3) quick, quill, quilt; 4) quack
  1) r, /r/: 2) rig; 3) rib, rim, rip; 4) rat, Ron

Introduce Sight Words
- Say: You are going to see some words today that you may not know, so you will need to keep them in your memory.
- Write the words *about* and *did* on the board. Read them both to students.
- Write the words *make, on,* and *see* on the board. Read the words, and have students choral read each word with you.
- Write the words *take, we,* and *went* on the board. Ask a volunteer to read them aloud, and have the class follow suit. Place the words on a sight-word bulletin board.
- The book also contains social studies words. Follow the steps above with these words, but this time provide a simple definition for words that may cause confusion: *horseshoe, quilt,* and *wax*. For example: A candle is made of wax. When you light a candle, the wax closest to the flame can melt from the heat. Show students the picture of the candles in the book.

Build Oral Language
- Say: Today we will be reading a book about what life was like long ago, in the past. Before I read, I like to look at the picture on the cover because that gives me an idea about what might be inside.
- Select a student and discuss some of the things we use today that didn't exist long ago, such as computers and cell phones. Discuss some other items that we use today that weren't available in the past. Consider adding vocabulary to your discussion,

such as *clipper, fabric, light, market, sewing machine, stove,* or *well.* Then have the student tell you about an item we use today that makes life easier for us.
- Say: With a partner, discuss what it would be like if you didn't have lightbulbs or electricity. Think about what you would do if there was no television or automobiles. How would your life be different?
- Pick five pairs of students, and encourage one student from each pair to share in the discussion. Recognize when students use previously taught key vocabulary.

DURING THE READING

Preview the Book
- Read the title of the book on the cover, and point to the picture. Turn to pages 2 and 3 and read the sentences. Point to each word as you read. Have students follow along.
- Say: Do you know what the people are doing in these pictures? How does the title help us know what the book will be about? What are the clues in the pictures that help you understand what this book is about?
- As needed, point out the words that have the sound-spellings taught: *Bill, clips, quick, ram,* and *trip.*

Read the Book
- Read the book to students as they follow along. Point out words that contain the sound-spellings taught. Tell students the names of the actions and tools if they don't know them: *anvil, clips, dip, hammer, horseshoe, needle.*
- Have students silently read the book. Ask a few students to whisper read the book to you, and help them sound out new words. When observing students, focus on the new words: *big, clips, dip, fit, is, it, Jill, kick, Kim, Lil, milks, quick, quilt, trip, will.*
- **Social Studies Connections:** Say: The people in these pictures are actors. They dress up like people who lived long ago and use the tools used by people in the past. They show that life was very different long ago than it is today.

AFTER THE READING

Check Comprehension
To check students' understanding of the book, ask the following:
- ✓ Look at the picture on page 3. What is Bill doing to the sheep? Why does he need to be quick? (Answers may include: Bill is clipping the sheep's hair. He must be quick so he doesn't cut the sheep's skin.)
- ✓ Look at the text on page 6. Use the picture to explain how Lil milks the cow. (Answers may include: She squeezes milk into a pail.)
- ✓ Look at page 7. How are horseshoes similar to your shoes? How are they different? (Answers may include: Horses and people wear shoes to protect their feet. Horseshoes are made of iron. My shoes are made of cloth or leather.)

Reread to Develop Fluency
- Say: Today you will read the book to each other to practice reading with fluency. This means that you read the book as the author meant for it to be read aloud.
- Model reading fluently by reading the book aloud to students. Focus on changing your voice when you read a question.
- Have partners reread the book to each other. Demonstrate how their voices should go up at the end of a sentence that ends in a question. Students may struggle with decoding, comprehension, or vocabulary. For students who are struggling with decoding, say: I noticed that you are working on reading this word. Let's read it together, slowly sounding out the letters of each word. Great job! Reread the sentence again now that you know this word.
- Send home a copy of *In the Past* for students to read to family members. Consider assessing a few students on fluency.

Connect to Written Language
↻ Review: Write the words *dill, will,* and *yip* on the board. As a class, read the words together as you point to the letters. Then encourage students to write a sentence for each word.

✓ Dictate the following words for students to spell: *big, is, kids, quilt, rib, about,* and *make.* When finished, write the words on the board. Have students self-correct their papers.

✓ Say: Some words tell us about the action happening in the picture. For example, the words *jumps, runs,* and *walk* explain how someone moves through the room. Write on the board: *Don hops.* Let's read this sentence together. Show me how Don is moving. The word *hops* tells us this. Write on the board: *Don skips.* Let's read this sentence. Show me how Don is moving. The word *skips* tells us how Don is moving. Write these sentences on the board: *Sam naps. Sam drinks. Bill stops. Bill sips.* Read the sentences as a class, and encourage group discussion about the meaning of each. Have students write a sentence using words that show action.

Animal Homes

SKILLS

PHONICS SKILLS INTRODUCED
- Short *e*
- Consonants *j, v, x, z*

SIGHT WORDS
- *an, does, fly, he, him, his, in, its, one, well*

VOCABULARY WORDS–
Science Words
- *bees, cliff, den, eagle, fox, hive, live(s), nest, pup*

CURRICULUM LINK–
Science Focus
- Animal Habitats

Animal Homes

BEFORE THE READING

Develop Phonemic Awareness and Phonics
Oral Segmentation
- Say: Today we are going to be segmenting words so that we can say them sound by sound. Segmenting means pulling words apart by their sounds.
- Write the words *egg* and *den* on the board, and model saying the words sound by sound: /e/ /g/, egg; /d/ /e/ /n/, den.
- Write *jet* and *fox* on the board. Sound out each word, and have students follow suit chorally: /j/ /e/ /t/, jet; /f/ /ä/ /ks/, fox.
- Write *vet* and *buzz* on the board. Have students segment the words out loud but independently. Walk around to support students. If a student is struggling to segment the sounds in each word, model saying each sound as you move a chip onto a line or sound box, and have the student follow suit.

Introduce Phonics Skills
Short *e* and Consonants *j, v, x, z*
- Say: We just practiced segmenting some words with the /e/ sound. Now we are going to read some words with this sound-spelling.
- Write the word *hen* on the board, and underline the *e*. Say: The letter *e* is the spelling for the /e/ sound. Model reading the word, one sound at a time, while pointing to the letters: /h/ /e/ /n/.
- Write the words *bet, pet,* and *set* on the board. Have students read the words as a class. Say: Slowly sound out each letter.
- Have students try reading the words *met* and *wet* independently, following the routine above. Walk around to support students. Students who are struggling may need extra modeling, practice, and feedback, such as: Let's look at the word *met.* Remember that the letter *e* is the spelling for the /e/ sound. Let's say the sounds of this word together as I point to each letter: /m/ /e/ /t/, met.
- Repeat the steps with consonants, using these exemplars:
  1) j, /j/: 2) job; 3) jet, jog, jab; 4) jot, jam
  1) v, /v/: 2) vet, vat; 3) van; 4) visit*
  1) x, /ks/: 2) fox; 3) box, tax, wax; 4) fix, mix
  1) z, /z/: 2) zap; 3) zig, zag; 4) zip
  *Write *visit* on the board and underline the two vowels. Explain that every syllable has only one vowel sound, such as /viz/ and /it/. Blend and segment the word parts.

Introduce Sight Words
- Say: You are going to see some words today that you may not know, so you will need to keep them in your memory.
- Write the words *does, fly,* and *one* on the board. Read them to students as you point to each letter.
- Write the words *him, his,* and *well* on the board. Read the words, and have students echo read each word.
- Write the words *an, he, in,* and *its* on the board. Ask a volunteer to read them aloud, and have the rest of the class follow suit. Place the words on a sight-word bulletin board.
- The book also contains science words. Follow the steps above with these words, but this time provide a simple definition for words that may cause confusion: *bees, cliff, den, eagle, fox, hive, lives, nest, pup.* For example: A hive is where bees live. Show students the picture of the hive in the book.

Build Oral Language
- Say: Today we will be reading a book about where animals live. Before I read, I often think about the topic and try to recall what I already know about it.
- Have a discussion with a student about where different animals live. Mention a few animals that are not kept as pets and where those animals live. Consider adding

vocabulary to your discussion, such as *underground*, *forest*, and *enemies*. Then have the student tell you what he or she knows about animal homes.

- Say: Interview a partner about what he or she knows about animal homes. Ask your partner to name animals that aren't people's pets, say where those animals live, and tell you what other animals live there. Then switch roles.
- Pick five pairs of students, and encourage one student from each pair to share what they learned. Recognize when students use previously taught key vocabulary.

DURING THE READING

Preview the Book
- Read the title of the book on the cover, and point to the picture. Turn to pages 2 and 3 and read the text, pointing to each word as you read. Also point out the picture. Have students follow along in their books.
- Say: Do you know what the book will be about based on the title and the first few pages that I read? How do you know what it will be about?
- As needed, point out the words that have the sound-spellings taught: *eggs, Let's, nest, visit.*

Read the Book
- Read the book to students as they follow along. Point out words that contain the sound-spellings taught. Tell students the names of the animal homes if they don't know them: *box hive, cliff, den, nest.*
- Have students silently read the book. Ask a few students to whisper read the book to you, and help them sound out new words. When observing students, focus on the new words: *den, eggs, let's, nest, red, job, visit, box, fox, zap, zag, zig.*
- **Science Connections:** Say: Every animal has a habitat, which is a place where the animal lives. A habitat also has the food and water an animal needs to survive.

AFTER THE READING

Check Comprehension
To check students' understanding of the book, ask the following:
- ✓Point to the word on page 3 that tells where the eagle lives. (Students should point to the word *cliff.*) What is on the cliff that belongs to the eagle? (The nest and the eggs belong to the eagle.) Do you think it would be difficult to live on a cliff? (Answers will vary but should focus on why it would or wouldn't be difficult to live in this habitat.)
- ✓Look at the den on page 4. What animals live in this den? Why do you think a den is a good home for a red fox? (A red fox and its pup live in this den. Answers will vary but should include why a den is a good habitat for a red fox.)
- ✓Look at the picture on page 6. How does the picture help you understand what you read? How does the text help you understand the picture? (Answers may include: The picture of the box hives on page 6 helps me understand what some bees' homes look like. The text helps me understand that bees live in these box hives.)

Reread to Develop Fluency
- Say: Today you will read the book to each other to practice reading with fluency. This means that you read the book as the author meant for it to be read aloud.
- Model reading fluently by reading the book aloud to students. Focus on making your voice rise at the end of questions. Demonstrate how to show a strong feeling, such as excitement, when a sentence ends with an exclamation point.
- Have partners reread the book to each other. Suggest that they pause when they come to the end of a sentence before starting the next one. Students may struggle with decoding, comprehension, or vocabulary. For students who are struggling with vocabulary, say: I noticed that you're not sure what that word means, which makes it hard to read the sentence. Let's look up the definition of the word.
- Send home a copy of *Animal Homes* for students to read to family members. Consider assessing a few students on fluency.

Connect to Written Language
↻Review: Write the words *big, Bill,* and *will* on the board. As a class, read the words together as you point to the letters. Have student volunteers replace the vowel in each word with an *e*, and read the new words together.

✓Dictate the following words for students to spell: *egg, red, fox, vet, jam, fly,* and *does.* When finished, write the words on the board. Have students self-correct their papers.

✓Say: Some words are made up of two different words. When the two words are put together, they make a new word with a new meaning. You can figure out this new meaning by thinking about the two different words. Write the word *cannot* on the board. Let's read this word together: *cannot.* Do you see two different words in the word *cannot*? With your finger trace a line under the word *can* and say can. Trace your finger under the word *not* and say not. The word *can* means to be able to do something. You use the word *not* to say that the opposite of something happened. So *cannot* means to be unable to do something. Write these words on the board: *firefighter, horseshoe,* and *sandbox.* Read the words as a class, and encourage group discussion about the meaning of each. Have students think of more compound words and write them on a piece of paper.

Finding Animals

SKILLS

PHONICS SKILL INTRODUCED
- Short *e*
- *r*-blends

SIGHT WORDS
- *into, white, yes, you*

VOCABULARY WORDS–
Science Words
- *bird, bug, crab, fish, grass, lizard, rabbit, shell, striped, tiger*

CURRICULUM LINK–
Science Focus
- Camouflage

Finding Animals

BEFORE THE READING

Develop Phonemic Awareness and Phonics
Oral Segmentation
- Say: Today we are going to be segmenting sounds to hear individual sounds in words. Segmenting means pulling words apart by their sounds.
- Write the words *red* and *wet* on the board. Model segmenting the sounds of the words as you point to each sound-spelling: /r/ /e/ /d/, red; /w/ /e/ /t/, wet.
- Write *jet* and *bed* on the board. Say these sounds while pointing to the sound-spellings, and have students echo you: /j/ /e/ /t/, jet; /b/ /e/ /d/, bed.
- Write *egg* and *lend* on the board. Have students try blending the words out loud but independently. Walk around to support students. If a student is struggling to blend the discrete sounds, model putting up one finger for each sound while saying it aloud, and have the student follow suit.

Introduce Phonics Skills
Short *e* and *r*-blends
- Say: We just practiced segmenting some words with the /e/ sound. Now we are going to read some words with this sound-spelling.
- Write the word *pen* on the board, and underline the *e*. Say: The letter *e* is the spelling for the /e/ sound. Model reading the word, one sound at a time, while pointing to the letters: /p/ /e/ /n/.
- Write the words *get, let,* and *met* on the board. Have students read the words as a class. Say: Slowly sound out each letter.
- Have students try reading the words *red, yet,* and *press* independently, following the routine above. Walk around to support students. Students who are struggling may need extra modeling, practice, and feedback, such as: Let's look at the word *press*. When two consonants appear together in a word, the sound of each consonant is blended together. For example, the letters *pr* in *press* stand for the /pr/ sound. Let's slowly say the sounds of this word together. Now you do it.
- Repeat the steps with *r*-blends, using these exemplars:
  1) cr, /cr/: 2) crab; 3) cram; 4) crib
  1) dr, /dr/: 2) dress, drab; 3) drip; 4) drag, drop
  1) gr, /gr/: 2) grass, grit; 3) grab, grip; 4) grin, gram
  1) tr, /tr/: 2) trap, trick; 3) tram, trot; 4) trip, trim

Introduce Sight Words
- Say: You are going to see some words today that you may not know, so you will need to keep them in your memory.
- Write the word *into* on the board. Read it to students as you point to each letter.
- Write the words *white* and *yes* on the board. Read the words, and have students echo read each word.
- Write the word *you* on the board. Ask a volunteer to read it aloud, and have the rest of the class follow suit. Place the words on a sight-word bulletin board.
- The book also contains science words. Follow the steps above with these words, but this time provide a simple definition for words that may cause confusion: *bird, crab, lizard, rabbit, shell, striped, tiger*. For example: The tiger is striped. Stripes are the up-and-down patches of color on its fur. The stripes help the tiger blend into the grass, making it hard to see. Show students the picture of the tiger on page 5.

Build Oral Language
- Say: Today we will be reading a book about animals that can hide in plain sight. Before I read, I like to imagine what the title means and see if it helps me make a guess on what the book will be about.
- Select a student, and discuss ways animals hide. Explain that some animals have fur or skin that helps protect them by blending into their environment. This is called camouflage. Consider adding vocabulary to your discussion, such as *stem, leaves,*

grass, shell, rock, hides, shy, scared, or *furry*. Then have the student tell you about ways animals hide.
- Say: With a partner, discuss why you think animals might need to hide. Think about how different animals have different ways they can stay safe.
- Pick five pairs of students, and have one student from each pair choose an animal. Then have the student interview his or her partner about ways that animal uses camouflage. Then have partners switch roles. Recognize when students use previously taught key vocabulary.

DURING THE READING

Preview the Book
- Read the title of the book on the cover, and point to the picture. Turn to pages 2 and 3 and read the sentences, pointing to each word as you read. Have students follow along in their books.
- Say: Do you know what the book will be about based on the title and the pages that I read? How do you know what it will be about?
- As needed, point out the words that have *r*-blends or the /e/ sound: *green, pretty, red, stem, tree.*

Read the Book
- Read the book to students as they follow along. Point out words that contain the sound-spellings taught. Have the group chorally read each page after you read it.
- Have students silently read the book. Listen to a few students as they partner read to each other, and help students sound out new words. When observing students, focus on the new decodable words: *crab, grass, red, rest, went, wet, yes.*
- **Science Connections:** Say: There are several ways animals use camouflage to hide or stay safe. Some use their natural coloring (an arctic fox), some can change their coloring (a chameleon), and some are shaped so that they can blend in with their surroundings (like the owl or the praying mantis). Can you think of other ways that animals use camouflage?

AFTER THE READING

Check Comprehension
To check students' understanding of the book, ask the following:
✓ Look at the insect on page 2. How is it hiding? (Answers may include: The insect's shape and color match the stem, so it isn't noticeable.)
✓ Look at the picture of the crab on page 6. How is the shell protecting the crab? (Answers may include: The shell is the same color as the sand.) Point to the word that shows where the crab hides. (Students should point to *shell*.)
✓ Look at the rabbit on page 7. How does the picture help you understand the word *camouflage*? (Answers may include: The white rabbit can hide in its snowy surroundings.) Which word in the text describes the color in the picture? (*white*)

Reread to Develop Fluency
- Say: Today you will read the book to each other to practice reading with fluency. This means that you read the book as the author meant for it to be read aloud.
- Model reading fluently by reading the book aloud to students. Focus on making your voice go up at the end of questions.
- Have partners reread the book to each other. Demonstrate how they need to make their voices go up when they ask a question. Students may struggle with decoding, comprehension, or vocabulary. For students who are struggling with decoding, say: I noticed that some of the words in these sentences are difficult to read. Let's slowly sound out the letters and tap to each sound. You did it! Now that you know the word, reread the sentence with proper expression.
- Send home a copy of *Finding Animals* for students to read to family members. Consider assessing a few students on fluency.

Connect to Written Language
↻ Review: Write the words *den, let,* and *vet* on the board. As a class, read the words together as you point to the letters. Then replace the vowel in each word with *o*, and read the new words together. Are any of these nonsense words?

✓ Dictate the following words for students to spell: *red, wet, hen, pet, grab, crab, into,* and *you.* When finished, write the words on the board. Have students self-correct their papers.

✓ Say: Some words, such as *into*, give us information about where something is happening. Write on the board: *The bug flies into a flower.* Let's read this sentence together. This tells me where the bug flew. This word is made up of two smaller words: *in* and *to.* Can you think of other compound words that are made up of smaller words?

Fun at the Fair

SKILLS

PHONICS SKILL INTRODUCED
- Short *u*
- *s*-blends

SIGHT WORDS
- *around, blue, they, yellow*

VOCABULARY WORDS–
Social Studies Words
- *fair, proud, ribbon, year*

CURRICULUM LINK–
Social Studies Focus
- Traditions

Fun at the Fair

BEFORE THE READING

Develop Phonemic Awareness and Phonics
Oral Segmentation
- Say: Today we are going to be listening to sounds and segmenting them to make words. Segmenting means pulling words apart by their sounds.
- Write the words *up* and *bus* on the board, and model segmenting the sounds of the words as you point to each sound-spelling: /u/ /p/, up; /b/ /u/ /s/, bus.
- Write *cup* and *bug* on the board. Say these sounds while pointing to the sound-spellings, and have students echo you: /k/ /u/ /p/, cup; /b/ /u/ /g/, bug.
- Write *sun, swim,* and *nest* on the board. Have students try segmenting the words out loud but independently. Walk around to support students. If a student is struggling to segment the discrete sounds, model clapping once for each sound.

Introduce Phonics Skills
Short *u* and *s*-blends
- Say: We just practiced segmenting some words with the /u/ sound. Now we are going to read some words with this sound-spelling.
- Write the word *fun* on the board, and underline the *u*. Say: The letter *u* is the spelling for the /u/ sound. Model reading the word, one sound at a time, while pointing to the letters: /f/ /u/ /n/.
- Write the words *fun, jut, run, sun, tug,* and *yum* on the board. Have students read the words as a class. Say: Slowly sound out each letter.
- Have students try reading the words *snub* and *stub* independently, following the routine above. Walk around to support students. Students who are struggling may need extra modeling, practice, and feedback. Say: Let's look at the word *snub.* Remember that often when two consonants appear together in a word, the sound of each consonant is blended together. Let's slowly say the sounds of this word together as I point to each letter. Now you do it.
- Repeat the steps with *s*-blends, using these exemplars:
  1) sk, /sk/: 2) skip; 3) skill; 4) skunk
  1) sl, /sl/: 2) slap, slit; 3) sled; slat; 4) slip; slot
  1) sm, /sm/: 2) small; 3) smell; 4) smog
  1) sn, /sn/: 2) snack, snap; 3) sniff, snip; 4) snub
  1) sp, /sp/: 2) span; 3) speck, spin; 4) spot, spun
  1) st, /st/: 2) stand; 2) stem, fast; 3) stick; 4) stop, stump
  1) sw, /sw/: 2) swap, swat; 3) swell; 4) swift

Introduce Sight Words
- Say: You are going to see some words today that you may not know, so you will need to keep them in your memory.
- Write the word *around* on the board. Read it to students as you point to each letter.
- Write the words *blue* and *they* on the board. Read the words, and have students echo read each word.
- Write the word *yellow* on the board. Ask a volunteer to read it aloud, and have the rest of the class follow suit. Place the words on a sight-word bulletin board.
- The book also contains social studies words. Follow the steps above with these words, but this time provide a simple definition for words that may cause confusion: *fair, proud,* and *year.* For example: A fair is a special place where you can go on rides, see animals, and eat yummy foods. Show students the picture of the fair.

Build Oral Language
- Say: Today we will be reading a book about going to a fair. Many states have fairs every year. At fairs, people display things they are proud of, such as animals they have raised or food they have grown.
- Select a student, and ask him or her to share what he or she knows about fairs. Build student's background knowledge and vocabulary by asking questions, such as

"Have you ever been to a fair? If so, what did you see there?" Consider incorporating words such as *celebrate, exhibits, fairgrounds,* and *tradition* into the discussion.

- Say: With a partner, discuss a time you went to a fair. Discuss what you saw, what you ate, and what things you did there.
- Divide the class into pairs. Have the pairs brainstorm what they know about fairs. Then have them share their observations with the class orally or on chart paper. Recognize when students use previously taught key vocabulary.

DURING THE READING

Preview the Book
- Read the title of the book on the cover, and point to the picture. Turn to pages 2 and 3 and read the sentences, pointing to each word as you read.
- Say: Do you know what the book will be about based on the title and the first two pages that I read? How do you know what it will be about?
- As needed, point out the words that have the /u/ and *s*-blend sounds: *fun, Justin, small,* and *slow.* Preteach the word *slow.*

Read the Book
- Read the book to students as they follow along. Point out words that contain the sound-spellings taught. Tell students the names of the items shown if they don't know them: *rides, pony, pig, jam, sweet corn.*
- Have students silently read the book. Ask a few students to whisper read the book to you, and help them sound out new words. When observing students, focus on the new words: *fast, fun, jump, run, slow, small, smell, snack, spin, stand, stop, sun, yum.*
- **Social Studies Connections:** Say: A state fair is an example of a community tradition. It celebrates different cultures in the community with events.

AFTER THE READING

Check Comprehension
To check students' understanding of the book, ask the following:
- ✓Which part of the fair would you like the best? Why? (Answers will vary, but may include: The rides because they're fun and scary at the same time.)
- ✓Look at the picture on page 5. What is the boy doing? (The boy is dancing.) What words in the text tell you what he is doing? (*jumps, runs, spins, dance.*) Why do you think the boy is wearing a costume? (Answers may include: The boy is in costume to show the traditions of his culture.)
- ✓Look at page 6. How does the picture help you understand the text? How does the text help you understand the picture? (Answers may include: The picture of the woman with the ribbon helps me understand that she won a prize for jam. The text helps me understand that she won first place.)

Reread to Develop Fluency
- Say: Today you will read the book to each other to practice reading with fluency. This means that you read the book as the author meant for it to be read aloud.
- Model reading fluently by reading the book aloud to students. Focus on changing the inflection of your voice to match the punctuation.
- Have partners reread the book to each other. Remind students to raise their voices at the end of a sentence with a question mark and show strong feeling when a sentence ends with an exclamation point. Students may struggle with decoding, comprehension, or vocabulary. For students who are struggling with comprehension, say: I noticed that you seem unsure how to read this sentence. What are some clues we can use to help us understand what we read? Now that we understand the sentence a little better, let's try reading it again with proper expression.
- Send home a copy of *Fun at the Fair* for students to read to family members. Consider assessing a few students on fluency.

Connect to Written Language
↺Review: Write the words *crab, grass,* and *rest* on the board. As a class, read the words together as you point to the letters. Then have students choose one word with which to write a sentence.

✓Dictate the following words for students to spell: *fast, fun, jump, must, run, blue,* and *they.* When finished, write the words on the board. Have students self-correct their papers.

✓Say: Some words have an *-ed* or *-s* at the end. They show that the action happened in the past or is still happening. If *-ed* appears, it happened in the past. If *-s* appears, it's still happening. Write on the board: *Don skips.* Let's read this sentence together. This means Don is still skipping. The *-s* tells us this. Write on the board: *Don skipped.* Let's read this sentence. This means Don is finished skipping. The *-ed* tells us this. Write these sentences on the board: *Sam slips. Sam slipped. Jill jumps. Jill jumped.* Read the sentences as a class, and encourage group discussion about the meaning of each. Have students write a sentence with a word that has the *-s* or *-ed* inflection.

Weather

SKILLS

PHONICS SKILLS INTRODUCED
- Short *u*
- *l*-blends

SIGHT WORDS
- *back, drink, light, now, them, up, us, warm, water, with*

VOCABULARY WORDS–
Science Words
- *clouds, hot, rain, sun, warm, weather, windy*

CURRICULUM LINK–
Science Focus
- Weather

Weather

BEFORE THE READING

Develop Phonemic Awareness and Phonics
Oral Blending
- Say: Today we are going to be listening to sounds and blending them to make words. Blending means putting sounds together to make words.
- Write the words *bus* and *rub* on the board. Model blending the sounds of the words as you point to each sound-spelling: /b/ /u/ /s/, bus; /r/ /u/ /b/, rub.
- Write *duck* and *mug* on the board. Say these sounds while pointing to the sound-spellings, and have students echo you: /d/ /u/ /k/, duck; /m/ /u/ /g/, mug.
- Write *hut, yum*, and *up* on the board. Have students try blending the words out loud but independently. Walk around to support students. If a student is struggling to blend the discrete sounds, model putting up one finger for each sound while saying it aloud, and have the student follow suit.

Introduce Phonics Skills
Short *u* and *l*-blends
- Say: We just practiced blending some words with the /u/ sound. Now we are going to read some words with this sound-spelling.
- Write the word *sun* on the board, and underline the *u*. Say: The letter *u* is the spelling for the /u/ sound. Model reading the word, one sound at a time, while pointing to the letters: /s/ /u/ /n/.
- Write the words *fun, gum*, and *run* on the board. Have students read the words as a class. Say: Slowly sound out each letter.
- Have students try reading the words *bug, plug*, and *rug* independently, following the routine above. Walk around to support students. Students who are struggling may need extra modeling, practice, and feedback, such as: Let's look at the word *plug*. When two consonants appear together in a word, the sound of each consonant is blended together. For example, the letters *pl* in *plug* stand for the /pl/ sound. Let's slowly say the sounds of this word together as I point to each letter. Now you do it.
- Repeat the steps with *l*-blends, using these exemplars:
  1) bl, /bl/: 2) black; 3) block, blunt, bluff; 4) blast
  1) fl, /fl/: 2) flap; 3) flip, flop, flock; 4) flick
  1) pl, /pl/: 2) plant; 3) pluck, plus, plump; 4) plot
  1) sl, /sl/: 2) slid; 3) slick, slap, slip; 4) slob, slot, slit

Introduce Sight Words
- Say: You are going to see some words today that you may not know, so you will need to keep them in your memory.
- Write the words *drink, light, them*, and *warm* on the board. Read them to students as you point to each letter.
- Write the words *now, water, back*, and *us* on the board. Read the words, and have students echo read each word.
- Write the words *with* and *up* on the board. Ask a volunteer to read them aloud, and have the rest of the class follow suit. Place the words on a sight-word bulletin board.
- The book also contains science words. Follow the steps above with these words, but this time provide a simple definition for words that may cause confusion: *clouds, hot, rain, sun, warm, weather, windy*. For example: Weather is what the outside air is like. It can be hot or cold, wet or dry, or clear or cloudy. Show students pictures of different types of weather from the book.

Build Oral Language
- Say: Today we will be reading a book about weather. Before I read, I often think about the topic and try to recall what I already know about it.
- Have a discussion with a student about what the weather is like today. Describe today's temperature. Explain that the weather isn't always like it is today. Describe

how else the weather could be. Consider adding vocabulary to your discussion, such as *rain, cool, windy, sunny, warm, chilly,* and *clouds.* Then have the student tell you what he or she knows about the weather.

- Say: Make a KWL chart with a partner. Model making a KWL chart on the board. In the first column, write what you both know about the weather. In the second column, write what you both want to know about the weather. In the third column, write what you both learned about the weather.
- Pick five pairs of students, and encourage one student from each pair to share what they wrote in their charts. Recognize when students use previously taught key vocabulary.

DURING THE READING

Preview the Book

- Read the title of the book on the cover, and point to the picture. Turn to page 2 and read the two sentences, pointing to each word as you read. Also point out the picture. Have students follow along in their books.
- Say: Do you know what the book will be about based on the title and the first page that I read? How do you know what it will be about?
- As needed, point out the words that have the /u/ sound: *sun, up, us.*

Read the Book

- Read the book to students as they follow along. Point out words that contain the sound-spellings taught. Tell students what the different types of weather are if they don't know them: *sun, rain, clouds, windy.*
- Have students silently read the book. Ask a few students to partner read the book to you, and help students sound out new words. When observing students, focus on the new words: *bugs, ducks, sun, up, us, block, plants.*
- **Science Connections:** Say: Clouds are made up of many tiny drops of water. The tiny drops join and make large drops. As the drops get larger and larger, they become heavier and heavier. When they get too heavy, they fall as rain. Rain is a type of weather we can experience.

AFTER THE READING

Check Comprehension

To check students' understanding of the book, ask the following:

✓ Point to the word on page 2 that tells how the weather feels. What makes the weather feel warm? (Students should point to the word *warm*. The weather feels warm because of the sun.)

✓ What is the weather like on page 4? How do you know that it will rain? (The weather is cloudy and rainy. The text tells us it will rain: Drip! Drip! Drop!)

✓ Look at page 7. How does the picture help you understand what you read? How does the text help you understand the picture? (Answers may include: The picture of the kite flying in the sky helps me understand that it is windy and not raining. The text helps me understand that the weather is hot and windy.)

Reread to Develop Fluency

- Say: Today you will read the book to each other to practice reading with fluency. This means that you read the book as the author meant for it to be read aloud.
- Model reading fluently by reading the book aloud to students. Focus on making your voice show excitement when a sentence ends with an exclamation point.
- Have partners reread the book to each other. Suggest that they pause when they come to the end of a sentence before starting the next one. Students may struggle with decoding, comprehension, or vocabulary. For students who are struggling with decoding, say: I see that you're working on reading this word. Let's read it together, slowly sounding out the letters of each word. You've got it!
- Send home a copy of *Weather* for students to read to family members. Consider assessing a few students on fluency.

Connect to Written Language

↻ Review: Write the words *fun, run,* and *snack* on the board. As a class, read the words together as you point to the letters. Have student volunteers replace the vowel in the first two words with an *a,* and read the new words together.

✓ Dictate the following words for students to spell: *bug, sun, run, block, flag, warm,* and *light.* When finished, write the words on the board. Have students self-correct their papers.

✓ Ask students whether they like rainy or sunny days better. Have them draw themselves in the sun or rain. Ask them to write one or two sentences telling what they like to do in the sun or rain. You may want to use one of the following sentence stems:
I like to _____ in the hot sun.
I like to _____ in the rain.

At the Vet

SKILLS

PHONICS SKILLS INTRODUCED
- Short Vowels
- *s*-blends

SIGHT WORDS
- *black, give(s), had, keep(s), much, out, soon, white, your*

VOCABULARY WORDS–
Social Studies Words
- *heal, healthy, paw, scale, shot, sick, well*

CURRICULUM LINK–
Social Studies Focus
- Service Providers

At the Vet

BEFORE THE READING

Develop Phonemic Awareness and Phonics
Rhyme
- Say: Today we are going to rhyme words. A rhyme is two words that have the same ending sounds.
- Write the words *cat, sat, vet,* and *met* on the board. Model rhyming the sounds of the words as you point to each sound-spelling: /k/ /a/ /t/, cat; /s/ /a/ /t/, sat; /v/ /e/ /t/, vet; /m/ /e/ /t/, met.
- Write *big, wig, hot,* and *dot* on the board. Say these sounds while pointing to the sound-spellings, and have students echo you: /b/ /i/ /g/, big; /w/ /i/ /g/, wig; /h/ /o/ /t/, hot; /d/ /o/ /t/, dot. After each rhyme set, ask students to say *yes* if the words rhyme.
- Write *pup* and *cast* on the board. Have students say rhyming words out loud but independently. Walk around to support students. If a student is struggling to find rhyming words, say: Say *pup.* Change /p/ to /c/. What word do you get? Yes, *cup.* Now say *cast.* Change /k/ to /f/. What word do you get? That's right, *fast.*

Introduce Phonics Skills
Short Vowels and *s*-blends
- Say: We just practiced rhyming some words with the /a/ /e/ /i/ /o/, and /u/ sounds. Now we are going to read some words with these sound-spellings.
- Write the word *cat* on the board, and underline the *a.* Say: The letter *a* is the spelling for the /a/ sound. Model reading the word, one sound at a time, while pointing to the letters: /k/ /a/ /t/.
- Write the words *hat, map,* and *tan* on the board. Have students read the words as a class. Say: Slowly sound out each letter.
- Have students try reading the words *slap, net, grip, mop,* and *truck* independently, following the routine above. Walk around to support students. Students who are struggling may need extra modeling, practice, and feedback, such as: Let's look at the word *slap.* When two consonants appear together in a word, the sound of each consonant is blended together. For example, the letters *sl* in *slap* stand for the /sl/ sound. Let's slowly say the sounds of this word together as I point to each letter. Now you do it.
- Repeat the steps with *s*-blends, using these exemplars:
  1) st, /st/: 2) stop; 3) stand, stun, stem; 4) staff, stuck, stick
  1) sm, /sm/: 2) smell; 3) smock, smack; 4) smug, smog
  1) sp, /sp/: 2) spill; 3) span, spin, spun; 4) spit, sped, spell
  1) sl, /sl/: 2) slam; 3) slab, slant, 4) slug

Introduce Sight Words
- Say: You are going to see some words today that you may not know, so you will need to keep them in your memory.
- Write the words *keep, much,* and *white* on the board. Read them to students as you point to each letter.
- Write the words *give, your,* and *soon* on the board. Read the words, and have students echo read each word.
- Write the words *had, out,* and *black* on the board. Ask a volunteer to read them aloud, and have the rest of the class follow suit. Place the words on a sight-word bulletin board.
- The book also contains social studies words. Follow the steps above with these words, but this time provide a simple definition for words that may cause confusion: *heal, healthy, paw, scale, shot, sick,* and *well.* For example: A paw is the foot of an animal that has four feet and claws. Show students pictures from the book.

Build Oral Language
- Say: Today we will be reading a book about going to the vet. Before I read, I often think about the topic and try to recall what I already know about it.

- Have a discussion with a student about the vet. Explain what a vet is and what he or she does. Consider adding vocabulary to your discussion, such as *doctor, healthy, examine, medicine*. Then have the student tell you what he or she knows about vets.
- Say: Talk with a partner about what you know about taking a pet to a vet. On a sticky note, write what you both know about going to the vet. When you are done, add the sticky note information to chart paper.
- Pick five pairs of students, and encourage one student from each pair to share what they wrote. Recognize when students use previously taught key vocabulary.

DURING THE READING

Preview the Book
- Read the title of the book on the cover, and point to the picture. Turn to page 2 and read the two sentences, pointing to each word as you read. Also point out the caption, and read that word as well. Have students follow along in their books.
- Say: Do you know what the book will be about based on the title and the first page that I read? How do you know what it will be about?
- As needed, point out words that have short vowel sounds: *vet, is, doctor, help, pets*.

Read the Book
- Read the book to students as they follow along. Point out words that contain the sound-spellings taught. Tell students what types of animals go to vets if they don't know them: *cats, rabbits, dogs, kittens, puppies*.
- Have students silently read the book. Ask a few students to echo read the book to you, and help them sound out new words. When observing students, focus on the new words: *pet, rabbit, vet, sick, glass, cast*.
- **Social Studies Connections:** Say: Vets care for pets that are sick or hurt. But vets also give healthy pets checkups so that they can stay healthy. Vets know what to do when an animal is sick. That's why you take your pet to the vet when it is not feeling well.

AFTER THE READING

Check Comprehension
To check students' understanding of the book, ask the following:
- ✓What is happening to the rabbit on page 4? Why do you think the rabbit is getting a shot? How will the shot help the rabbit? (The vet is giving the rabbit a shot. The rabbit is getting a shot because it is sick. The shot will make it well.)
- ✓What is happening to the cat on page 5? How will the cast help the cat? (The vet is putting a cast on the cat's leg. The cast will help the cat's leg heal.)
- ✓Look at the picture on page 6. How does the picture help you understand what you read? How does the text help you understand the picture? (Answers may include: The picture of the dog getting its paw wrapped in a bandage helps me understand that there is something wrong with the dog's paw. The text helps me understand that the dog had glass in its paw.)

Reread to Develop Fluency
- Say: Today you will read the book to each other to practice reading with fluency. This means that you read the book as the author meant for it to be read aloud.
- Model reading fluently by reading the book aloud to students. Focus on pausing between sentences.
- Have partners reread the book to each other. Suggest that they pause when they come to the end of a sentence before starting the next one. Students may struggle with decoding, comprehension, or vocabulary. For students who are struggling with comprehension, say: I noticed that you seem unsure how to read this sentence. What are some clues we can use to help us understand what we read? Now that we understand the sentence a little better, let's try reading it again.
- Send home a copy of *At the Vet* for students to read to family members. Consider assessing a few students on fluency.

Connect to Written Language
- ↻Review: Write the words *bugs, ducks,* and *sun* on the board. As a class, read the words together as you point to the letters. Have student volunteers replace the vowel in each word with an *o*, and read the new words together.

- ✓Dictate the following words for students to spell: *vet, big, spot, cast, stand, keeps,* and *your*. When finished, write the words on the board. Have students self-correct their papers.

- ✓Have students draw a picture of a pet at the vet. Ask them to write or dictate 2–3 sentences, telling how the vet is helping the pet. You may want to use the following sentence stem: *A _____ is at the vet.*

At a Fire

SKILLS

PHONICS SKILL INTRODUCED
- Final *e* (*a_e, i_e, o_e, u_e*)
- *r*-blends

SIGHT WORDS
- *from, he, look, no, out, their, up, uses, with*

VOCABULARY WORDS—
Social Studies Words
- *engine, firefighters, heroes, ladder, smoke, water*

CURRICULUM LINK—
Social Studies Focus
- Everyday Heroes

At a Fire

BEFORE THE READING

Develop Phonemic Awareness and Phonics
Rhyme
- Say: Today we are going to be listening for sounds that rhyme. A rhyme is two words that have the same ending sounds.
- Write the words *save* and *brave* on the board. Model blending the sounds of the words as you point to each sound-spelling: /s/ /ā/ /v/, save; /br/ /ā/ /v/, brave.
- Write *fine* and *line* on the board. Say these sounds while pointing to the sound-spellings, and have students echo you: /f/ /ī/ /n/, fine; /l/ /ī/ /n/, line.
- Write *hole* and *pole* on the board. Have students try blending the words out loud but independently. Walk around to support students. If a student is struggling to rhyme, model saying just the rhyming sound and then inserting the onset.

Introduce Phonics Skills
Final *e* (*a_e, i_e, o_e, u_e*) and *r*-blends
- Say: We just practiced blending some words with the final *e*. Now we are going to read some words with these sound-spellings.
- Write the word *same* on the board, and underline the *a*. Say: When you see the letters *a_e*, these represent the spelling for the /ā/ sound. Model reading the word while pointing to the letters: /s/ /ā/ /m/. Ask students to name other words that have the long *a, i, o,* or *u* sounds, spelled *a_e, i_e, o_e, u_e*. List these words on the board, and have students circle the final *e* spelling in each word.
- Write the words *fame, time,* and *lime* on the board. Have students read the words as a class. Say: Slowly sound out each letter. Which words rhyme?
- Have students try reading the words *broke, joke,* and *yoke* independently, following the routine above. Walk around to support students. Students who are struggling may need extra modeling and practice, such as: Let's look at the words *time* and *lime*. When you see the letters *i_e*, we use the /ī/ sound. Let's just say the last sounds, /ī/ /m/. Let's slowly say the sounds of the words together.
- Repeat the steps with *r*-blends, using these exemplars:
  1) gr, /gr/: 2) grab; 3) grove, grip, grin; 4) grate, grit
  1) br, /br/: 2) brave; 3) brim; 4) brag, bride
  1) cr, /cr/: 2) crib; 3) crate, crime; 4) crane, crop
  1) tr, /tr/: 2) trap; 3) tram; 4) trip, trim

Introduce Sight Words
- Say: You are going to see some words today that you may not know, so you will need to keep them in your memory.
- Write the words *from* and *he* on the board. Read them to students as you point to each letter.
- Write the words *look, no, out,* and *their* on the board. Read the words, and have students echo read each word.
- Write the words *up, uses,* and *with* on the board. Ask a volunteer to read them aloud, and have the rest of the class follow suit. Place the words on a sight-word bulletin board.
- The book also contains social studies words. Follow the steps above with these words, but this time provide a simple definition for words that may cause confusion: *engine, firefighters, heroes, ladder, smoke,* and *water.* For example: A hero is someone who thinks of other people before thinking of him- or herself. Show students the pictures of the firefighters from the book, and explain how they work to help other people.

Build Oral Language
- Say: Today we will be reading a book about firefighters. I like to look at the cover before I read to see if it will tell me what the book will be about.

- Select a student and discuss a time you saw a firefighter. Ask what that person was wearing and whether he or she had any tools. Consider adding vocabulary to your discussion, such as *help, save, coat, race, drive, blaze, smoke, ladder,* or *hose.* Then have the students tell you what they know about fire engines and firefighters. List their answers on a KWL chart.
- Say: What do you want to know about firefighters and about heroes?
- List their questions in the W column of the KWL chart. Recognize when students use previously taught key vocabulary.

DURING THE READING

Preview the Book
- Read the title of the book on the cover, and point to the picture. Turn to pages 2 and 3, and point to each word as you read the sentences. Have students follow along.
- Say: Do you know what the book will be about based on the title and the first page that I read? What do you think the men are doing?
- As needed, point out the words that have *r*-blends or the final *e* sound: *brave, fire, flames, home, save.*

Read the Book
- Read the book to students as they follow along. Point out words that contain the sound-spellings taught. Tell students the names of the words in the pictures if they don't know them: *firefighters, coat, race, fire engine, drive, smell, ladder, heroes.*
- Have students silently read the book. Ask a few students to echo read the book with you, and help students sound out new words. When observing students, focus on the new words: *blaze, brave, flames, race, save, drive, fire, hose, pole, smoke, use.*
- **Social Studies Connections:** Say: Firefighters work together in teams to fight fires. Someone on the team drives the fire engine, someone else operates the hoses, and some firefighters search the building to save people inside. Firefighters are everyday heroes.

AFTER THE READING

Check Comprehension
To check students' understanding of the book, ask the following:
- ✓Look at the pictures on pages 2 and 3. What is happening? (The firefighters have to put out the fire.) What makes firefighters brave? (Answers may include: They are brave because they will put out a dangerous fire.)
- ✓Put your finger on the word on page 4 that shows how firefighters move quickly. (Students should be pointing to the word *race.*) The firefighters slide down a pole to get downstairs quickly. What else helps them move quickly? (Answers may include: They use a fire engine.)
- ✓Look at the text on page 6. How does the picture help you understand how to use a ladder? (Answers may include: The picture shows the firefighter using the ladder to get to the windows and fire.)

Reread to Develop Fluency
- Say: Today you will read the book to each other to practice reading with fluency. This means that you read the book as the author meant for it to be read aloud.
- Model reading fluently by reading the book aloud to students. Focus on pausing between sentences.
- Have partners reread the book to each other at least two times. Suggest that they alternate reading one page at a time. Students may struggle with decoding, comprehension, or vocabulary. For students who are struggling with vocabulary, say: I noticed that you're not quite sure about the meanings of some of the words in this sentence. Let's look up the definitions of the words you don't know.
- Send home a copy of *At a Fire* for students to read to family members. Consider assessing a few students on fluency.

Connect to Written Language
↻Review: Write the words *stop* and *leg* on the board. As a class, read the words together as you point to the letters. Then have students rewrite the words by replacing the vowel sounds in each word (/o/ with /e/ and vice versa), and read the new words together.

✓Dictate the following words for students to spell: *drive, hide, broke, grab, take, out,* and *look.* When finished, write the words on the board. Have students self-correct their papers.

✓Say: Some words are made up of two smaller words. These are called compound words. The word *firefighter* is a compound word. It includes *fire* and *fighter.* What other compound words can you name? Write a sentence with a compound word.

Amazing Magnets

SKILLS

PHONICS SKILL INTRODUCED
- Final *e* (*i_e, o_e, u_e*)
- *l*-blends

SIGHT WORDS
- *and, are, be, made, or, they, what*

VOCABULARY WORDS–
Science Words
- *iron, magnet, metal*

CURRICULUM LINK–
Science Focus
- Magnets

Amazing Magnets

BEFORE THE READING

Develop Phonemic Awareness and Phonics
Oral Substitution
- Say: Today we are going to be substituting sounds in words. When you substitute a sound, it means you can replace a sound in a word to make new words.
- Write the words *rope* and *ride* on the board. Substitute the first sound in each word with /h/. Model blending the sounds of the words as you point to each sound-spelling: /r/ /ō/ /p/, rope; /h/ /ō/ /p/, hope; /r/ /ī/ /d/, ride; /h/ /ī/ /d/, hide.
- Write *bike* and *Mike* on the board. Say these sounds while pointing to the sound-spellings. Point out the long /ī/ sound, and have students echo you: /b/ /ī/ /k/, bike; /m/ /ī/ /k/, Mike.
- Write *flip* and *glide* on the board. Out loud but independently, have students try substituting the blend in each word with the /s/ sound. Walk around to support students. If a student is struggling to blend the discrete sounds, model extending the sounds in the word. Have students slow down their speech while trying it independently.

Introduce Phonics Skills
Final *e* (*i_e, o_e, u_e*) and *l*-blends
- Say: We just practiced substituting sounds in words to make new words. Some of these words had long vowel sounds, like /ī/, /ō/, and /ū/. When a word ends in *e*, the vowel sound is usually long and the *e* is silent. Now we are going to read some words with these sound-spellings.
- Write the words *ride, stone,* and *cute* on the board, and underline the *i, o,* and *u*. Say: When you see the letters *i, o,* and *u* with a final *e*, they make the long vowel sound, like /ī/ in *kite*, /ō/ in *home*, and /ū/ in *mute*. Model reading the words, one sound at a time while pointing to the letters: /k/ /ī/ /t/, kite; /h/ /ō/ /m/, home; and /m/ /ū/ /t/, mute.
- Write the words *note, ride,* and *fume* on the board. Have students read the words as a class. Say: Slowly sound out each letter, and notice that the final *e* is silent.
- Have students try reading the words *size, cube,* and *stove* independently, following the routine above. Walk around to support students. Students who are struggling may need extra modeling and practice, such as: Let's look at the word *stove*. When we blend /s/ and /t/ together, they make the /st/ sound. Let's say the sounds of this word together as I point to each letter.
- Repeat the steps with *l*-blends, using these exemplars:
  1) cl, /kl/: 2) clip; 3) clap, clan; 4) clot, class
  1) gl, /gl/: 2) glass; 3) glide, gloss, glad; 4) glade
  1) bl, /bl/: 2) black; 3) blame, blaze; 4) blade, blast
  1) pl, /pl/: 2) plate; 3) plan, plot; 4) plane

Introduce Sight Words
- Say: You are going to see some words today that you may not know, so you will need to keep them in your memory.
- Write the words *and* and *are* on the board. Read each word to students.
- Write the words *be* and *made* on the board. Read the words, and have students echo read them.
- Write the words *or, they,* and *what* on the board. Ask a volunteer to read them aloud, and have the rest of the class follow suit. Place the words on a sight-word bulletin board.
- The book also contains science words. Follow the steps above with these words, but this time provide a simple definition for words that may cause confusion: *iron, magnet,* and *metal*. For example: A metal is a type of material that is used to make bridges, cars, and other objects. Iron is a kind of metal. It is very hard and strong. Show students pictures of metal from the book.

Build Oral Language

- Say: Today we will be reading a book about magnets. When I look at the cover of a book, the picture gives me clues about what the book is about.
- Select a student and discuss what is happening in the picture. Explain how the metal items are attracted to the big magnet. Consider adding vocabulary to your discussion, such as *pick*, *magnets*, and *attract*.
- Say: With a partner, predict what a magnet can do. Write or draw your ideas on a sticky note, and post it on a sheet of chart paper.
- Pick five pairs of students, and encourage one student from each pair to explain their ideas. Recognize when students use previously taught key vocabulary.

DURING THE READING

Preview the Book

- Read the title of the book on the cover, and point to the picture. Turn to page 2 and read the two sentences, pointing to each word as you read. Have students follow along in their books.
- Say: I'm wondering about the picture on page 2 of this book. The nails are sticking to the magnet. From the words on the first page, I think this book is going to tell me more about magnets. What do you think it will be about?
- As needed, point out the words that have the final *e* or *l*-blends: *clips*.

Read the Book

- Read the book to students as they follow along. Help students read the captions. Point out words that contain the sound-spellings taught: *clip, nail, big, small, rope, plastic, wood, cloth*.
- Have students silently read the book. Ask a few students to whisper read the book to you, and help them sound out new words. When observing students, focus on the new words: *made, note, rope, size, slide, slip, use, clip, glass*.
- **Science Connections:** Say: Magnets can pull or attract many kinds of metals. If metal is covered in cloth or glass, a magnet can still attract it or pick it up. Look at the magnets on page 4. The magnets are inside the toys. That is how they stick to the metal on the refrigerator door.

AFTER THE READING

Check Comprehension

To check students' understanding of the book, ask the following:
- ✓ Look at the magnets on page 4. How are these magnets being used? (Answers may include: Magnets are holding notes and pictures to the door.)
- ✓ Point to the magnet on page 5. Why do you think large magnets are needed? (Answers may include: A larger magnet is needed to pick up heavy pieces of metal.)
- ✓ The picture on page 8 shows a few different objects. The magnet can pick up the objects that are made of metal. How do you know if an object is made of metal? (Answers may include: Metal objects are usually silver; they are also hard. The other objects are different colors and are made of softer materials.)

Reread to Develop Fluency

- Say: Today you will read the book to each other to practice reading with fluency. This means that you read the book as the author meant for it to be read aloud.
- Model reading fluently by reading the book aloud to students. Focus on pausing between sentences and raising your voice at the end of a question.
- Have partners reread the book to each other. Tell them to raise their voices at the end of a question. Students may struggle with decoding, comprehension, or vocabulary. For students who are struggling with decoding, say: I see that you're working on reading this word. Read it with me, and let's slowly sound out the letters. We did it! Now you try it on your own.
- Send home a copy of *Amazing Magnets* for students to read to family members. Consider assessing a few students on fluency.

Connect to Written Language

↻ **Review:** Write the words *blaze*, *drive*, and *fire* on the board. As a class, read the words together as you point to the letters. Then have students rewrite the words by replacing the first sound or blend in each word with *h*, and read the new words together.

✓ Dictate the following words for students to spell: *clip, made, note, rope, size, they*, and *what*. When finished, write the words on the board. Have students self-correct their papers.

✓ Say: Some words have more than one meaning. We can tell what they mean by thinking about the words around them, and by using clues from the picture to help. Write on the board: *Kim slides on the metal slide*. Let's read this sentence together. In this sentence, the word *slide* describes how Kim moved, but it also describes something to play on at the park. The word *iron* can also mean two things. Write on the board: *Pam has an iron, and she has a new iron table*. Let's read these sentences. This means Pam has an appliance (an iron), and she has a table made of iron (a kind of metal). Ask: Can you think of another word that has more than one meaning? Encourage students to write or dictate a sentence with a word that has two meanings.

The U.S. Flag

SKILLS

PHONICS SKILL INTRODUCED
- Final *e* (*a_e, e_e, i_e, o_e*)
- Digraph *wh*

SIGHT WORDS
- *also, blue, each, even, first, look, one, our, that, there, this, up*

VOCABULARY WORDS–
Social Studies Words
- *flagpole, free, July 4*

CURRICULUM LINK–
Social Studies Focus
- Symbols of America

The U.S. Flag

BEFORE THE READING

Develop Phonemic Awareness and Phonics
Rhyme
- Say: Today we are going to rhyme words. A rhyme is two words that have the same ending sound.
- Write the words *game, same, these,* and *cheese* on the board. Model rhyming the sounds of the words as you point to each sound-spelling: /g/ /ā/ /m/, game; /s/ /ā/ /m/, same; /th/ /ē/ /z/, these; /ch/ /ē/ /z/, cheese.
- Write *white* and *hope* on the board. Say these sounds while pointing to the sound-spellings, and have students echo you: /w/ /ī/ /t/, white; /h/ /ō/ /p/, hope. Give rhyming words for each. After each rhyme set, ask students to say "yes" if the words rhyme.
- Write *five* and *pole* on the board. Have students say rhyming words out loud but independently. Walk around to support students. If a student is struggling to find rhyming words, say: Say *five*. Change /f/ to /d/. What word do you get? That's right, *dive*. Now say *pole*. Change /p/ to /h/. What do you get? Correct, *hole*.

Introduce Phonics Skills
Final *e* (*a_e, e_e, i_e, o_e*) and Digraph *wh*
- Say: We just practiced blending some words with the final *e*. Now we are going to read some words with these sound-spellings.
- Write the word *space* on the board, and underline the *a_e*. Say: The letters *a_e* stand for the /ā/ sound. Model reading the word, one sound at a time, while pointing to the letters: /sp/ /ā/ /s/. Ask students to name other words that have the long *a, e, i,* or *o* sounds, spelled *a_e, e_e, i_e, o_e*. List these words on the board, and have students circle the final *e* spelling in each word.
- Write the words *states, stripes,* and *homes* on the board. Have students read the words as a class. Say: Slowly sound out each letter.
- Have students try reading the words *wave, ride,* and *bone* independently, following the routine above. Walk around to support students. Students who are struggling may need extra modeling, practice, and feedback.
- Repeat the steps with digraph *wh*, using these exemplars:
1) wh, /w/: 2) whale; 3) while; 4) whiff

Introduce Sight Words
- Say: You are going to see some words today that you may not know, so you will need to keep them in your memory.
- Write *blue, one,* and *there* on the board. Read them to students as you point to each letter.
- Write *also, each, look,* and *this* on the board. Read the words, and have students echo read each word.
- Write *even, first,* and *our* on the board. Ask a volunteer to read them aloud, and have the rest of the class follow suit. Place the words on a sight-word bulletin board.
- The book also contains social studies words. Follow the steps above with these words, but this time provide a simple definition for words that may cause confusion: *flagpole, free,* and *July 4*. For example: A flagpole is a pole from which a flag flies. Show students the picture of the flagpole from the book.

Build Oral Language
- Say: Today we will be reading a book about the U.S. flag. Before I read, I often think about the topic and try to recall what I already know about it.
- Select a student and discuss the U.S. flag. Have the student explain what it looks like. Consider adding vocabulary to your discussion, such as *flagpole, free,* and *July 4*.

- Say: With a partner, discuss the U.S. flag. Describe how it looks and what it stands for.
- Pick five pairs of students, and encourage one student from each pair to share in the discussion. Recognize when students use previously taught key vocabulary.

DURING THE READING

Preview the Book
- Read the title of the book on the cover, and point to the picture. Turn to pages 2 and 3 and read the sentences, pointing to each word as you read. Also point out the caption and read those words as well. Have students follow along in their books.
- Say: Do you know what the book will be about based on the title and the first pages that I read? How do you know what it will be about?
- As needed, point out the words that have the /ā/ and /ī/ sounds: *states, united,* and *white*.

Read the Book
- Read the book to students as they follow along. Point out words that contain the sound-spellings taught.
- Have students silently read the book. Ask a few students to whisper read the book to you, and help them sound out new words. When observing students, focus on the new words: *flagpole, homes, space, states, stripes, wave, white*.
- **Social Studies Connections:** Say: The flag is a symbol of our country. It reminds us of what is important about the United States. It is the land of the free. Some other symbols of our country are the bald eagle and the Statue of Liberty.

AFTER THE READING

Check Comprehension
To check students' understanding of the book, ask the following:
- ✓ Look at page 3. Why do you think the American flag is so important. (Answers may include: It is a symbol for our country.)
- ✓ Look at page 4. How many stars does our flag have? (Our flag has 50 stars.) What do the stars on our flag stand for? (Each star stands for one of the 50 states.) Why do you think we still represent the first 13 states? (Answers may include: So we understand how the United States of America got its start.)
- ✓ Look at page 5. How does the picture help you understand the text? How does the text help you understand the picture? (Answers may include: The picture shows a U.S. flag from long ago. The text helps us understand that this was a flag for the first 13 states.)

Reread to Develop Fluency
- Say: Today you will read the book to each other to practice reading with fluency. This means that you read the book as the author meant for it to be read aloud.
- Model reading fluently by reading the book aloud to students. Focus on pausing briefly when a comma appears in a sentence.
- Have partners reread the book to each other. Suggest that they pause briefly when they see a comma in a sentence. Students may struggle with decoding, comprehension, or vocabulary. For students who are struggling with comprehension, say: I noticed that you seem unsure how to read this sentence. What are some clues we can use to help us understand what we read? Now that we understand the sentence a little better, let's try reading it again with proper expression.
- Send home a copy of *The U.S. Flag* for students to read to family members. Consider assessing a few students on fluency.

Connect to Written Language
↻ Review: Write the words *time, woke,* and *cube* on the board. As a class, read the words together as you point to the letters. Then have students replace the vowel in the first two words with *a,* and read the new words together.

✓ Dictate the following words for students to spell: *eve, homes, were, stripes, each,* and *white*. When finished, write the words on the board. Have students self-correct their papers.

✓ Have students make U.S. flags using a variety of materials, such as markers, paint, colored paper, or fabric. Ask each student to write or dictate 2–3 sentences describing the flag and what it means to him or her. You may suggest that students use the following sentence stem: *This is the U.S. flag. To me, it means _____.* Display the children's flags around the school or classroom.

Homes

SKILLS

PHONICS SKILL INTRODUCED
- Final *e* (*a_e, e_e, i_e, o_e, u_e*)
- Digraph *th*

SIGHT WORDS
- *her, his, live, many, play, small, where*

VOCABULARY WORDS–
Social Studies Words
- *cabs, country, mules*

CURRICULUM LINK–
Social Studies Focus
- Communities

Homes

BEFORE THE READING

Develop Phonemic Awareness and Phonics
Oral Segmentation
- Say: Today we are going to be listening to sounds and segmenting them to make words. Segmenting means pulling words apart by their sounds.
- Write the words *drive* and *skate* on the board. Model segmenting the sounds of the words as you point to each sound-spelling: /dr/ /ī/ /v/, drive; /sk/ /ā/ /t/, skate.
- Write *home* and *ride* on the board. Say these sounds while pointing to the sound-spellings, and have students echo you: /h/ /ō/ /m/, home; /r/ /ī/ /d/, ride.
- Write *late* and *Pete* on the board. Have students try segmenting the words out loud but independently. Walk around to support students. If a student is struggling to segment the discrete sounds, model clapping once for each sound while saying it aloud, and have the student follow suit.

Introduce Phonics Skills
Final *e* (*a_e, e_e, i_e, o_e, u_e*) and Digraph *th*
- Say: We just practiced segmenting some words with the final *e*. Now we are going to read some words with these sound-spellings.
- Write the word *late* on the board, and underline the *a_e*. Say: The letters *a_e* stand for the /ā/ sound. Model reading the word, one sound at a time, while pointing to the letters: /l/ /ā/ /t/. Ask students to name other words that have the long *a, e, i, o,* or *u* sounds, spelled *a_e, e_e, i_e, o_e, u_e*. List these words on the board, and have students circle the final *e* spelling in each word.
- Write the words *rake, gene, like, close,* and *mule* on the board. Have students read the words as a class. Say: Slowly sound out each letter.
- Have students try reading the words *bake, Pete, miles,* and *home* independently, following the routine above. Walk around to support students. Students who are struggling may need extra modeling and practice, such as: Let's look at the words *bake* and *cake*. Remember that *a_e* makes the /ā/ sound. Let's just say the last sounds, /ā/ /k/. Now replace the first sound with some different letters. Do the words still rhyme? Yes! Let's slowly say the sounds of more words together as I point to each letter. Now you do it.
- Repeat the steps with digraph *th*, using these exemplars. Tell students that the two consonants *t* and *h* together make one new sound, /th/:
  1) th, /th/: 2) that, then; 3) this; 4) those

Introduce Sight Words
- Say: You are going to see some words today that you may not know, so you will need to keep them in your memory.
- Write the words *her, his,* and *live* on the board. Read them to students as you point to each letter.
- Write the words *many* and *where* on the board. Read the words, and have students echo read each word.
- Write the words *play* and *small* on the board. Ask a volunteer to read them aloud, and have the class follow suit. Place the words on a sight-word bulletin board.
- The book also contains social studies words. Follow the steps above with these words, but this time provide a simple definition for words that may cause confusion: *cabs, country,* and *mules*. For example: A cab is a car with a driver whom you pay to take you where you want to go. Show students the picture of the cab from the book.

Build Oral Language
- Say: Today we will be reading a book about communities. Before I read, I often think about the topic and try to recall what I already know about it.

- Select a student, and discuss the type of community in which you live. Describe your neighborhood and how big it is. Consider adding vocabulary to your discussion, such as *city, community, country, noise, quiet, skyscrapers, town*. Then have the student tell you about the neighborhood in which he or she lives.
- Say: With a partner, discuss your neighborhood or community. Describe how it looks, sounds, and smells.
- Pick five pairs of students, and encourage one student from each pair to share in the discussion. Recognize when students use previously taught key vocabulary.

DURING THE READING

Preview the Book
- Read the title of the book on the cover, and point to the picture. Turn to page 2 and read the sentences, pointing to each word as you read. Have students follow along in their books.
- Say: Do you know what the book will be about based on the title and the first page that I read? How do you know what it will be about?
- As needed, point out the words that have the /ā/, /ē/, /and /th/ sounds: *place, Pete, the*.

Read the Book
- Read the book to students as they follow along. Point out words that contain the sound-spellings taught.
- Have students silently read the book. Ask a few students to whisper read the book to you, and help them sound out new words. When observing students, focus on the new words: *bake, bones, cake, homes, ice, Kate, lakes, likes, makes, mules, Pete, place, rides, Rose, sale, skates, take, these*.
- **Social Studies Connections:** Say: A community is the place where people live, work, and go to school. Some people live in big cities. Some live in small towns, and others live in the country surrounded by farms and fields full of crops.

AFTER THE READING

Check Comprehension
To check students' understanding of the book, ask the following:
✓Look at pages 5 and 6. In what type of community does Kate live? Describe Kate's community. (Answers may include: Kate lives in a town. It has many buildings and homes. It has an ice rink. Kate has a backyard.)
✓How is Pete's community different from where Rose lives? (Answers may include: Pete lives in a big city. It is very noisy. It has lots of tall buildings, and many people live there. Rose lives on a farm in the country. It is very quiet. Not many people live in the country, but there are many animals on Rose's family's farm.)
✓In which community would you like to live? Why? Use the pictures and text from the book in your response. (Answers will vary.)

Reread to Develop Fluency
- Say: Today you will read the book to each other to practice reading with fluency. This means that you read the book as the author meant for it to be read aloud.
- Model reading fluently by reading the book aloud to students. Focus on reading at a consistent pace.
- Have partners reread the book to each other. Suggest that they read at a consistent pace. Students may struggle with decoding, comprehension, or vocabulary. For students who are struggling with comprehension, say: I noticed that you seem unsure how to read this sentence. What are some clues we can use to help us understand what we read? Now that we understand the sentence a little better, let's try reading it again with proper expression.
- Send home a copy of *Homes* for students to read to family members. Consider assessing a few students on fluency.

Connect to Written Language
↻Review: Write the words *stripe, white,* and *states* on the board. As a class, read the words together as you point to the letters. Then replace the *r*-blend in *stripe* with *w* and the *s*-blend in *states* with *d*. Have students write the words, and then read the new words together.

✓Dictate the following words for students to spell: *bone, homes, late, take, these, play,* and *small*. When finished, write the words on the board. Have students self-correct their papers.

✓Have students draw pictures of the communities in which they live. Ask each student to write or dictate 2–3 sentences describing what makes his or her community special. You may suggest that students use the following sentence stem: *My community is _____.* You may wish to make students' pictures into a bulletin board advertising your community.

Safe at Play

SKILLS

PHONICS SKILL INTRODUCED
- Long *a* (*ai*, *ay*)
- Digraph *sh*

SIGHT WORDS
- *all, far, how, may, or, walk, way*

VOCABULARY WORDS—
Social Studies Words
- *rules, stay safe, take your turn*

CURRICULUM LINK—
Social Studies Focus
- Need for Rules

Safe at Play

BEFORE THE READING

Develop Phonemic Awareness and Phonics
Oral Segmentation
- Say: Today we are going to be segmenting words. Segmenting means pulling words apart by their sounds.
- Write the words *may* and *wait* on the board. Model segmenting the sounds of the words as you point to each sound-spelling: /m/ /ā/, may; /w/ /ā/ /t/, wait.
- Write *play* and *ship* on the board. Say these sounds while pointing to the sound-spellings, and have students echo you: /pl/ /ā/, play; /sh/ /i/ /p/, ship.
- Write *stay* and *fish* on the board. Have students try segmenting the words out loud but independently. Walk around to support students. If a student is struggling with the blends, model saying just the blending sound and ask the student to watch what your mouth is doing. Have the student follow suit as he or she slowly says the sounds.

Introduce Phonics Skills
Long *a* (*ai*, *ay*) and Digraph *sh*
- Say: We just practiced segmenting some words with the /ā/ sound. Now we are going to read some words with this sound-spelling.
- Write the words *wait* and *may* on the board, and underline the *ai* and the *ay*. Say: The *ai* is one spelling for the /ā/ sound. Model reading the word, one sound at a time, while pointing to the letters: /w/ /ā/ /t/. Say: The *ay* is another spelling for the /ā/ sound. Model reading the word, one sound at a time, while pointing to the letters: /m/ /ā/.
- Write the words *pail* and *play* on the board. Have students read the words as a class. Say: Slowly sound out each letter or blend.
- Have students try reading the words *stay* and *fray* independently, following the routine above. Walk around to support students. Students who are struggling may need extra modeling and practice, such as: Let's look at the word *stay*. Remember that the together letters *st* make one sound. What sound is that? Right, the /st/ sound. Let's slowly say the sounds of this word together as I point to the letters.
- Repeat the steps with the digraph *sh*, using these exemplars. Tell students that the two consonants *s* and *h* together make one new sound, /sh/:
  1) sh, /sh/: 2) shell, ship; 3) shop, shut; 4) fish, splash

Introduce Sight Words
- Say: You are going to see some words today that you may not know, so you will need to keep them in your memory.
- Write *all* and *far* on the board. Read them to students as you point to each letter.
- Write *how, may,* and *or* on the board. Read the words, and have students echo read each word.
- Write *walk* and *way* on the board. Ask a volunteer to read them aloud, and have the rest of the class follow suit. Place the words on a sight-word bulletin board.
- The book also contains social studies words. Follow the steps above with these words, but this time provide a simple definition for words that may cause confusion: *beach, follow, look out, play, playground, pool, rules, safe, stay safe, swim,* and *take your turn.* For example: *Look* means "to try to see something," and *look out* means "to be careful." Show students the picture on page 5, and ask why the girl needs to be careful.

Build Oral Language
- Say: Today we will be reading a book about safety rules. Before I read, I like to think about what I already know about the topic to see if it matches the story.
- Select a student and discuss some safety rules for the class. Explain why these rules are important to keep us safe while we're having fun. Consider adding vocabulary to

your discussion, such as *swim, safe, safely, fall, careful, fair, cooperate, skate,* or *share.* Then have the student tell you about other rules they follow at school or at home.

- Say: With a partner, discuss what it looks like to follow a rule and what might happen if someone is not being safe. Why is it important to have rules?
- Pick five pairs of students, and encourage one student from each pair to share in the discussion. Recognize when students use previously taught key vocabulary.

DURING THE READING

Preview the Book

- Read the title of the book on the cover, and point to the picture. Turn to page 2 and read the sentences, pointing to each word as you read. Have students follow along.
- Say: I wonder what this book will be about? The title and the picture make me think it will be about having fun and also about being safe. Do you think we can have fun and still be safe?
- As needed, point out the words that have the /sh/ sound or the /ā/ sound spelled *ai* or *ay: play, may, splash.*

Read the Book

- Read the book to students as they follow along. Point out words that contain the sound-spellings taught. Tell students the names of the activities if they don't know them: swimming in a pool, spinning on a ride, digging and running on the beach, skating, and riding a bike.
- Have students silently read the book. Ask a few students to partner read the book to each other, and help students sound out new words. When observing students, focus on the new words: *fish, may, pail, play, shells, splash, stay, wait, way.*
- **Social Studies Connections:** Say: Everyone is responsible for following rules. Rules help us stay safe. Rules also help us cooperate so we can play and work together in a way that is fair. Why is it important to obey the rules?

AFTER THE READING

Check Comprehension

To check students' understanding of the book, ask the following:

✓Look at the children on page 3. What words in the text help you know the rules? (Answers may include: The words *wait* and *take your turn* tell how children should enter the pool.)

✓Look at the picture on page 5. What could happen if the girl gets in the way? (Answers may include: The girl might fall or get hurt.)

✓The text on page 8 says the kids are safe. Point to something in the picture that is safe. (The kids are wearing helmets or floaties.) What do you think are the rules for these activities? (Answers may include: Use safety equipment.)

Reread to Develop Fluency

- Say: Today you will read the book to each other to practice reading with fluency. This means that you read the book as the author meant for it to be read aloud.
- Model reading fluently by reading the book aloud to students. Focus on adding emphasis or excitement to sentences that end with an exclamation point.
- Have partners reread the book to each other. Suggest that they pause when they come to the end of a sentence before starting the next one. Students may struggle with decoding, comprehension, or vocabulary. For students who are struggling with comprehension, say: I noticed that you seem unsure how to read this sentence. What are some clues we can use to help us understand what we read? Now that we understand the sentence a little better, let's try reading it again with proper expression.
- Send home a copy of *Safe at Play* for students to read to family members. Consider assessing a few students on fluency.

Connect to Written Language

↻Review: Write the words *bake, bones,* and *ice* on the board. As a class, read the words together as you point to the letters. Then have student volunteers replace the long vowels with new vowels and say the new words together. Ask students to give a thumbs-down when the new words are nonsense words.

✓Dictate the following words for students to spell: *may, play, shells, wish, day, home, all,* and *far.* When finished, write the words on the board. Have students self-correct their papers.

✓Say: Sometimes one word is actually two words put together, like the word *playground.* Write on the board: *foot* and *ball.* Let's read these two words together. Can you guess the compound word? Write on the board: *Jake plays football in the backyard.* Let's read this sentence. Which words are the compound words? How do compound words help you visualize as you read? Now write a sentence using the compound word.

Holidays

SKILLS

PHONICS SKILL INTRODUCED
- Long *a* (*ai, ay*)
- Digraph *ch*

SIGHT WORDS
- *about, clean, eat, good, thank, think, too, what*

VOCABULARY WORDS–
Social Studies Words
- *celebrate, holiday, thankful, Thanksgiving*

CURRICULUM LINK–
Social Studies Focus
- Holidays

Holidays

BEFORE THE READING

Develop Phonemic Awareness and Phonics
Oral Segmentation
- Say: Today we are going to be listening to sounds and segmenting them to make words. Segmenting means pulling words apart by their sounds.
- Write the words *day* and *such* on the board. Model segmenting the sounds of the words as you point to each sound-spelling: /d/ /ā/, day; /s/ /u/ /ch/, such.
- Write *rain* and *which* on the board. Say these words while pointing to the sound-spellings, and have students echo you: /r/ /ā/ /n/, rain; /w/ /i/ /ch/, which.
- Write *lay* and *Chuck* on the board. Have students try segmenting the words out loud but independently. Walk around to support students. If a student is struggling to segment the discrete sounds, model clapping once for each sound while saying it aloud, and have the student follow suit.

Introduce Phonics Skills
Long *a* (*ai, ay*) and Digraph *ch*
- Say: We just practiced segmenting some words with the long *a*. Now we are going to read some words with these sound-spellings.
- Write the word *paint* on the board, and underline the *ai*. Say: The letters *ai* make the /ā/ sound. Model reading the word, one sound at a time, while pointing to the letters: /p/ /ā/ /n/ /t/.
- Write the words *may, pay,* and *stain* on the board. Say: Notice that the /ā/ sound can also be spelled with *ay*. Have students read the words as a class. Say: Slowly sound out each letter.
- Have students try reading the words *drain, gray, pain,* and *stay* independently, following the routine above. Walk around to support students. Students who are struggling may need extra modeling and practice, such as: Let's look at the word *drain*. Remember that together the letters *dr* make one sound. What sound is that? Right, the /dr/ sound. Let's slowly say the sounds of this word together as I point to the letters. Now you try it.
- Repeat the steps with the digraph *ch*, using these exemplars. Tell students that the two consonants *c* and *h* together make one new sound, /ch/:
  1) ch, /ch/: 2) chat; 3) chest, chips; 4) chill, crunch

Introduce Sight Words
- Say: You are going to see some words today that you may not know, so you will need to keep them in your memory.
- Write the words *clean* and *thank* on the board. Read them to students as you point to each letter.
- Write the words *about, eat, too,* and *what* on the board. Read the words, and have students echo read each word.
- Write the words *good* and *think* on the board. Ask a volunteer to read them aloud, and have the class follow suit. Place the words on a sight-word bulletin board.
- The book also contains social studies words. Follow the steps above with these words, but this time provide a simple definition for words that may cause confusion: *celebrate, holiday, thankful,* and *Thanksgiving*. For example: Thanksgiving is a holiday in November when we spend time with family and think about all the things for which we are thankful. Show students the picture of the family celebrating Thanksgiving from the book.

Build Oral Language
- Say: Today we will be reading a book about holidays. Before I read, I often think about the topic and try to recall what I already know about it.
- Select a student and discuss your favorite holiday. Explain what you do on that day and why it's your favorite. Consider adding vocabulary to your discussion, such as

celebrate, family, feast, freedom, holiday, parade, and *Thanksgiving.* Then have the student tell you about his or her favorite holiday.

- Say: With a partner, discuss your favorite holiday. Describe what you do on that particular day and why it's your favorite.
- Pick five pairs of students, and encourage one student from each pair to share in the discussion. Recognize when students use previously taught key vocabulary.

DURING THE READING

Preview the Book
- Read the title of the book on the cover, and point to the picture. Turn to pages 2 and 3 and read the sentences, pointing to each word as you read. Have students follow along in their books.
- Say: Do you know what the book will be about based on the title and the first pages that I read? How do you know what it will be about?
- As needed, point out the words that have the /ā/ (*ai, ay*) and /ch/ sounds: *chicken, chips, day, holiday, may, watch, which.*

Read the Book
- Read the book to students as they follow along. Point out words that contain the sound-spellings taught.
- Have students silently read the book. Ask a few students to whisper read the book to you, and help them sound out new words. When observing students, focus on the new words: *chicken, chips, day, may, paint, say, which.*
- **Social Studies Connections:** Say: Some holidays help us remember people from long ago and the things that they did. Thanksgiving reminds us of the Pilgrims who moved to America from another land and the American Indians who helped them plant food. July 4 reminds us that long ago, our country was not free, but now it is.

AFTER THE READING

Check Comprehension
To check students' understanding of the book, ask the following:
✓Which three holidays did we read about? (the Fourth of July, Earth Day, and Thanksgiving)
✓Look at pages 5 and 6. What are some things people do to celebrate Earth Day? Why do you think these actions help our planet? (Answers may include: plant flowers and trees, pick up trash, paint, clean up outdoors. These activities help make sure that we are not polluting our planet. They also help beautify it.)
✓What is your favorite holiday? Why? Use the pictures and text in the book in your answer. (Answers will vary.)

Reread to Develop Fluency
- Say: Today you will read the book to each other to practice reading with fluency. This means that you read the book as the author meant for it to be read aloud.
- Model reading fluently by reading the book aloud to students. Model raising your voice at the end of a sentence to denote a question.
- Have partners reread the book to each other. Suggest that they raise their voices when they come to the end of a sentence that ends in a question mark. Students may struggle with decoding, comprehension, or vocabulary. For students who are struggling with comprehension, say: I noticed that you seem unsure how to read this sentence. What are some clues we can use to help us understand what we read? Now that we understand the sentence a little better, let's try reading it again with proper expression.
- Send home a copy of *Holidays* for students to read to family members. Consider assessing a few students on fluency.

Connect to Written Language

↻Review: Write the words *shells, stay,* and *splash* on the board. As a class, read the words together as you point to the letters. Then replace the *sh* in *shells* with *t* and the *sp* in *splash* with *f.* Encourage students to write the words, and then read the new words together.

✓Dictate the following words for students to spell: *paint, drain, may, play, which, eat,* and *good.* When finished, write the words on the board. Have students self-correct their papers.

✓Have students draw pictures of themselves celebrating their favorite holiday with their family members. Suggest that students add a caption to their pictures using the following sentence stem: *I like to _____ on _____.* Send the students' pictures home to share with their families.

How Plants Grow

SKILLS

PHONICS SKILL INTRODUCED
- Final *e* (*e_e*), Long *e* (*e, ea, ee*)
- Plurals

SIGHT WORDS
- *give, many, new, next, pretty, then*

VOCABULARY WORDS–
Science Words
- *bloom, fruits, grow, soil*

CURRICULUM LINK–
Science Focus
- Plant Life

How Plants Grow

BEFORE THE READING

Develop Phonemic Awareness and Phonics
Oral Segmentation
- Say: Today we are going to be segmenting words. Segmenting means pulling words apart by their sounds.
- Write the words *met* and *meet* on the board. Model segmenting the sounds of the words as you point to each sound-spelling: /m/ /e/ /t/, met; /m/ /ē/ /t/, meet.
- Write *set* and *seat* on the board. Say these sounds while pointing to the sound-spellings, and have students echo you: /s/ /e/ /t/, set; /s/ /ē/ /t/, seat.
- Write *weak, sheet,* and *feel* on the board. Have students try segmenting the words out loud but independently. Walk around to support students. If a student is struggling with the digraph *sh*, model saying just the /sh/ sound, and ask the student to watch what your mouth is doing. Have the student repeat the sounds slowly.

Introduce Phonics Skills
Final *e* (*e_e*), Long *e* (*e, ea, ee*), and Plurals
- Say: We just practiced segmenting some words with the /ē/ sound. Now we are going to read some words with this sound-spelling.
- Write the words *we, bean,* and *see* on the board, and underline the *e, ea,* and *ee*. Say: These are some of the spellings for the /ē/ sound. Model reading the words, one sound at a time, while pointing to the letters: /w/ /ē/, /b/ /ē/ /n/, and /s/ /ē/.
- Write the words *eat* and *seeds* on the board. Have students read the words as a class. Say: Slowly sound out each letter. Have students try reading the words *be* and *leaves* independently, following the routine above.
- Write the word *seed* on the board. Tell students that this means one seed. If there is more than one, we call it a plural and add an *–s* to the word: *seeds*. When a word ends in *s, ss, ch, sh,* or *x*, we add *–es*. Write the word *dress* on the board, and make it a plural: *dresses*. Model reading the words, one sound at a time, while pointing to the letters: seed, seeds; dress, dresses.
- Have students try reading the words *bean, beans, dish,* and *dishes* independently, following the routine above. Walk around to support students. Students who are struggling may need extra modeling and practice, such as: Let's look at the word *dishes*. Remember that the letters *sh* make one sound. What sound is that? Right, the /sh/ sound. Let's slowly say the sounds of this word together.
- Repeat the steps with the plurals, using these exemplars:
  1) s, /s/: 2) ship, ships; 3) trap, traps; pea, peas; 4) meet, meets
  1) es, /es/: 2) wash, washes; 3) peach, peaches; 4) box, boxes

Introduce Sight Words
- Say: You are going to see some words today that you may not know, so you will need to keep them in your memory.
- Write *give* and *many* on the board. Read them to students as you point to each letter.
- Write *new* and *next* on the board. Read the words, and have students echo read them.
- Write *pretty* and *then* on the board. Ask a volunteer to read them aloud and have the rest of the class follow suit. Place the words on a sight-word bulletin board.
- The book also contains science words. Follow the steps above with these words, but this time provide a simple definition for words that may cause confusion: *bloom, flowers, fruits, grow, leaves, plants, rain, seeds, soil, sun, vines, water*. For example: The word *bloom* describes how a flower opens when it is fully grown. Show students pictures of flowers from the book.

Build Oral Language
- Say: Today we will be reading a book about plants and how they grow. Before I read, I look at the picture on the cover and think about what I already know.
- Select a student and discuss what grows from the ground. Explain how plants need food to grow just like we do. Consider adding vocabulary to your discussion, such

as *soil, water, leaves, sunlight, vines, bloom,* or *seeds.* Then have the student tell you about any plants or food they have seen growing.

- Say: With a partner, use sticky notes to draw or write some of the parts of a plant you know. Post your words or pictures on a chart at the front of the room. What did you and your partner add?
- Pick five pairs of students, and encourage one student from each pair to share in the discussion. Recognize when students use previously taught key vocabulary.

DURING THE READING

Preview the Book
- Read the title of the book on the cover, and point to the picture. Turn to page 2 and read the sentences, pointing to each word as you read. Have students follow along.
- Say: When I look at the pictures, I understand what this book will be about. The title and the words give me more clues. There are pictures of fruit and flowers. I think these are different types of plants. I wonder if they grow the same way?
- As needed, point out the words that have the long *e* (*e_e, e, ea, ee*) sounds or words that are plurals: *seeds, flowers.*

Read the Book
- Read the book to students as they follow along. Point out words that contain the sound-spellings taught. Tell students the parts of the plants or the planting process if they don't know them: *stem, leaves, fruit, flower, water, begin, grow, pick, farmer, bloom, inside, wait.*
- Have students silently read the book. Ask a few students to whisper read the book to you, and help them sound out new words. When observing students, focus on the new words: *be, beans, each, eat, leaves, peach, peas, see, seeds, plants, pumpkins, shapes, sizes, vines, we.*
- **Science Connections:** Say: If we plant a seed, a new plant will grow that looks just like the plant it came from.

AFTER THE READING

Check Comprehension
To check students' understanding of the book, ask the following:
✓ Look at the fruit on pages 2 and 3. Can you point to the seeds that are inside the apple? Where are the seeds in the peas? How are they different? (Answers may include: The seeds are inside the apple and the peas. You can eat seeds in peas, but you can't eat the seeds in an apple.)
✓ Look at the picture on page 5. Where do the seeds get planted? (Answers may include: The seeds are planted in soil.)
✓ The text on page 6 describes how the pumpkins grow. Point to the words that tell what happens first. (Students should point to *vines grow*.) Read the last two sentences. Notice the words *next* and *then*. Which picture shows each step? (Students should indicate the picture of the flower first, then the pumpkins.)

Reread to Develop Fluency
- Say: Today you will read the book to each other to practice reading with fluency. This means that you read the book as the author meant for it to be read aloud.
- Model reading fluently by reading the book aloud to students. Focus on changing your voice depending on the punctuation at the end of the sentence.
- Have partners reread the book to each other. Remind them to change their voices to go up for a question or add excitement for an exclamation point. Students may struggle with decoding, comprehension, or vocabulary. For students who are struggling with comprehension, say: I noticed that you aren't sure what that word means. Let's look at the picture and see if it helps. Now that we understand the word, let's reread the sentence and add some expression to show we understand.
- Send home a copy of *How Plants Grow* for students to read to family members. Consider assessing a few students on fluency.

Connect to Written Language
↻ Review: Write the words *chicken, chips,* and *drain* on the board. As a class, read the words together as you point to the letters. Emphasize the /ch/ sounds. Ask students to write a sentence using one of the words.

✓ Dictate the following words for students to spell: *bean, we, see, me, beads, give,* and *many.* When finished, write the words on the board. Have students self-correct their papers.

✓ Say: The word *leaves* means two things. It can mean more than one leaf on a plant, but it can also be used to show that someone is going away. When two words sound the same and are spelled the same but have different meanings, they are called homonyms. Write on the board: *They will fire him for starting the fire.* Let's read this sentence together. The first instance of the word *fire* means "to be let go from a job." The second use of the word means "a flame that burns things." Write on the board: *They had to duck to get out of the way of the low-flying duck.* Let's read this sentence. In this sentence the two uses of the word *duck* are homonyms. Can you tell what they mean? Encourage students to brainstorm some homonyms, and chart their ideas. Then have them write two sentences that use homonyms.

Terrific Teeth

SKILLS

PHONICS SKILL INTRODUCED
- Long *e* (*e, ea, ee*)
- *r-, l-,* and *s*-blends

SIGHT WORDS
- *also, come, her, long, open, very, why*

VOCABULARY WORDS–
Science Words
- *bite(s), chew(s), eat, food, front, sharp, smile, teeth*

CURRICULUM LINK–
Science Focus
- Teeth

Terrific Teeth

BEFORE THE READING

Develop Phonemic Awareness and Phonics
Rhyme
- Say: Today we are going to work with words that rhyme. A rhyme is two words that have the same ending sound.
- Write the words *he, we, meal,* and *real* on the board, and model saying each rhyming pair: he/we; meal/real.
- Write *need, seed, be,* and *me* on the board. Say these words while pointing to the sound-spellings, and have students echo you: need/seed; be/me.
- Write *team* and *knee* on the board. Have students say rhyming words out loud but independently. Walk around to support students. If a student is struggling to find rhyming words, say: Say: *team.* Change /t/ to /s/. What word do you get? That's right, *seam.* Now try it with *knee.*

Introduce Phonics Skills
Long *e* (*e, ea, ee*) and *r-, l-,* and *s*-blends
- Say: We just practiced rhyming some words with the /ē/ sound. Now we are going to read some words with this sound-spelling.
- Write the word *teeth* on the board, and underline the *ee.* Say: The letters *ee* are one spelling for the /ē/ sound. Model reading the word, one sound at a time, while pointing to the letters: /t/ /ē/ /th/.
- Write the words *she, meat,* and *seed* on the board. Focus on the different spellings for /ē/, and have students read the words as a class.
- Have students try reading the words *steal, fleet,* and *street* independently, following the routine above. Walk around to support students. Students who are struggling may need extra modeling, practice, and feedback, such as: Let's look at the word *street.* When three consonants appear together in a word, the sound of each consonant is blended together. The letters *str* make up the /str/ sound. Let's slowly say the sounds of *street* together as I point to each letter. Now you do it.
- Repeat the steps with *r-, l-,* and *s*-blends, using these exemplars:
  1) cr, /kr/: 2) cream; 3) creed, creak, crush; 4) crease, creep, cram
  1) fl, /fl/: 2) flea; 3) fleet, fleece, flat 4) flee, flick, flip
  1) st, /st/: 2) steep; 3) steal, stem; 4) steel, stone, still
  1) spr, /spr/: 2) spree; 3) sprint, spring; 4) sprung

Introduce Sight Words
- Say: You are going to see some words today that you may not know, so you will need to keep them in your memory.
- Write *also, come,* and *her* on the board. Read them to students as you point to each letter.
- Write *long* and *very* on the board. Read the words, and have students echo read each.
- Write the words *open* and *why* on the board. Ask a volunteer to read them aloud, and have the rest of the class follow suit. Place the words on a sight-word bulletin board.
- The book also contains science words. Follow the steps above with these words, but this time provide a simple definition for words that may cause confusion: *bite(s), chew(s), eat, food, front, sharp, smile,* and *teeth.* For example: Something that is sharp has an edge or a point that cuts easily. Show the sharp teeth in the book.

Build Oral Language
- Say: Today we will be reading a book about teeth. Before I read, I often think about the topic and try to recall what I already know about it.
- Have a discussion with a student about teeth. Describe what your teeth look like, what you use them for, and what you eat. Consider adding vocabulary to your discussion, such as *sharp, bite, crack, chew, gnaw, front,* and *back.* Then have the student tell you what he or she knows about teeth.

- Say: Interview a partner about what he or she knows about animals' teeth. Then switch roles.
- Encourage five students from different pairs to share what they learned during the interviews. Recognize when students use previously taught key vocabulary.

DURING THE READING

Preview the Book
- Read the title of the book on the cover, and point to the picture. Turn to page 2 and read it, pointing to each word as you read. Also point to the picture and describe what is shown. Have students follow along in their books.
- Say: Do you know what the book will be about based on the title and the first page that I read? How do you know what it will be about?
- As needed, point out the words with the focused skills: *see, teeth, we, need.*

Read the Book
- Read the book to students as they follow along. Point out words that contain the sound-spellings taught. As needed, explain the words that describe how people use their teeth to eat: *bites, squashes, chews.*
- Have students silently read the book. Ask a few students to whisper read the book to you, and help them sound out new words. When observing students, focus on the new words: *she, eat, meat, peach, need, see, seeds, teeth, crush, flat.*
- **Science Connections:** Say: You are growing and changing in several ways. One way is that your teeth are changing. When you were babies, your first teeth grew in. Now you are losing those baby teeth, and new, permanent teeth are growing in. These are the teeth you will have for the rest of your lives.

AFTER THE READING

Check Comprehension
To check students' understanding of the book, ask the following:
✓ Look at the woman on page 3. Point to the word that describes her teeth. (*sharp*) How do her sharp teeth help her while she eats? What would happen if her teeth weren't sharp? (Her sharp teeth help her bite into the peach. If her teeth weren't sharp, she might have trouble chewing food.)
✓ Look at the squirrel's and horse's teeth on pages 5 and 6. Why do you think the horse's teeth are shaped differently from the squirrel's teeth? (The horse's teeth are different because it eats food that needs to be chewed with big, wide, flat teeth.)
✓ Look at the picture on page 7. How does the picture help you understand what you read? How does the text help you understand the picture? (Answers may include: The picture of the tiger's teeth helps me understand that its teeth are long and sharp. The text helps me understand that the tiger's teeth help it eat meat.)

Reread to Develop Fluency
- Say: Today you will read the book to each other to practice reading with fluency. This means that you read the book as the author meant for it to be read aloud.
- Model reading fluently by reading the book aloud to students. Focus on expressing excitement when reading sentences that end with an exclamation point.
- Have partners reread the book to each other, focusing on reading with expression. Students may struggle with decoding, comprehension, or vocabulary. For students who are struggling with comprehension, say: I noticed that you seem unsure how to read this sentence. What are some clues we can use to help us understand what we read? Now that we understand the sentence a little better, let's try reading it again with proper expression.
- Send home a copy of *Terrific Teeth* for students to read to family members. Consider assessing a few students on fluency.

Connect to Written Language
↻ Review: Write the words *each, flowers,* and *see* on the board. As a class, read the words together as you point to the letters. Have students replace the vowels in *see* with *ea,* write a sentence with that word, and read the new word together.

✓ Dictate the following words for students to spell: *we, eat, see, he, cream, long,* and *why.* When finished, write the words on the board. Have students self-correct their papers.

✓ Have students draw pictures of their favorite animal eating. Ask them to write 2–3 sentences telling about the animal. You may wish to use the following sentence stems telling what the animal eats and describing what its teeth look like: *This animal eats _____. It has _____ teeth.*

Frogs

SKILLS

PHONICS SKILL INTRODUCED
- Long *o* (*o, oa, ow*)
- Digraphs (*ch, sh, th, wh*)

SIGHT WORDS
- *about, comes, from, has, now, out, very*

VOCABULARY WORDS–
Science Words
- *air, breathe, egg(s), frog, gills, grow(s), lungs, swim, tadpole(s), tail, water*

CURRICULUM LINK–
Science Focus
- Frog Life Cycle

Frogs

BEFORE THE READING

Develop Phonemic Awareness and Phonics
Oral Blending
- Say: Today we are going to be listening to sounds and blending them to make words. Blending means putting sounds together to make words.
- Write the words *go, soap,* and *low* on the board. Model blending the sounds of the words as you point to each sound-spelling: /g/ /ō/, go; /s/ /ō/ /p/, soap; /l/ /ō/, low.
- Write *cold, show,* and *boat* on the board. Say these sounds while pointing to the sound-spellings, and have students echo you.
- Write *throw* and *coach* on the board. Have students try blending the words out loud but independently. Walk around to support students. If a student is struggling to blend the discrete sounds, model putting up one finger for each sound while saying it aloud, and have the student follow suit.

Introduce Phonics Skills
Long *o* (*o, oa, ow*) and Digraphs
- Say: We just practiced blending some words with the /ō/ sound. Now we are going to read some words with this sound-spelling.
- Write the word *no* on the board, and underline the *o*. Say: The letter *o* is the spelling for the /ō/ sound. Model reading the word, one sound at a time, while pointing to the letters: /n/ /ō/.
- Write the words *croak, grow,* and *bow* on the board. Point out the spellings for /ō/. Have students read the words as a class. Say: Slowly sound out each letter.
- Have students try reading the words *go, soak,* and *show* independently, following the routine above. Walk around to support students. Students who are struggling may need extra modeling, practice, and feedback, such as: Let's look at the word *show.* Remember that when two consonants appear together, they sometimes make one sound. For example, together the letters *sh* make the /sh/ sound. Let's slowly say the sounds of this word together as I point to each letter. Now you do it.
- Repeat the steps with digraphs *ch, sh, th,* and *wh* using these exemplars:
  1) ch, /ch/: 2) chin; 3) chat, cheat, chain; 4) chant
  1) sh, /sh/: 2) shut; 3) ship, shape; 4) shade, shift
  1) th, /th/: 2) thin; 3) throat, three; 4) think, thank
  1) wh, /w/: 2) when; 3) what, white; 4) whip, while, whine

Introduce Sight Words
- Say: You are going to see some words today that you may not know, so you will need to keep them in your memory.
- Write the words *about, comes,* and *from* on the board. Read the words to students as you point to each letter.
- Write the words *has* and *now* on the board. Read the words, and have students echo read each word.
- Write the words *out* and *very* on the board. Ask a volunteer to read them aloud, and have the rest of the class follow suit. Place the words on a sight-word bulletin board.
- The book also contains science words. Follow the steps above with these words, but this time provide a simple definition for words that may cause confusion: *air, breathe, egg(s), frog, gills, grow(s), lungs, swim, tadpole(s), tail, water.* For example: A tadpole is a baby frog. Show students pictures of tadpoles from the book.

Build Oral Language
- Say: Today we will be reading a book about how frogs grow. Before I read, I often think about the topic and try to recall what I already know about it.

- Select a student, and discuss a time you saw a frog. Explain where you saw it and describe what the frog looked like. Compare the frog's appearance to how a tadpole looks. Consider adding vocabulary to your discussion, such as *pond, lake, land, tadpole,* and *leap.* Then have the student tell you about how frogs grow.
- Say: Interview a partner about what he or she knows about how frogs grow. Ask your partner if he or she has ever seen a tadpole or a frog.
- Pick five pairs of students, and encourage one student from each pair to share in the discussion. Recognize when students use previously taught key vocabulary.

DURING THE READING

Preview the Book
- Read the title of the book on the cover, and point to the picture. Turn to page 2 and read the sentences, pointing to each word as you read. Also point out the caption and read that as well. Have students follow along in their books.
- Say: Do you know what the book will be about based on the title and the first page that I read? How do you know what it will be about?

Read the Book
- Read the book to students as they follow along. Point out words that contain the sound-spellings taught. Tell students the parts of a tadpole if they don't know them: *tail* and *gills.*
- Have students silently read the book. Ask a few students to whisper read the book to you, and help them sound out new words. When observing students, focus on the new words: *go, grow(s), grown, croak, throat, breathe, change(s), fish, shrinks.*
- **Science Connections:** Say: Tadpoles' bodies go through changes quickly. A tadpole has gills and a tail to breathe and move underwater. As an adult, it lives on land, so it needs lungs and legs. These changes happen as the tadpole grows into an adult frog.

AFTER THE READING

Check Comprehension
To check students' understanding of the book, ask the following:
- ✓Read page 3. From what does a tadpole grow? Why does a tadpole look more like a fish than a frog? (A tadpole grows from a frog egg. A tadpole looks like a fish because it has a tail and gills. Fish have tails and gills but frogs don't.)
- ✓How does the picture on page 5 help you understand what you read? How does the text help you understand the picture? (Answers may include: The picture helps me understand the changes a tadpole goes through before it becomes a frog. The text helps me understand that these changes, such as the front legs growing and the tail shrinking, happen very fast.)
- ✓How are the frogs on pages 6 and 7 different from a tadpole? (The frogs have lungs so they can live on land. A tadpole has gills so it can live underwater. The frog has legs. A tadpole has a tail. The frog is an adult. A tadpole is a baby.)

Reread to Develop Fluency
- Say: Today you will read the book to each other to practice reading with fluency. This means that you read the book as the author meant for it to be read aloud.
- Model reading fluently by reading the book aloud to students. Focus on reading the questions and exclamations with expression.
- Have partners reread the book to each other. Remind students how to read sentences that end with question marks and exclamation points. Students may struggle with decoding, comprehension, or vocabulary. For students who are struggling with vocabulary, say: I noticed that you're not quite sure what that word means, which makes it hard to read the sentence. Let's look up the definition.
- Send home a copy of *Frogs* for students to read to family members. Consider assessing a few students on fluency.

Connect to Written Language
↻Review: Write the words *crush, flat,* and *teeth* on the board. As a class, read the words together as you point to the letters. Then replace the vowel in *crush* with *a.* Have students write the new word, and read it together.

✓Dictate the following words for students to spell: *grow, go, croak, boat, throw, comes,* and *now.* When finished, write the words on the board. Have students self-correct their papers.

✓Say: Some words have an *-s* at the end. They show that the action is happening now. Write on the board: *A frog lays its eggs.* Let's read this sentence together. This means the frog is laying its eggs right now. The *-s* tells us this. Write these two sentences on the board: *It grows back legs. Its body changes very fast.* Read the sentences as a class, and encourage group discussion about the meaning of each. Encourage students to use a word that has an inflection to write a sentence about a tadpole as it changes. You may wish to use the following sentence stem: *The tadpole's tail _____ as it grows.*

Astronauts in Space

SKILLS

PHONICS SKILL INTRODUCED
- Long *o* (*o, oa, ow*)
- Soft *c*

SIGHT WORDS
- *away, be, cold, could, day(s), down, one, walk, works, would*

VOCABULARY WORDS—
Social Studies Words
- *air pack, astronaut(s), backpack, Earth, float, helmet, move, rockets, space, spacecraft, space suit*

CURRICULUM LINK—
Social Studies Focus
- Space Explorers

Astronauts in Space

BEFORE THE READING

Develop Phonemic Awareness and Phonics
Oral Substitution
- Say: Today we are going to be substituting sounds in words. Substitution means replacing a sound in a word to make new words.
- Write the words *goat* and *hold* on the board. Model substituting the first sounds of each word with the /b/ sound as you point to each sound-spelling: /b/ /ō/ /t/, boat; /b/ /ō/ /l/ /d/, bold.
- Write *cent* and *pace* on the board. Say these sounds while pointing to the sound-spellings. Then have students echo you as you substitute the first sound with the /r/ sound: /r/ /e/ /n/ /t/, rent; /r/ /ā/ /s/, race.
- Write *row* and *boast* on the board. Out loud but independently, have students substitute the first sound with the /t/ sound. Walk around to support students. If a student is struggling, model moving colored chips into boxes for each sound. Replace the first chip with a chip of a different color as you substitute the new sound.

Introduce Phonics Skills
Long *o* (*o, oa, ow*) and Soft *c*
- Say: We just practiced substituting the first sound in some words. Now we are going to read some words with the sound-spellings we just heard.
- Write the words *go, boat,* and *tow* on the board, and underline the *o, oa,* and *ow.* Say: The *o* is one spelling for the /ō/ sound. Model reading the word *go*, one sound at a time, while pointing to the letters: /g/ /ō/. Say: The *oa* is also a spelling for the /ō/ sound. Model reading the word *boat*, one sound at a time, while pointing to the letters: /b/ /ō/ /t/. Say: The *ow* is another spelling for the /ō/ sound. Model reading the word *tow*, one sound at a time, while pointing to the letters: /t/ /ō/.
- Write the words *slow, loan, robe,* and *bold* on the board. Have students read the words as a class. Say: Slowly sound out each letter, and notice the different spellings for the /ō/ sound.
- Have students try reading the words *no, float,* and *window* independently, following the routine above. Walk around to support students. Students who are struggling may need extra support and practice. Let's look at the word *window*. This word has two syllables. Let's say the word together and then try reading it. The /ō/ sound appears at the end of this word.
- Repeat the steps with the soft *c*. Explain that the letter *c* usually makes the /s/ sound when it comes right before *e, i,* or *y.*
  1) c, /s/: 2) race, rice, space; 3) face, city, ice; 4) place, cell

Introduce Sight Words
- Say: You are going to see some words today that you may not know, so you will need to keep them in your memory.
- Write the words *away* and *be* on the board. Read them, and point to each letter.
- Write the words *cold, could,* and *day* on the board. Read the words, and have students echo read each word.
- Write the word *down* on the board. Ask a volunteer to read it aloud, and have the rest of the class follow suit. Place the words on a sight-word bulletin board.
- The book also contains social studies words. Follow the steps above with these words, but this time provide a simple definition for words that may cause confusion: *air pack, astronaut(s), backpack, Earth, float, helmet, move, rockets, space, spacecraft,* and *space suit.* For example: *Space* describes the area where a rocket soars above Earth. Show students the pictures of space on pages 2–4.

Build Oral Language
- Say: Today we will be reading a book about astronauts. I wonder what an astronaut does? I like to ask a question before I read and then see if the book answers my question.

- Select a student and discuss some things an astronaut does. Explain how astronauts need special equipment to breathe when they are in space. Consider adding vocabulary to your discussion, such as *Earth, ride, float, breathe, helmet, Velcro, sticks, tray, weightless,* or *moon*. Then have the student tell you what they know about astronauts and space.
- Say: With a partner, think of a question you would like to ask about astronauts. You might want to know what they see in space, or what they eat. What is a question you have that this book might answer?
- Pick five pairs of students, and encourage one student from each pair to share in the discussion. Recognize when students use previously taught key vocabulary.

DURING THE READING

Preview the Book
- Read the title of the book on the cover, and point to the picture. Turn to page 2 and read the sentences, pointing to each word as you read. Have students follow along.
- Say: This book is about astronauts in space. The title and the pictures make me want to know more about what astronauts do in space. What do they eat? How do they sleep? I think this book will tell me some of the things I want to know.
- As needed, point out the words that have the long *o* (*o, oa, ow*) and soft *c* sounds: *astronaut, space, spacecraft, window*.

Read the Book
- Read the book to students as they follow along. Point out words that contain the sound-spellings taught. Tell students words related to space if they don't know them: *spacecraft, weightless, gravity, space suit, air pack, Earth, helmet, rockets, straps, float*.
- Have students silently read the book. Ask a few students to whisper read the book to you, and help them sound out new words. When observing students, focus on the new words: *cold, go, hold, Velcro, float, pillow, window, space, spacecraft, space suit*.
- **Social Studies Connections:** Say: As astronauts explore space, they do important work in space, including science experiments and maintaining the spacecraft. They truly are space explorers.

AFTER THE READING

Check Comprehension
To check students' understanding of the book, ask the following:
- ✓Look at the astronaut on page 3. Why do you think the astronaut is wearing a space suit and air pack? (Answers may include: There is no air in space, so astronauts need to wear the suits to breathe.)
- ✓The astronaut on page 5 is wearing different clothes when he is inside the spacecraft. How is his clothing different? (There is no spacesuit, air pack, or helmet.)
- ✓Look at the picture on page 6. The text says that astronauts sleep while floating. Why do you think they sleep that way? (Answers may include: Astronauts are weightless in space, so they will float.)

Reread to Develop Fluency
- Say: Today you will read the book to each other to practice reading with fluency. This means that you read the book as the author meant for it to be read aloud.
- Model reading fluently by reading the book aloud to students. Focus on pausing at the end of a sentence before starting a new one.
- Have partners reread the book to each other. Suggest that they pause when they come to the end of a sentence before starting the next one. Students may struggle with decoding, comprehension, or vocabulary. For students who are struggling with comprehension, say: I noticed that you seem unsure about the meaning of this sentence. Are there clues that we can use to help us understand what we read? Now that we understand the sentence a little better, let's try reading it again.
- Send home a copy of *Astronauts in Space* for students to read to family members. Consider assessing a few students on fluency.

Connect to Written Language
- ↻Review: Write the words *change, fish,* and *grow* on the board. As a class, read the words together as you point to the letters. Then have students practice writing the words and underlining the digraphs (*ch, sh*). Say the words together. Ask students to write a sentence that uses all three words, and draw a picture to go with the sentence. Offer a sentence starter, such as, "*The fish will ____ and ____.*"

- ✓Dictate the following words for students to spell: *bowl, cold, float, go, race, works,* and *would*. When finished, write the words on the board. Have students self-correct their papers.

- ✓Say: Sometimes we put two words together to make a new word. For example, see how the word *spacecraft* has two words, *space* and *craft*. Write on the board: *backpack*. Let's read this word together. Can you see the two words that were put together? Yes, the words are *back* and *pack*. Encourage students to write or dictate more compound words.

Animals of the Rain Forest

SKILLS

PHONICS SKILL INTRODUCED
- Long *i* (*i*, *–igh*, *–y*)
- Soft *g*

SIGHT WORDS
- *every, fall, find, green, grow, read, sleep*

VOCABULARY WORDS–
Science Words
- *jaguar, orangutan, rain forest*

CURRICULUM LINK–
Science Focus
- Rain Forest Animals

Animals of the Rain Forest

BEFORE THE READING

Develop Phonemic Awareness and Phonics
Phonemic Manipulation
- Say: Today we are going to substitute one letter in some words and make them into new words.
- Write the words *by* and *tag* on the board. Model replacing the first sound in each word with /dr/ as you point to each sound-spelling: /dr/ /ī/, dry; /dr/ /a/ /g/, drag.
- Write *bake, cave,* and *bin* on the board. Say these sounds while pointing to the sound-spellings, and have students echo you as you substitute the first sound with the /w/ sound.
- Write *vest* and *pig* on the board. Out loud but independently, have students replace the first sound in each word with the /b/ sound. Walk around to support students. If a student is struggling, model moving colored chips into boxes for each sound. Replace the first chip with a chip of a different color as you substitute the new sound.

Introduce Phonics Skills
Long *i* (*i*, *–igh*, *–y*) and Soft *g*
- Say: Today we are going to learn about the /ī/ sound. Sometimes the /ī/ sound is spelled with the letter *i* as in *kind*. The letters *igh* can also make the /ī/ sound as in *night*. The letter *y* sometimes makes the /ī/ sound as in *cry*.
- Write the word *night* on the board, and underline the *igh*. Say: The letters *igh* make the /ī/ sound. Have students say the sound as you point to the letters. Repeat with *kind* and *cry*.
- Ask students to name other words that contain the /ī/ sound. List those words on the board. For each word, have a volunteer come to the board and circle the letters that make the /ī/ sound.
- Repeat the steps with the soft *g* sound, using the exemplars below. Say: The letter *g* can make a hard sound as in *game* or a soft sound as in *gem*. The soft *g* makes the /j/ sound like the letter *j*. Usually, when *g* comes before *e, i,* or *y* in a word, it will make the soft *g* or /j/ sound.
  1) g, /j/: 2) gentle, germ; 3) giant, giraffe; 4) gym, huge

Introduce Sight Words
- Say: You are going to see some words today that you may not know, so you will need to keep them in your memory.
- Write *every* and *fall* on the board. Read them to students as you point to each letter.
- Write *grow* and *read* on the board. Read each, and have students echo read them.
- Write *find, green,* and *sleep* on the board. Ask a volunteer to read them aloud, and have the rest of the class follow suit. Place the words on a sight-word bulletin board.
- The book also contains science words. Follow the steps above with these words, but this time provide a simple definition for words that may cause confusion: *jaguar, orangutan,* and *rain forest*. For example: An orangutan is a type of ape that has long arms and reddish-brown hair. Orangutans eat plants and live mostly in trees. Show students the picture of the orangutan on page 5 of the book.

Build Oral Language
- Say: Today we will be reading a book about animals that live in the rain forest. Before I read, I often think about the topic and try to recall what I already know about it.
- Select a student and discuss what you know about rain forests. Explain that a rain forest is an area with many tall trees. It rains every day in the rain forest, and the

weather there is always very warm. Consider adding vocabulary to your discussion, such as *apes, canopy, damp, forest floor, insects, jaguars, lizards, noisy, orangutans, rainy, vines, wet.*

- Say: With a partner, discuss what you know about the rain forest and name some animals that live there.
- Pick five pairs of students, and encourage one student from each pair to share in the discussion. Recognize when students use previously taught key vocabulary.

DURING THE READING

Preview the Book
- Read the title of the book on the cover, and point to the picture. Turn to pages 2 and 3 and read the text, pointing to each word as you read. Also point out the captions and read those words as well. Have students follow along in their books.
- Say: Do you know what the book will be about based on the title and the first pages that I read? How do you know what it will be about?
- As needed, point out the words that have the /ī/ sound: *daytime, kinds, nighttime, viper, wild.*

Read the Book
- Read the book to students as they follow along. Point out words that contain the sound-spellings taught. Tell students the names of the animals if they don't know them: *pit viper, red-eyed tree frog, monkey, orangutan, crocodile, jaguar, fruit bat.*
- Have students silently read the book. Ask a few students to whisper read the book to you, and help them sound out new words. When observing students, focus on the new words: *dry, find, giant, high, huge, kinds, might, night, quiet, wild.*
- **Science Connections:** Say: There are rain forests all over the world. Birds, lizards, insects, and other animals live in rain forests. Many of the animals depend on the trees to live and sleep in, for protection, and for food, such as leaves and fruit. Orangutans are huge apes that live in the trees. Jaguars often take naps in trees.

AFTER THE READING

Check Comprehension
To check students' understanding of the book, ask the following:
✓ From looking at the pictures in the book, which animals do you think spend time in trees in the rain forest? (Answers may include: snakes, pit vipers, monkeys, orangutans, fruit bats.)
✓ Which word on page 3 has the /ī/ sound and means "not tame"? (*wild*)
✓ What do you think is the most interesting part of the rain forest? (Answers will vary. Accept all reasonable responses.)

Reread to Develop Fluency
- Say: Today you will read the book to each other to practice reading with fluency. This means that you read the book as the author meant for it to be read aloud.
- Model reading fluently by reading the book aloud to students. Focus on expressing excitement with your voice when a sentence ends in an exclamation point.
- Have partners reread the book to each other. Suggest that they express excitement when an exclamation point ends a sentence. Students may struggle with decoding, comprehension, or vocabulary. For students who are struggling with comprehension, say: I noticed that you seem unsure how to read this sentence. What are some clues we can use to help us understand what we read? Now that we understand the sentence a little better, let's try reading it again with proper expression.
- Send home a copy of *Animals of the Rain Forest* for students to read to family members. Consider assessing a few students on fluency.

Connect to Written Language
↻ Review: Write the words *cent, hold,* and *race* on the board. As a class, read the words together as you point to the letters. Then replace the *c* in *cent* and *race* with *t* and the *h* in *hold* with *g.* Read the new words together, and have students write sentences with them.

✓ Dictate the following words for students to spell: *fly, giant, green, grow, kite, right,* and *stage.* When finished, write the words on the board. Have students self-correct their papers.

✓ Have students fold a sheet of unlined paper in half and hold it like a book. Then have them draw a picture of their favorite rain forest animal on the "cover" and label it. Ask them to write three sentences about the animal, one sentence on each of the other pages. You may suggest that students use the following sentence stems: *The _____ lives in the rain forest. In the daytime, it _____. At night, it _____.* You may wish to display students' books in the classroom or school library.

All About Bats

SKILLS

PHONICS SKILL INTRODUCED
- Long *i* (*i, –igh, –y*)

SIGHT WORDS
- *have, here, may, new, only, other(s), so, two, well*

VOCABULARY WORDS–
Science Words
- *bat, caves, fingers, fly, fur, hour, mammal*

CURRICULUM LINK–
Science Focus
- Bats

All About Bats

BEFORE THE READING

Develop Phonemic Awareness and Phonics
Oral Segmentation
- Say: Today we are going to segment words so that we can say them sound by sound. Segment means to pull apart words by their sounds.
- Write the words *my* and *cry* on the board. Model saying the words sound by sound: /m/ /ī/, my; /kr/ /ī/, cry.
- Write *might* and *sight* on the board. Sound out each word, and have students follow suit chorally: /m/ /ī/ /t/, might; /s/ /ī/ /t/, sight. Ask students to say *yes* if the words rhyme.
- Write *bind* and *kind* on the board. Have students segment the words out loud but independently. Walk around to support students. If a student is struggling to segment the sounds in each word, model saying each sound as you move a chip onto a line or sound box and have the student follow suit.

Introduce Phonics Skills
Long *i* (*i, –igh, –y*)
- Say: We just practiced blending some words with the /ī/ sound. Now we are going to read some words with this sound-spelling.
- Write the words *find* and *bind* on the board, and underline the *i*. Say: Sometimes the letter *i* is the spelling for the /ī/ sound. Model reading the words, one sound at a time, while pointing to the letters: /f/ /ī/ /n/ /d/; /b/ /ī/ /n/ /d/.
- Write the words *fight* and *light* on the board. Say: Sometimes the letters *igh* stand for the /ī/ sound. Point out the spellings for /ī/. Have students read the words as a class. Say: Slowly sound out each letter.
- Write the words *by* and *sky* on the board. Say: Sometimes the letter *y* makes the /ī/ sound. Point out the spellings for /ī/. Choose a student and ask him or her to read the words with you.
- Have students try reading the words *mind, tight,* and *try* independently, following the routine above. Walk around to support students. Students who are struggling may need extra support and practice, such as: Let's look at the word *try*. Remember that when two consonants appear together, they sometimes make one sound. For example, together the letters *tr* stand for the /tr/ sound. Let's slowly say the sounds of this word together as I point to each letter. Now you do it.

Introduce Sight Words
- Say: You are going to see some words today that you may not know, so you will need to keep them in your memory.
- Write the words *have, here,* and *may* on the board. Read the words to students as you point to each letter.
- Write the words *new, only,* and *other* on the board. Read the words, and have students echo read each word.
- Write the words *so, two,* and *well* on the board. Ask a volunteer to read them aloud, and have the rest of the class follow suit. Place the words on a sight-word bulletin board.
- The book also contains science words. Follow the steps above with these words, but this time provide a simple definition for words that may cause confusion: *bat, caves, fingers, fly, fur, hour, mammal.* For example: A mammal is a warm-blooded animal with hair or fur. People, dogs, and cows are mammals. Show students pictures of bats from the book and tell them that bats are also mammals.

Build Oral Language
- Say: Today we will be reading a book about bats. Before I read, I often think about the topic and try to recall what I already know about it.

- Select a student and discuss what you know about bats. Say if you've ever seen a bat or a photo of a bat, and describe what it looked like. Talk about where bats live and what they eat. Add vocabulary to your discussion, such as *mammals, insects, fur, caves, wings*. Then have the student tell you what he or she knows about bats.
- Say: Talk with your partner about what you know about bats. Write what you both know on a sticky note. When you are done, add the sticky note information to chart paper.
- Pick five pairs of students, and encourage one student from each pair to share what they wrote on their chart paper. Recognize when students use previously taught key vocabulary.

DURING THE READING

Preview the Book
- Read the title of the book on the cover, and point to the picture. Turn to page 2, and read the sentences, pointing to each word as you read. Also point to the image and discuss that as well. Have students follow along in their books.
- Say: Do you know what the book will be about based on the title and the first page that I read? How do you know what it will be about?

Read the Book
- Read the book to students as they follow along. Point out words that contain the sound-spellings taught. Tell students where bats live and how they sleep: caves, upside down.
- Have students silently read the book. Ask a few students to whisper read the book to you, and help them sound out new words. When observing students, focus on the new words: *find, kind, high, light, night, fly, sky*.
- **Science Connections:** Say: Bats are mammals because their babies are born live. They do not hatch from eggs. The babies get milk from their mothers. Bat babies are called pups. Many people are afraid of bats, but they don't need to be. Bats usually leave people alone.

AFTER THE READING

Check Comprehension
To check students' understanding of the book, ask the following:
- ✓How does the picture on page 5 help you understand what you read? How does the text help you understand the picture? (Answers may include: The picture helps me understand what bats look like when they sleep. The text helps me understand that many bats sleep upside down inside caves during the day.)
- ✓Read page 6. Why do bats hunt for food at night? How is a bat different from you? (Bats hunt for food at night because they see very well in the dark, and they are also awake at night. A bat is awake while I am asleep.)
- ✓Read page 7. Why do more fruit trees grow when bats eat fruit? (When bats eat fruit, they drop the fruit's seeds. When those seeds land on soil, new fruit trees grow from them.)

Reread to Develop Fluency
- Say: Today you will read the book to each other to practice reading with fluency. This means that you read the book as the author meant for it to be read aloud.
- Model reading fluently by reading the book aloud to students. Focus on pausing at periods and reading exclamations with excitement.
- Have partners reread the book to each other. Remind students how to read sentences that end with exclamation points and periods. Students may struggle with decoding, comprehension, or vocabulary. For students who are struggling with vocabulary, say: I noticed that you're not quite sure what that word means, which makes it hard to read the sentence. Let's look up the definition of the word.
- Send home a copy of *All About Bats* for students to read to family members. Consider assessing a few students on fluency.

Connect to Written Language
↻Review: Write the words *huge, might,* and *night* on the board. As a class, read the words together as you point to the letters. Then replace the *igh* in *might* and *night* with *e*. Have students write the new words, and read them together.

✓Dictate the following words for students to spell: *fly, night, sky, child, my, have,* and *only*. When finished, write the words on the board. Have students self-correct their papers.

✓Say: Some words are pronounced the same way but have different meanings and spellings. These are called homophones. Write on the board: *It can fly fast too.* Read the sentence as a class and say: The word *too* in this sentence means "also." Write on the board: *Bats have two legs.* Read the sentence as a class and say: The word *two* in this sentence means "the number 2." Encourage students to write additional sentences using the homophones *too* and *two*. You may wish to use the following sentence frames about bats: *Bats have _____ feet. Bats have fur _____.*

Push and Pull

SKILLS

PHONICS SKILL INTRODUCED
- Long *u* (*u_e, ew*)
- Inflectional Ending *–ed*

SIGHT WORDS
- *her, if, just, may, pull(ed), she*

VOCABULARY WORDS–
Science Words
- *away, fast, force, hard, move, presses, pull(ed), push(ed)(es), slowly, tugs*

CURRICULUM LINK–
Science Focus
- Pushes and Pulls

Push and Pull

BEFORE THE READING

Develop Phonemic Awareness and Phonics
Oral Segmentation
- Say: Today we are going to be segmenting the sounds in words. Segmenting means pulling words apart by their sounds. We will listen for the /ū/ sound.
- Write the words *human* and *cube* on the board. Model segmenting the sounds of each word as you point to the sound-spellings: /h/ /ū/ /m/ /a/ /n/, human; /k/ /ū/ /b/, cube. Then, clap once for each syllable.
- Write *bugle* and *menu* on the board. Say these words while pointing to the sound-spellings. Have students echo you as you segment the sounds and clap the syllables: /b/ /ū/ /g/ /l/, bugle; /m/ /e/ /n/ /ū/, menu.
- Write *few* and *review* on the board. Have students try segmenting the sounds out loud but independently. Walk around to support students. If a student is struggling with segmenting, model touching your hand under your chin to count each syllable. Have the student follow suit as he or she says the sounds slowly.

Introduce Phonics Skills
Long *u* (*u_e, ew*) and Inflectional Ending *–ed*
- Say: We just practiced segmenting the sounds in some words. Now we are going to read some words as we point out each sound-spelling.
- Write the words *cute* and *few* on the board, and underline the *u_e* and *ew*. Say: The *u_e* and *ew* are two spellings for the /ū/ sound. Model reading each word, one sound at a time, while pointing to the letters: /k/ /ū/ /t/, cute; /f/ /ū/, few.
- Write the words *use* and *review* on the board. Have students read the words as a class. Say: Sound out each letter, and notice the spellings for the /ū/ sound.
- Have students try reading the words *mule, mew,* and *cube* independently, following the routine above. Walk around to support students. Students who are struggling may need extra modeling and practice, such as: Let's look at the word *mule*. Remember that the letters *u_e* make the long *u* sound. Let's slowly say each of the sounds together as I point to the letters. Now you try it.
- Repeat the steps with the ending *–ed*, using these exemplars. Explain that *–ed* can stand for the /d/ sound (*used*), the /t/ sound (*kicked*), or the /ed/ sound (*landed*):
  1) –ed, /d/: 2) used; 3) tugged, blamed, tuned; 4) chewed, trimmed
  1) –ed, /t/: 2) kicked; 3) fixed, asked, licked; 4) pressed, baked
  1) –ed, /ed/: 2) landed; 3) planted, needed, painted; 4) mended, fitted

Introduce Sight Words
- Say: You are going to see some words today that you may not know, so you will need to keep them in your memory.
- Write *her* and *if* on the board. Read them to students as you point to each letter.
- Write *just* and *may* on the board. Read the words, and have students echo read them.
- Write *she* on the board. Ask a volunteer to read it aloud, and have the rest of the class follow suit. Place the words on a sight-word bulletin board.
- The book also contains science words. Follow the steps above with these words, but this time provide a simple definition for words that may cause confusion: *force, hard, push,* and *slowly*. For example: A force is something that acts on another thing to make it move. Show students the picture of the soccer player on page 7.

Build Oral Language
- Say: Today we will be reading a book about forces called pushing and pulling. I think I understand the difference between pushing and pulling.
- Select a student, and discuss some things you push, like a door or a ball. Explain how a push works, and model how the harder you push, the more something moves. Then describe some things you pull, like a rope. Consider adding vocabulary to your

discussion, such as *object, tug, pressed, away, toward, close, hard, more, less, up,* or *back.* Then have the student show you an example of a push and a pull.

- Say: With a partner, role-play something you push and something you pull. How can you show if you are pushing hard, or just a little?
- Pick five pairs of students, and encourage each pair to share their role-play. See if other students can guess what they are pushing or pulling. Recognize when students use previously taught key vocabulary.

DURING THE READING

Preview the Book
- Read the title of the book on the cover, and point to the picture. Turn to pages 2 and 3 and read the sentences, pointing to each word as you read. Have students follow along.
- Say: This book is about two forces called pushing and pulling. I can tell from the cover that the kids are pulling. The title and the pictures help me know what the book will be about. I wonder what the pictures will show for pushing?
- As needed, point out the words that have the long *u* (*u_e, ew*) sounds or the inflectional ending *–ed*: *huge, pulled, tugged, use.*

Read the Book
- Read the book to students as they follow along. Point out words that contain the sound-spellings taught. Explain the actions in the pictures if students aren't sure about them: *lift, roll, pull, tug, press, kick, swing.*
- Have students silently read the book. Ask a few students to whisper read the book to you, and help them sound out new words. When observing students, focus on the new words: *huge, use, pulled, tugged, few, pushed, pressed, needed.*
- **Science Connections:** Say: Sometimes we use wheels to help us pull or push something that is heavy. Think about a suitcase with wheels. Why would wheels help make it easier to pull? Think about a chair with wheels. Imagine pushing the chair. Would it be hard or easy to push?

AFTER THE READING

Check Comprehension
To check students' understanding of the book, ask the following:
✓Look at page 2. What are some ways the children in the picture can make the tube move? (Answers may include: They can lift it, push it, or pull it.)
✓Page 5 describes two different forces: pushing and pulling. What kind of force is this player using? (Answers may include: He is using the bat to push the ball away.)
✓Look at the picture on page 7. Is a kick a push or a pull? (a push) Which clue in the picture helps you know? (Answers may include: When she kicks she will push the ball away.) Point to the word that describes how she kicks the ball. (Answers may include: She pushes it with her feet.)

Reread to Develop Fluency
- Say: Today you will read the book to each other to practice reading with fluency. This means that you read the book as the author meant for it to be read aloud.
- Model reading fluently by reading the book aloud to students. Focus on pausing slightly when you come to a comma.
- Have partners reread the book to each other. Suggest that they pause when they come to a comma within a sentence. Students may struggle with decoding, comprehension, or vocabulary. For students who are struggling with comprehension, say: I noticed that you seem unsure about the meaning of this sentence. Are there clues in the other words or in the pictures that we can use to help us understand what we read? Now that we understand the sentence a little better, let's try reading it again with proper expression.
- Send home a copy of *Push and Pull* for students to read to family members. Consider assessing a few students on fluency.

Connect to Written Language
↻Review: Write the words *daytime, light,* and *sky* on the board. As a class, read the words together as you point to the letters. Then practice writing the words and underline the /ī/ sound in each word. Have students write a sentence for each word.

✓Dictate the following words for students to spell: *cute, cube, use, few, mule, her,* and *pulled.* When finished, write the words on the board. Have students self-correct their papers.

✓Say: Sometimes words have an *–ed* or an *–s* at the end. If *–ed* is used, it shows that the action happened in the past; if *–s* is used, it shows the action is still happening. Write on the board: *Kim kicks the ball.* This means Kim is kicking now. Write on the board: *Kim kicked the ball.* This means Kim finished kicking the ball. Encourage students to write a sentence and draw a picture showing past or present actions.

Using Maps

SKILLS

PHONICS SKILL INTRODUCED
- Long Vowels (Long *a, e, i, o,* and *u*)
- Inflectional Ending –*ing*

SIGHT WORDS
- *day, drawing(s), little, where*

VOCABULARY WORDS–
Social Studies Words
- *city, compass rose, directions, east, Florida, key, map, Miami Beach, north, roads, south, state, streets, symbols, United States, west*

CURRICULUM LINK–
Social Studies Focus
- Maps

Using Maps

BEFORE THE READING

Develop Phonemic Awareness and Phonics
Phonemic Manipulation
- Say: Today we are going to be changing some of the sounds in words to make new words.
- Write the words *may, me, might,* and *go* on the board. Model replacing the first sound of each word with the /s/ sound as you point to each sound-spelling: /s/ /ā/, say; /s/ /ē/, see; /s/ /ī/ /t/, sight; /s/ /ō/, so.
- Write *train, sale,* and *rose* on the board. Replace the first sound or blend with the /p/ sound. Have students echo you as you segment each word: /p/ /ā/ /n/, pain; /p/ /ā/ /l/, pale; /p/ /ō/ /z/, pose.
- Write *day, bee, fine,* and *show* on the board. Have students try replacing the first sound or digraph with the /l/ sound. Walk around to support students. If a student is struggling with replacing sounds, model how you shape your mouth for each sound. Have the student follow suit as he or she says the sounds slowly.

Introduce Phonics Skills
Long vowels (long *a, e, i, o,* and *u*) and Inflectional Ending –*ing*
- Say: We just practiced segmenting the sounds in some words. Now we are going to read some words as we point out each sound-spelling.
- Write the words *lake, east, sign, no,* and *few* on the board. Say: Today we are reviewing long vowel sounds. Model reading the words, one sound at a time, while pointing to the letters: /l/ /ā/ /k/, lake; /ē/ /st/, east; /s/ /ī/ /n/, sign; /n/ /ō/, no; /f/ /ū/, few.
- Write the words *place, need, light, bone,* and *duke* on the board. Have students read the words as a class. Say: Slowly sound out each letter, and notice the different spellings for the long vowel sounds.
- Have students try reading the words *state, real, wide, toad,* and *mute* independently, following the routine above. Walk around to support students. Students who are struggling may need extra modeling and practice, such as: Let's look at the word *toad*. Remember the spelling *oa* is one spelling for the long *o* sound. Let's slowly say each of the sounds together as I point to the letters. Now you try it.
- Repeat the steps with the ending –*ing*, using these exemplars. Explain that when adding –*ing* to a word that ends in *e*, you drop the *e* before adding the –*ing*. 1) –ing, /ing/: 2) taking; 3) dining, waving, yelling; 4) sailing, kicking

Introduce Sight Words
- Say: You are going to see some words today that you may not know, so you will need to keep them in your memory.
- Write the word *day* on the board. Read it to students as you point to each letter.
- Write the words *drawing* and *drawings* on the board. Read the words, and have students echo read each word.
- Write the words *little* and *where* on the board. Ask a volunteer to read them aloud, and have the class follow suit. Place the words on a sight-word bulletin board.
- The book also contains social studies words. Follow the steps above with these words, but this time provide a simple definition for words that may cause confusion: *city, compass rose, directions, east, Florida, key, map, Miami Beach, north, roads, south, state, streets, symbols, United States,* and *west*. For example: A compass rose is a symbol on a map that shows each direction. Show students the compass rose on the map on page 2.

Build Oral Language
- Say: Today we will be reading a book about maps. I have seen maps before. Let's see what this book can teach us about maps.

- Select a student and discuss how you might use a map to find your way to a friend's house or to the store. Explain how maps represent streets, buildings, parks, and lakes. Consider adding vocabulary to your discussion, such as *flat, road, symbol, rectangle, flag, circle, directions, right, left, state,* or *dot.* Then have the student give an example of a map he or she has used.
- Say: With a partner, brainstorm some words that relate to maps and directions. Post your words on a sheet of chart paper.
- Pick five pairs of students, and encourage each pair to share their words. Recognize when students use previously taught key vocabulary.

DURING THE READING

Preview the Book
- Read the title of the book on the cover, and point to the picture. Turn to page 2, and read the sentences, pointing to each word as you read. Have students follow along.
- Say: This book is about maps. The picture on the cover shows one kind of map, and the picture on page 2 shows another kind of map. I'm predicting that this book will teach me about different kinds of maps and how to use them.
- As needed, point out the words that have long vowel sounds (*a, e, i, o, u*) and the inflectional ending *–ing*: *drawing, show(s), place(s), streets, roads.*

Read the Book
- Read the book to students as they follow along. Point out words that contain the sound-spellings taught. Explain the characteristics of maps: *flat drawing, symbols, key, flag, driving directions, compass rose, north, south, east, west, big city.*
- Have students silently read the book. Ask a few students to partner read the book to each other, and help them sound out new words. When observing students, focus on the new words: *be, day, drawing(s), drivers, driving, east, find(ing), inside, lake, Miami Beach, need, place(s), read, real, right, roads, rose, show(s), size, state, use.*
- **Social Studies Connections:** Say: Sometimes maps are printed on paper, and sometimes we read them from a computer or a phone screen. If you made a map of your neighborhood, what would you include?

AFTER THE READING

Check Comprehension
To check students' understanding of the book, ask the following:
✓There are symbols on the map on page 2. What do the symbols represent? (Answers may include: The symbols show a school, house, tree, and playground.)
✓Page 4 describes a map that helps drivers know when to turn. Find the symbol that shows a left turn. On which street is the turn? (Raintree Road.)
✓Find the word *north* in the map on page 5. Which landmarks are north of Spencer Road? (The town of Cypress and Cypress Creek.) Which word in the text explains the location of south on the map? (*bottom*)

Reread to Develop Fluency
- Say: Today you will read the book to each other to practice reading with fluency. This means that you read the book as the author meant for it to be read aloud.
- Model reading fluently by reading the book aloud to students. Focus on pausing slightly when you come to a comma.
- Have partners reread the book to each other. Have students focus on reading sentences with commas. Students may struggle with decoding, comprehension, or vocabulary. For students who are struggling with vocabulary, say: I noticed that you seem unsure about the meaning of this word. Are there clues in the pictures that can help you understand the word? Or we can look up the meaning in a dictionary. Now that we understand the word, let's try reading the sentence again.
- Send home a copy of *Using Maps* for students to read to family members. Consider assessing a few students on fluency.

Seasons

SKILLS

PHONICS SKILL INTRODUCED
- *r*-controlled vowels (*er, ir, ur*)

SIGHT WORDS
- *best, cold, fly, four, I, which, why*

VOCABULARY WORDS–
Science Words
- *early, season, weather*

CURRICULUM LINK–
Science Focus
- Seasons

Seasons

BEFORE THE READING

Develop Phonemic Awareness and Phonics
Oral Segmentation
- Say: Today we are going to be listening to sounds and segmenting them to make words. Segmenting means pulling apart words by their sounds.
- Write the words *girl, nurse,* and *term* on the board. Model segmenting the sounds of the words as you point to each sound-spelling: /g/ /ir/ /l/, girl; /n/ /ur/ /s/, nurse; /t/ /er/ /m/, term.
- Write *burn* and *fern* on the board. Say these sounds while pointing to the sound-spellings, and have students echo you: /b/ /ur/ /n/, burn; /f/ /er/ /n/, fern.
- Write *sir* and *third* on the board. Have students try segmenting the words out loud but independently. Walk around to support students. If a student is struggling to segment the discrete sounds, model clapping once for each sound while saying it aloud, and have the student follow suit.

Introduce Phonics Skills
r-controlled vowels (*er, ir, ur*)
- Say: We just practiced blending some words with *r*-controlled vowels spelled with *er, ir,* and *ur*. Now we are going to read some words with these sound-spellings.
- Write the words *germ, skirt,* and *curl* on the board, and underline the *er, ir,* and *ur*. Say: The letters *er, ir,* and *ur* all make the same sound. Model reading the words, one sound at a time while pointing to the letters: /j/ /er/ /m/, germ; /sk/ /ir/ /t/, skirt; /k/ /ur/ /l/, curl.
- Write the words *bird, hurt,* and *serve* on the board. Have students read the words as a class. Say: Slowly sound out each letter.
- Have students try reading the words *herd, purse,* and *shirt* independently, following the routine above. Walk around to support students. Students who are struggling may need extra modeling and practice, such as: Let's look at the word *shirt*. Remember that together the letters *sh* make one sound, the /sh/ sound. Let's slowly say each of the sounds together as I point to the letters. Now you try it.

Introduce Sight Words
- Say: You are going to see some words today that you may not know, so you will need to keep them in your memory.
- Write the words *best, cold,* and *fly* on the board. Read them to students as you point to each letter.
- Write the words *four, I,* and *which* on the board. Read the words, and have students echo read each word.
- Write the word *why* on the board. Ask a volunteer to read it aloud, and have the rest of the class follow suit. Place the words on a sight-word bulletin board.
- The book also contains science words. Follow the steps above with these words, but this time provide a simple definition for words that may cause confusion: *early, season,* and *weather*. For example: The word *weather* refers to the condition of the outside air at a particular time or place. Weather can be hot, cold, wet, dry, sunny, clear, cloudy, calm, or windy.

Build Oral Language
- Say: Today we will be reading a book about the seasons. Before I read, I often think about the topic and try to recall what I already know about it.
- Select a student and discuss what you know about the seasons. Consider adding vocabulary to your discussion, such as *air, fall, hibernate, puddles, snow, spring, summer, temperature, winter*. Have the student tell you about his or her favorite season.

- Say: With a partner, discuss your favorite season. What is the weather like during that season? What do you like to do during that season?
- Pick five pairs of students, and encourage one student from each pair to share in the discussion. Recognize when students use previously taught key vocabulary.

DURING THE READING

Preview the Book
- Read the title of the book on the cover, and point to the picture. Turn to pages 2 and 3 and read the text, pointing to each word as you read. Have students follow along in their books.
- Say: Do you know what the book will be about based on the title and the first pages that I read? How do you know what it will be about?
- As needed, point out the words that have r-controlled vowels spelled with er, ir, or ur: winter, turn.

Read the Book
- Read the book to students as they follow along. Point out words that contain the sound-spellings taught.
- Have students silently read the book. Ask a few students to whisper read the book to you, and help them sound out new words. When observing students, focus on the new words: birds, burst, chirp, colder, colors, dirt, every, turn(s), twirl.
- **Science Connections:** Say: The seasons don't always occur at the same time around the world. In addition, depending on the part of the world in which you live, you may not experience all the seasons in the same way. For example, in Southern California, children do not experience snow in winter.

AFTER THE READING

Check Comprehension
To check students' understanding of the book, ask the following:
✓ Look at the pictures on page 2. Which season do you think is shown in each picture. (Answers clockwise from left to right: spring, summer, winter, fall.)
✓ Which word on page 4 has an r-controlled vowel spelled with er, ir, or ur and describes a sound birds make. (chirp) What is something new that you learned from this page? (Answers may vary.)
✓ What type of clothing do you wear in the winter? spring? summer? fall? (Answers may vary.)

Reread to Develop Fluency
- Say: Today you will read the book to each other to practice reading with fluency. This means that you read the book as the author meant for it to be read aloud.
- Model reading fluently by reading the book aloud to students. Focus on raising or dropping your voice depending on the end punctuation of the sentence.
- Have partners reread the book to each other. Remind students to raise their voices at the end of a sentence that ends in a question mark. Students may struggle with decoding, comprehension, or vocabulary. For students who are struggling with vocabulary, say: I noticed that you're not quite sure what that word means, which makes it hard to read the sentence. Let's look up the definition of the word in the dictionary.
- Send home a copy of Seasons for students to read to family members. Consider assessing a few students on fluency.

Connect to Written Language
↻ Review: Write the words rake, sign, and state on the board. As a class, read the words together as you point to the letters. Then add the ending –ing to each word, and read the new words together.

✓ Dictate the following words for students to spell: birth, lurch, cold, stir, surf, verb, and why. When finished, write the words on the board. Have students self-correct their papers.

✓ Divide the class into four groups, and assign one season to each group. Have each student in the group draw a picture of the assigned season and write 2–3 sentences about that season. You may suggest that students use the following sentence stems: In _____ the weather is _____. I wear _____ in the _____. I like to _____ in the _____. Ask one student from each group to share what they wrote with the class.

Bears

SKILLS

PHONICS SKILL INTRODUCED
- *r*-controlled vowels (*er, ir, ur*)

SIGHT WORDS
- *black, bring, keep, long, must, warm*

VOCABULARY WORDS–
Science Words
- *berries, cubs, den, mother, stream, twigs*

CURRICULUM LINK–
Science Focus
- Animals

Bears

BEFORE THE READING

Develop Phonemic Awareness and Phonics
Oral Segmentation
- Say: Today we are going to be segmenting the sounds in words. Segmenting means pulling apart words by their sounds.
- Write the words *her, dirt,* and *turn* on the board. Model saying each word sound by sound as you point to each sound-spelling: /h/ /er/, her; /d/ /ir/ /t/, dirt; /t/ /ur/ /n/, turn. Ask students to clap when they hear an *r*-controlled vowel.
- Write *fern, stir,* and *nurse* on the board. Clap at each *r*-controlled vowel sound while pointing to the sound-spellings. Have students echo you as you segment the sounds: /f/ /er/ /n/, fern; /st/ /ir/, stir; /n/ /ur/ /s/, nurse.
- Write *term, first,* and *hurt* on the board. Have students try segmenting the sounds out loud but independently. Walk around to support students. If a student is struggling with segmenting, model how you slow down your speech for each sound. Have the student follow suit as he or she slowly says each sound.

Introduce Phonics Skills
r-controlled vowels (*er, ir, ur*)
- Say: We just practiced segmenting the sounds in some words. Now we are going to read some words as we point out each sound-spelling.
- Write the words *verb, bird,* and *curb* on the board, and underline the *er, ir,* and *ur*. Say: The letters *er, ir,* and *ur* all make the same sound. Model reading the words, one sound at a time, while pointing to the letters: /v/ /er/ /b/, verb; /b/ /ir/ /d/, bird; /k/ /ur/ /b/, curb.
- Write the words *purge, third,* and *stern* on the board. Have students read the words as a class. Say: Slowly sound out each letter, and notice the different spellings for the *r*-controlled vowel sound.
- Have students try reading the words *nurse, girl,* and *perch* independently, following the routine above. Walk around to support students. Students who are struggling may need extra modeling and practice, such as: Let's look at the word *perch*. Remember that together the letters *ch* make the /ch/ sound. Let's slowly say each of the sounds together as I point to the letters. Now you try it.

Introduce Sight Words
- Say: You are going to see some words today that you may not know, so you will need to keep them in your memory.
- Write the words *black* and *bring* on the board. Read them to students as you point to each letter.
- Write the words *keep* and *long* on the board. Read the words, and have students echo read each word.
- Write the words *must* and *warm* on the board. Ask a volunteer to read them aloud, and have the rest of the class follow suit. Place the words on a sight-word bulletin board.
- The book also contains social studies words. Follow the steps above with these words, but this time provide a simple definition for words that may cause confusion: *berries, cubs, den, mother, stream,* and *twigs*. For example: A den is the name of the home where bears live. Show students the picture of the den on page 7.

Build Oral Language
- Say: Today we will be reading a book about bears. Have you ever seen a real bear? I wonder what bears do and how they live. I think this book will answer some of my questions.
- Select a student and discuss what bears eat, where they sleep, and how they grow. Explain how bears hibernate or sleep during the coldest part of the winter. Explain how even though they sleep a long time, they don't get hungry because they store the food they eat as fat. Consider adding vocabulary to your discussion, such as *January,*

February, March, April, May, June, July, August, September, October, November, December, cubs, berries, or *mother.* Then have the student share what he or she knows about bears and hibernation.

- Say: With a partner, conduct an interview about eating and sleeping habits of different animals.
- Pick five pairs of students, and encourage each pair to share what they learned. How many students had similar descriptions? Recognize when students use previously taught key vocabulary.

DURING THE READING

Preview the Book
- Read the title of the book on the cover, and point to the picture. Read page 2, pointing to each word as you read. Have students follow along in their books.
- Say: This book is about bears. The picture on the cover shows a family of bears. I would like to know what life is like for this family.
- As needed, point out the words that have *r*-controlled vowel sounds (*er, ir, ur*): *her, birth.*

Read the Book
- Read the book to students as they follow along. Point out words with the sound-spellings taught. Explain the months of the year if students are unsure about them.
- Have students silently read the book. Ask a few students to whisper read the book to you, and help them sound out new words. When observing students, focus on the new words: *birth, curl, fur, her,* and *nurse.*
- **Science Connections:** Say: Black bears are a species that live in many places in North America. Most bears hibernate in the winter, and the cubs drink milk, or nurse, from their mother. The mother lives off the food it ate during the spring and summer months.

AFTER THE READING

Check Comprehension
To check students' understanding of the book, ask the following:
✓Page 2 says that bears are born in January or February. What is the season when they are born? (winter)
✓Page 4 describes how the cubs leave the den in April. What is happening outside the den that draws the bears out? (Answers may include: The cold weather is over, and plants are growing again for food.)
✓Page 5 describes the food that bears eat. Which word describes the food in the picture? (*berries*) How does the bear eat the berries? (Answers may include: It holds the branch with its paw and eats the berries off the branch.)

Reread to Develop Fluency
- Say: Today you will read the book to each other to practice reading with fluency. This means that you read the book as the author meant for it to be read aloud.
- Model reading fluently by reading the book aloud to students. Focus on pausing briefly at commas and ending sentences with a slightly longer pause.
- Have partners reread the book to each other. Suggest that they reread any sentences in which they have trouble reading one or more words. Have them reread the words until they can read the sentence with ease. Students may struggle with decoding, comprehension, or vocabulary. For students who are struggling with decoding, say: I notice that you're working on reading this word. Let's read it together, slowly sounding out the letters of the word. You've got it! Now that you know the word, reread the sentence with proper expression.
- Send home a copy of *Bears* for students to read to family members. Consider assessing a few students on fluency.

Connect to Written Language
↻Review: Write the words *birds, chirp,* and *twirl* on the board. As a class, read the words together as you point to the letters. Then practice writing the words, and underline the *r*-controlled vowel sound in each word. Have students write a sentence for each word.

✓Dictate the following words for students to spell: *birth, curl, fur, her, nurse, black,* and *warm.* When finished, write the words on the board. Have students self-correct their papers.

✓Say: We don't always have to say "the bears" or "the mother bear." We can use special words called pronouns to substitute. Pronouns are words like *they, their, it, his, her,* or *them.* Write on the board: *The bears take a nap. They stay warm.* The word *they* replaces "the bears." Write on the board: *The mother bear looks for food. She finds berries.* We use the word *she* to represent "the mother bear." Encourage students to write two sentences, using pronouns in at least one of the sentences.

People at Work

SKILLS

PHONICS SKILL INTRODUCED
- *r*-controlled vowels (*ar*)

SIGHT WORDS
- *call, come, home, leave, near, owns, people*

VOCABULARY WORDS–
Social Studies Words
- *bus, community, drives, farm, fields, fixes, jobs, makes, market, nurse, people, school, sells, teacher, work(ers)*

CURRICULUM LINK–
Social Studies Focus
- Community Workers

People at Work

BEFORE THE READING

Develop Phonemic Awareness and Phonics
Rhyming
- Say: Today we are going to be listening for rhyming sounds in words. A rhyme is two words that have the same ending sound.
- Write the words *far, yard,* and *harm* on the board. Model saying each word sound by sound as you point to each sound-spelling: /f/ /ar/, far; /y/ /ar/ /d/, yard; /h/ /ar/ /m/, harm. Ask students to think of a rhyme for each word.
- Write *lark* and *smart* on the board. Clap at each *r*-controlled sound while pointing to the sound-spellings. Have students echo you as you say each sound: /l/ /ar/ /k/, lark; /sm/ /ar/ /t/, smart.
- Write *jar, yarn,* and *sharp* on the board. Have students try saying the sounds out loud but independently and come up with a rhyming word for each. Walk around to support students. If a student is struggling with rhyming, use a magnet board, and model substituting beginning sounds by changing out letters. Have the student follow suit as he or she slowly says the sounds.

Introduce Phonics Skills
***r*-controlled vowels (*ar*)**
- Say: We just practiced rhyming the sounds in some words. Now we are going to read some words as we point out each sound-spelling.
- Write the words *car, barn,* and *dart* on the board, and underline the *ar*. Say: The *ar* is the spelling for the /är/ sound. Model reading the words, one sound at a time, while pointing to the letters: /k/ /ar/, car; /b/ /ar/ /n/, barn; /d/ /ar/ /t/, dart.
- Write the words *hard, March,* and *shark* on the board. Have students read the words as a class. Say: Sound out each letter, and notice the spelling for the /är/ sound.
- Have students try reading the words *arm, arch,* and *dark* independently, following the routine above. Walk around to support students. Students who are struggling may need extra modeling and practice, such as: Let's look at the word *arch.* Remember that together the letters *ch* make the /ch/ sound. Let's slowly say each of the sounds together as I point to the letters. Now you try it.

Introduce Sight Words
- Say: You are going to see some words today that you may not know, so you will need to keep them in your memory.
- Write *call* and *come* on the board. Read them as you point to each letter.
- Write *home* and *leave* on the board. Read each word, and have students echo read.
- Write *owns, near,* and *people* on the board. Ask a volunteer to read them aloud, and have the rest of the class follow suit. Place the words on a sight-word bulletin board.
- The book also contains social studies words. Follow the steps above with these words, but this time provide a simple definition for words that may cause confusion: *bus, community, drives, farm, fields, fixes, jobs, makes, market, nurse, people, school, sells, teacher,* and *work(ers)*. For example: A community is a group of people who live and work together. Show students the picture of the people on page 8.

Build Oral Language
- Say: Today we will be reading a book about people who work in our community. What types of work do people do? I think this book will explain some of the ways people work together.
- Select a student, and discuss the definition of a job. Explain that a job is how people earn money to buy things and pay for a place to live. Describe how some people work outside, and others work in offices or buildings. Consider adding vocabulary to your discussion, such as *community, farm, fields, fixes, makes, market, nurse, school, sells, teacher,* or *work(ers)*. Then have the student share what kind of job he or she would like to have in the future.

- Say: Tell a partner about a job you would like to have and why. Then listen as your partner tells you about the job he or she would like to have.
- Pick five pairs of students, and encourage each pair to share what they discussed. On the board write the names of some of the jobs discussed. Recognize when students use previously taught key vocabulary.

DURING THE READING

Preview the Book
- Read the title of the book on the cover, and point to the picture. Turn to page 2 and read the sentences, pointing to each word as you read. Have students follow along.
- Say: When I read the title of this book, I think about people who work. The picture on the cover shows a teacher. I am wondering about other kinds of work. I bet this book will tell me something about different jobs people have.
- As needed, point out the words that have the /är/ sound: *are*.

Read the Book
- Read the book to students as they follow along. Point out words that contain the sound-spellings taught. Explain the types of jobs pictured if students aren't sure about them: *police officer, farmer, grocer, nurse, driver, waiter, manufacturer, computer teacher, coffee-shop worker.*
- Have students silently read the book. Ask a few students to partner read the book to each other, and help them sound out new words. When observing students, focus on the new words: *barn, cars, far, farm, hard, large, March, market, starts.*
- **Social Studies Connections:** Say: It takes a lot of people doing many different jobs to build a strong community. Each job is important. A teacher and a nurse help take care of the children. A grocer brings in fresh food for people to eat. What are some other jobs that help a community?

AFTER THE READING

Check Comprehension
To check students' understanding of the book, ask the following:
- ✓ Page 2 introduces a few workers who help a community. How many is a few? (Answers may include: A few is more than two or three.)
- ✓ Page 5 shows Mr. Medina's market. Does Mr. Medina start work early or late? (early) Why do you think he gets to work at this time? (Answers may include: He has to set out all the food before people come to shop.)
- ✓ Can you point to the lights that flash on page 7? (Students should point to the lights on the bus at the top right of the picture.) What do the flashing lights tell other cars? (Answers may include: The lights mean that children are boarding or exiting the bus, so other cars need to be careful.)

Reread to Develop Fluency
- Say: Today you will read the book to each other to practice reading with fluency. This means that you read the book as the author meant for it to be read aloud.
- Model reading fluently by reading the book aloud to students. Focus on reading with expression.
- Have partners reread the book to each other. Suggest that they reread any sentences in which they have trouble reading one or more words. Have them reread the words until they can read the sentence with expression. Students may struggle with decoding, comprehension, or vocabulary. For students who are struggling with vocabulary, say: I notice that you're not quite sure about the meaning of this word. Let's see if there are any clues in the picture or the words around it to help us. If not, we can look up the definition. Now that we know the word, let's reread the sentence. Use expression to show you understand the meaning.
- Send home a copy of *People at Work* for students to read to family members. Consider assessing a few students on fluency.

Connect to Written Language
↻ Review: Write the words *fern, girl,* and *nurse* on the board. As a class, read the words together as you point to the letters. Then practice writing the words and underline the *r*-controlled vowel sounds in each word. Have students write a sentence for each word.

✓ Dictate the following words for students to spell: *barn, cars, Clark, farm, March, near,* and *people.* When finished, write the words on the board. Have students self-correct their papers.

✓ Say: Some words are pronounced the same way but have different meanings and spellings. These are called homophones. For example, the words *their* and *there* sound the same, but *their* means "belonging to them," and *there* means "where something is." Write on the board: *The teacher goes to school. Kids go to school too.* The word *to* in the first sentence tells where the teacher goes. The word *too* in the second sentence means "also." Encourage students to think of other homophones. Have them write homophone pairs and try to write a sentence that uses each homophone.

Plants and Animals

SKILLS

PHONICS SKILL INTRODUCED
- *r*-controlled vowels (*ar*)

SIGHT WORDS
- *eat, four, grow, most, some, these, things*

VOCABULARY WORDS–
Science Words
- *air, animals, den, drinking, food, grass, grow, home, leaves, light, live, meat, nest, plants, soil, sun, sunlight, water*

CURRICULUM LINK–
Science Focus
- Plant and Animal Needs

Plants and Animals

BEFORE THE READING

Develop Phonemic Awareness and Phonics
Oral Segmentation
- Say: Today we are going to segment words so that we can say them sound by sound. Segment means to pull apart words by their sounds.
- Write the words *car* and *hard* on the board. Model saying the words sound by sound: /k/ /ar/, car; /h/ /ar/ /d/, hard.
- Write *dark* and *farm* on the board. Sound out each word, and have students follow suit chorally: /d/ /ar/ /k/, dark; /f/ /ar/ /m/, farm.
- Write *smart* and *barn* on the board. Have students segment the words out loud but independently. Walk around to support students. If a student is struggling to segment the sounds in each word, model saying each sound as you move a chip onto a line or sound box, and have the student follow suit.

Introduce Phonics Skills
r-controlled vowels (ar)
- Say: We just practiced blending some words with *r*-controlled vowels spelled with *ar*. Now we are going to read some words with this sound-spelling.
- Write the word *art* on the board, and underline the *ar*. Say: The letters *ar* make the /är/ sound. Model reading the word, one sound at a time, while pointing to the letters: /ar/ /t/.
- Write the words *park, bark,* and *mark* on the board. Have students read the words as a class. Say: Slowly sound out each letter.
- Have students try reading the words *dart, spark,* and *large* independently, following the routine above. Walk around to support students. Students who are struggling may need extra modeling, practice, and feedback, such as: Let's look at the word *large.* Remember that when the letter *g* comes before an *e,* the *g* often has the /j/ sound. Let's slowly say the sounds of this word together as I point to each letter: /l/ /ar/ /j/, large. Now you do it.

Introduce Sight Words
- Say: You are going to see some words today that you may not know, so you will need to keep them in your memory.
- Write the words *eat* and *four* on the board. Read the words to students as you point to each letter.
- Write the words *grow* and *most* on the board. Read the words, and have students echo read each word.
- Write the words *some, these,* and *things* on the board. Ask a volunteer to read them aloud, and have the rest of the class follow suit. Place the words on a sight-word bulletin board.
- The book also contains science words. Follow the steps above with these words, but this time provide a simple definition for words that may cause confusion: *air, animals, den, drinking, food, grass, grow, home, leaves, light, live, meat, nest, plants, soil, sun, sunlight, water.* For example: A nest is a place that birds build to live in and take care of their babies. Show students the picture of the nest from the book.

Build Oral Language
- Say: Today we will be reading a book about what plants and animals need in order to grow. Before I read, I often think about the topic and try to recall what I already know about it.
- Select a student and discuss what you know about plant and animal needs. Describe a pet or a plant that you have. Explain what your pet or plant needs to grow. Add vocabulary to your discussion, such as *food, soil,* and *water.* Then have the student tell you what he or she knows about plant and animal needs.

- Say: Make a KWL chart with a partner. Model making a KWL chart on the board. In the first column, write what you both know about plant and animal needs. In the second column, write what you both want to know about plant and animal needs. In the third column, write what you both learned about plant and animal needs.
- Pick five pairs of students, and encourage one student from each pair to share what they wrote. Recognize when students use previously taught key vocabulary.

DURING THE READING

Preview the Book
- Read the title of the book on the cover, and point to the picture. Turn to page 2, and read the sentences, pointing to each word as you read. Also point to the image and discuss that as well. Have students follow along in their books.
- Say: Do you know what the book will be about based on the title and the first page that I read? How do you know what it will be about?
- As needed, point out the words with the *r*-controlled vowel sound spelled with *ar*: *yard, garden*.

Read the Book
- Read the book to students as they follow along. Point out words that contain the sound-spellings taught. Tell students where plants can grow if they don't know: *garden, jar, yard*.
- Have students silently read the book. Ask a few students to whisper read the book to you, and help them sound out new words. When observing students, focus on the new words: *dark, garden, jar, larger, yard*.
- **Science Connections:** Say: Plants and animals have special parts to get what they need to live and grow. Plants have roots for getting water. Some animals have a nose and lungs for breathing air. Other animals, such as fish, have gills that take in air from water.

AFTER THE READING

Check Comprehension
To check students' understanding of the book, ask the following:
- ✓Read page 4. How does a plant get water? Where does this water come from? (A plant gets water from the soil. The water comes from rain and melted snow.)
- ✓How are plants and animals alike and different? (Plants and animals are alike because both need water and air to live and grow. They are different because plants need soil for their homes, but animals can live in places like nests and dens.)
- ✓How does the picture on page 8 help you understand what you read? How does the text help you understand the picture? (Answers may include: The picture helps me understand that a nest is a safe home for a baby bird. The text helps me understand that animals need air, water, food, and a safe home to live and grow.)

Reread to Develop Fluency
- Say: Today you will read the book to each other to practice reading with fluency. This means that you read the book as the author meant for it to be read aloud.
- Model reading fluently by reading the book aloud to students. Focus on raising your voice when a sentence ends with a question mark.
- Have partners reread the book to each other. Remind children how to read sentences that end with question marks. Students may struggle with decoding, comprehension, or vocabulary. For students struggling with decoding, say: I see that you're trying to read this word. Let's read it together, slowly sounding out the letters of each word. You've got it! Reread the sentence now that you know the word.
- Send home a copy of *Plants and Animals* for students to read to family members. Consider assessing a few students on fluency.

Connect to Written Language
↻Review: Write the words *barn*, *far*, and *market* on the board. As a class, read the words together as you point to the letters. Then replace the *a* in *barn* and *far* with *u*. Have students write the new words, and read them together.

✓Dictate the following words for students to spell: *jar, yard, smart, car, dark, things*, and *four*. When finished, write the words on the board. Have students self-correct their papers.

✓Say: Some words are made up of two different words. When these words are put together, they make a new word with a new meaning. You can figure out this new meaning by thinking about the meanings of the two different words. Write the word *sunlight* on the board. Do you see two different words? Trace a line under *sun* and say: *sun*. Trace a line under *light* and say: *light*. The sun is the star that gives us warmth. Light is the brightness you see when you turn on a lamp. So *sunlight* means "the light of the sun." Write *sunflower, grasshopper*, and *bookshelf* on the board. Read the words as a class, and encourage group discussion about their meanings. Ask students to think of more compound words and to write them on a piece of paper.

*Peanuts to
Peanut Butter*

SKILLS

PHONICS SKILL INTRODUCED
- *r*-controlled vowels (*or, ore, our*)

SIGHT WORDS
- *best, buy(s), each, grow, know, put, take(s), under, what, where*

VOCABULARY WORDS–
Social Studies Words
- *crushed, factory, farmer, harvesting, jar, lids, machine(s), oil, peanuts, plants, roasted, salt, shells, soil, sugar*

CURRICULUM LINK–
Social Studies Focus
- Buy and Sell

Peanuts to Peanut Butter

BEFORE THE READING

Develop Phonemic Awareness and Phonics
Oral Blending
- Say: Today we are going to be listening to sounds and blending them to make words. Blending means putting sounds together to make words.
- Write the words *for* and *form* on the board. Model blending the sounds of the words as you point to each sound-spelling: /f/ /or/, for; /f/ /or/ /m/, form.
- Write *more* and *sort* on the board. Say these sounds while pointing to the sound-spellings, and have students echo you: /m/ /ore/, more; /s/ /or/ /t/, sort.
- Write *four* and *pour* on the board. Have students try blending the words out loud but independently. Walk around to support students. If a student is struggling to blend the discrete sounds, model putting up one finger for each sound while saying it aloud, and have the student follow suit.

Introduce Phonics Skills
r-controlled vowels (*or, ore, our*)
- Say: We just practiced blending some words with *r*-controlled vowels spelled with *or, ore,* and *our*. Now we are going to read some words with these sound-spellings.
- Write the word *fort* on the board, and underline the *or*. Say: The letters *or, ore,* and *our* all make the same sound. Model reading the word, one sound at a time, while pointing to the letters: /f/ /or/ /t/.
- Write the words *short, sore,* and *pour* on the board. Point out the different spellings for the *r*-controlled vowel sounds. Have students read the words as a class. Say: Slowly sound out each letter.
- Have students try reading the words, *sport, bore,* and *court* independently, following the routine above. Walk around to support students. Students who are struggling may need extra modeling, practice, and feedback, such as: Let's look at the word *sport*. Remember that when two consonants appear together, they are blended together. For example, the letters *sp* together make the /sp/ sound. Let's slowly say the sounds of this word together as I point to each letter. Now you do it.

Introduce Sight Words
- Say: You are going to see some words today that you may not know, so you will need to keep them in your memory.
- Write the words *best, buys,* and *each* on the board. Read the words to students as you point to each letter.
- Write the words *grow, know,* and *put* on the board. Read the words, and have students echo read each word.
- Write the words *take, under,* and *where* on the board. Ask a volunteer to read them aloud, and have the class follow suit. Place the words on a sight-word bulletin board.
- The book also contains social studies words. Follow the steps above with these words, but this time provide a simple definition for words that may cause confusion: *crushed, factory, farmer, harvesting, jar, lids, machines, oil, peanuts, plants, roasted, salt, shells, soil, sugar.* For example: Shells are hard outer coverings or cases. Show students the picture of peanut shells from the book.

Build Oral Language
- Say: Today we will be reading a book about the steps peanuts go through before they become peanut butter and are sold at the grocery store. Before I read, I often think about the topic and try to recall what I already know about it.
- Select a student and discuss what you know about where foods originally come from and how they end up in stores. For example, milk comes from cows and bread comes

from wheat. When they are ready to be sold, these items are taken to stores. Add vocabulary to your discussion: *farm, factory, machine, store, market, sell, buy.* Then have the student tell you what he or she knows about where food comes from.

- Say: Interview a partner about peanuts and peanut butter. Ask your partner to name some things that are made with peanuts. Ask if your partner knows how peanut butter is made and how it gets to the store. Then switch roles.
- Pick five pairs of students, and encourage one student from each pair to share what they learned during the interviews. Recognize when students use previously taught key vocabulary.

DURING THE READING

Preview the Book
- Read the title of the book on the cover, and point to the picture. Turn to page 2 and read the sentences, pointing to each word as you read. Also point to the image and discuss that as well. Have students follow along in their books.
- Say: Do you know what the book will be about based on the title and the first page that I read? How do you know what it will be about?

Read the Book
- Read the book to students as they follow along. Point out words that contain the sound-spellings taught. Tell students what equipment farmers use to collect peanuts if they don't know: *tractor.*
- Have students silently read the book. Ask a few students to whisper read the book to you, and help them sound out new words. When observing students, focus on the new words: *for, tractor, store(s), four, pour.*
- **Social Studies Connections:** Say: Peanut butter is a very popular food. Americans buy enough peanut butter in a year to make over 10 billion peanut butter and jelly sandwiches. Stores sell almost 90 million jars of peanut butter each year.

AFTER THE READING

Check Comprehension
To check students' understanding of the book, ask the following:
✓How does the picture on page 3 help you understand what you read? How does the text help you understand the picture? (Answers may include: The picture helps me understand what peanuts look like when they grow in a field. The text helps me understand that little green plants grow from the planted peanuts. The plants' branches grow into the soil where more peanuts grow.)
✓Look at page 4. How do you think a tractor helps a farmer who grows peanuts? (The tractor helps peanut farmers by picking up a lot of peanuts at once. The tractor can pick up more peanuts in less time than a farmer can.)
✓Look at page 6. What happens to peanuts after they are cleaned and roasted? (After peanuts are roasted, they are crushed. Then salt, oil, and sugar are added to the crushed peanuts. After machines pour peanut butter into jars, the jars are taken to stores.)

Reread to Develop Fluency
- Say: Today you will read the book to each other to practice reading with fluency. This means that you read the book as the author meant for it to be read aloud.
- Model reading fluently by reading the book aloud to students. Focus on reading with excitement when a sentence ends with an exclamation point.
- Have partners reread the book to each other. Remind children how to read sentences that end with exclamation points. Students may struggle with decoding, comprehension, or vocabulary. For students struggling with comprehension, say: I noticed that you seem unsure how to read this sentence. What are some clues we can use to help us understand what we read? Now that we understand the sentence a little better, let's try reading it again with proper expression.
- Send home a copy of *Peanuts to Peanut Butter* for students to read to family members. Consider assessing a few students on fluency.

Connect to Written Language
↻Review: Write the words *dark, for,* and *yard* on the board. As a class, read the words together as you point to the letters. Then replace the *o* in *for* with *a.* Have students write the new word, and read it together.

✓Dictate the following words for students to spell: *or, more, store, four, pour, grow,* and *under.* When finished, write the words on the board. Have students self-correct their papers.

✓Say: Some words are pronounced the same way but have different meanings and spellings. These are called homophones. Write on the board: *In the fall the farmer uses a big tractor for harvesting.* Read the sentence as a class and say: The word *for* in this sentence means "to meet the needs of something." Write on the board: *These four things make peanut butter.* Read the sentence as a class and say: The word *four* in this sentence means "the number 4." Encourage students to write additional sentences using the homophones *for* and *four.* You may wish to use the following sentence frames about peanut butter: *My dad bought _____ jars of peanut butter. He is going to use the peanut butter _____ our family's sandwiches.*

All Kinds of Sounds

SKILLS

PHONICS SKILL INTRODUCED
- Diphthong /ou/ (*ou, ow*)

SIGHT WORDS
- *around, back, falling, laughing, more*

VOCABULARY WORDS–
Science Words
- *hear, high, loud, low, move, pitch, quiet, sounds, speak, throat, vibrate(s)*

CURRICULUM LINK–
Science Focus
- Sound

All Kinds of Sounds

BEFORE THE READING

Develop Phonemic Awareness and Phonics
Oral Segmentation
- Say: Today we are going to be segmenting the sounds in words. Segmenting means pulling words apart by their sounds. We will listen for the /ou/ sound.
- Write the words *cow* and *out* on the board. Model saying each word sound by sound as you point to each sound-spelling: /k/ /ou/, cow; /ou/ /t/, out. Tap the desk once for each sound.
- Write *loud* and *town* on the board. Say these sounds while pointing to the sound-spellings. Have students echo you as you segment the sounds and clap the syllables: /l/ /ou/ /d/, loud; /t/ /ou/ /n/, town.
- Write *cloud* and *mouth* on the board. Have students try segmenting the sounds out loud but independently. Walk around to support students. If a student is struggling with segmenting, model using a colored chip for each sound, and push one chip forward as you say each sound. Have the student follow suit as he or she slowly says the sounds.

Introduce Phonics Skills
Diphthong /ou/ (*ou, ow*)
- Say: We just practiced segmenting the sounds in some words. Now we are going to read some words as we point out each sound-spelling.
- Write the words *round* and *how* on the board, and underline the *ou* and the *ow*. Say: The *ou* and *ow* are two spellings for the /ou/ sound. Model reading the words, one sound at a time, while pointing to the letters: /r/ /ou/ /n/ /d/, round; /h/ /ou/, how.
- Write the words *owl* and *shout* on the board. Have students read the words as a class. Say: Sound out each letter, and notice the different spellings for the /ou/ sound.
- Have students try reading the words *crowd, vow, couch,* and *mouth* independently, following the routine above. Walk around to support students. Students who are struggling may need extra modeling and practice, such as: Let's look at the words *couch* and *mouth*. Remember the letters *ch* and *th* each make one sound, /ch/ and /th/. Let's slowly say each of the sounds together as I point to the letters.

Introduce Sight Words
- Say: You are going to see some words today that you may not know, so you will need to keep them in your memory.
- Write the words *around* and *back* on the board. Read them to students as you point to each letter.
- Write *falling* on the board. Read the word, and have students echo read it to you.
- Write *laughing* and *more* on the board. Ask a volunteer to read them aloud, and have the rest of the class follow suit. Place the words on a sight-word bulletin board.
- The book also contains science words. Follow the steps above with these words, but this time provide a simple definition for words that may cause confusion: *hear, high, loud, low, move, pitch, quiet, sounds, speak, throat,* and *vibrate(s)*. For example: The word *pitch* describes the range of sounds. Sounds can be high or low. Show students the pictures of the cow and the bird on page 8 and discuss which makes a higher sound.

Build Oral Language
- Say: We will be reading a book about sounds. Some sounds are pleasant, like music, and some are hard to listen to, like a siren. How do sounds happen? What are other kinds of sounds? Let's see if this book helps me learn more.
- Select a student and discuss some soft sounds, like falling rain, or loud sounds, like a beating drum. Explain how sound comes in waves that hit our ears like a bouncing ball. A soft sound wave is gentle, and a loud sound wave is fast and strong. Describe some sounds you like. Consider adding vocabulary to your discussion, such as *hear,*

high, loud, low, move, pitch, quiet, sounds, speak, throat, or *vibrate(s).* Then have the student demonstrate a loud and a soft sound.

- Say: With a partner, brainstorm some loud and soft sounds. Write your ideas on sticky notes, and put them on the board.
- Pick five pairs of students, and encourage each pair to share their sounds. See if other students think the sounds are loud or soft. Recognize when students use previously taught key vocabulary.

DURING THE READING

Preview the Book

- Read the title of the book on the cover, and point to the picture. Turn to page 2 and read the sentences, pointing to each word as you read. Have students follow along.
- Say: This book is about different kinds of sounds. The picture on the cover shows a band, which makes a loud sound. Look at the picture on page 2. This boy is trying hard to hear something. I wonder what other sounds will be described in this book.
- As needed, point out the words that have the diphthong /ou/ (*ou, ow*): *house, sounds, around.*

Read the Book

- Read the book to students as they follow along. Point out words that contain the sound-spellings taught. Explain the types of sounds if students aren't sure about them: *quiet, thunder, loud, whisper, drum, throat, squeak, growl, pitch.*
- Have students silently read the book. Ask a few students to whisper read the book to you, and help them sound out new words. When observing students, focus on the new words: *around, clown, crowd, ground, growl, house, mouse, pound, sound(s).*
- **Science Connections:** Say: Sound comes from a vibration. If I stretch a rubber band around an open container, and pluck at it, it will vibrate and you will hear a sound. Think about a guitar. What is vibrating on the guitar to make the sound? Think about a car. What is vibrating inside the car to make a sound?

AFTER THE READING

Check Comprehension

To check students' understanding of the book, ask the following:

✓ Look at page 3. The lightning shows how strong the thunder is. What sound does a thunderstorm make? (Answers may include: A loud rumbling sound, or a boom.)

✓ The boy on page 5 is about to hit the drum. Do you think he will make a loud sound or a soft sound? (loud) What makes you think so? (Answers may include: He is going to hit the drum hard with the sticks.)

✓ Point to the word on page 6 that describes where the boy has put his hands. (*throat*) How do you know he is saying "Ahhh?" (Answers may include: His mouth is open like he is making an "ahhh" sound.)

Reread to Develop Fluency

- Say: Today you will read the book to each other to practice reading with fluency. This means that you read the book as the author meant for it to be read aloud.
- Model reading fluently by reading the book aloud to students. Focus on raising your voice slightly when you come to a question mark.
- Have partners reread the book to each other. Suggest that they raise their voices when they come to a question mark at the end of a sentence. Students may struggle with decoding, comprehension, or vocabulary. For students who are struggling with decoding, say: I can tell you are trying to read this word. Let's try it together, slowly sounding out the letters of each word. Watch what my mouth is doing. Now you try it. You did it! Now reread the whole sentence a little more quickly.
- Send home a copy of *All Kinds of Sounds* for students to read to family members. Consider assessing a few students on fluency.

Connect to Written Language

↻ Review: Write the words *four, pour,* and *store* on the board. As a class, read the words together as you point to the letters. Then practice writing the words and underline the *r*-controlled vowel sound (*ore, our*) in each word. Have students draw a picture and write a sentence for each word.

✓ Dictate the following words for students to spell: *around, clown, growl, loud, mouse, owl,* and *laughing.* When finished, write the words on the board. Have students self-correct their papers.

✓ Say: Words that have the same ending sounds are called rhymes. For example, the words *clown* and *town* have the same ending sounds. Write on the board: *Rain on the ground makes a quiet sound.* Can you hear the rhyme in the sentence? Which two words rhyme? Write on the board: *When I pound, it makes a loud ____.* Can you finish this sentence with a rhyming word? Encourage students to write a sentence with two rhyming words.

SKILLS

PHONICS SKILL INTRODUCED
- Diphthong /ou/ (*ou, ow*)

SIGHT WORDS
- *find, go, had, long, look, much, only, over, were*

VOCABULARY WORDS–
Social Studies Words
- *coach(es), computers, electric*

CURRICULUM LINK–
Social Studies Focus
- Now/Long Ago

Life Now and Long Ago

BEFORE THE READING

Develop Phonemic Awareness and Phonics
Phonemic Manipulation: Deletion
- Say: Today we are going to remove one letter from some words to make them into new words.
- Write the words *couch* and *cloud* on the board, and model removing the first sound in each word: couch, ouch; cloud, loud.
- Write *ground, amount, sour, shout, spout, cow,* and *howl* on the board. Have students say each word without its beginning sound.

Introduce Phonics Skills
Diphthong /ou/ (*ou, ow*)
- Say: We just practiced creating some new words with the /ou/ sound. Now we are going to read some words with this sound-spelling.
- Write the words *mouth* and *cow* on the board, and underline the *ou* and *ow*. Say: The letters *ou* and *ow* are the spellings for the /ou/ sound. Model reading the words, one sound at a time, while pointing to the letters: /m/ /ou/ /th/, /k/ /ow/.
- Write the words *flour, how,* and *round* on the board. Have students read the words as a class. Say: Slowly sound out each letter.
- Have students try reading the words *about, around,* and *mouse* independently, following the routine above. Walk around to support students. If students are struggling with words that begin with the schwa sound /ə/, say: Let's look at the word *around*. Notice that this word begins with the letter *a*, but it doesn't make the /a/ or /ā/ sound. Instead it makes the /ə/ sound. Let's slowly say the sounds of this word together as I point to each letter. Now you do it.

Introduce Sight Words
- Say: You are going to see some words today that you may not know, so you will need to keep them in your memory.
- Write the words *find, go,* and *had* on the board. Read them to students as you point to each letter.
- Write the words *long, look, much,* and *only* on the board. Read the words, and have students echo read each word.
- Write the words *over* and *were* on the board. Ask a volunteer to read them aloud, and have the rest of the class follow suit. Place the words on a sight-word bulletin board.
- The book also contains social studies words. Follow the steps above with these words, but this time provide a simple definition for words that may cause confusion: *coach(es), computers,* and *electric*. For example: A coach is a large four-wheeled carriage that is drawn by horses and has a raised seat in front for the driver. Show students a picture of a coach from the book.

Build Oral Language
- Say: Today we will be reading a book comparing what it was like to live long ago to what life is like now. Before I read, I often think about the topic and try to recall what I already know about it.
- Select a student, and discuss what you know about life long ago. Consider adding vocabulary to your discussion, such as *artifacts, history, modern, past, technology,* and *tools*. Then have the student tell you what they know about how life was different when their parents or grandparents were children.

- Say: With a partner, discuss some things your parents or grandparents have told you about what life was like when they were young. What are some things you have that your parents or grandparents didn't have when they were children?
- Pick five pairs of students, and encourage one student from each pair to share in the discussion. Recognize when students use previously taught key vocabulary.

DURING THE READING

Preview the Book
- Read the title of the book on the cover, and point to the picture. Turn to page 2 and read the sentences, pointing to each word as you read. Have students follow along in their books.
- Say: Do you know what the book will be about based on the title and the first page that I read? How do you know what it will be about?
- As needed, point out the words that have the /ou/ sounds: *now, our*.

Read the Book
- Read the book to students as they follow along. Point out words that contain the sound-spellings taught. Tell students the names of items if they don't know them: *carriage, coach, horse-drawn plow*.
- Have students silently read the book. Ask a few students to whisper read the book to you, and help them sound out new words. When observing students, focus on the new words: *about, cow, down, found, house, how, now, our, out, plow, town*.
- **Social Studies Connections:** Say: The greatest source of change from long ago to today is technology. As you grow up and get older, you will see new inventions that do not exist today.

AFTER THE READING

Check Comprehension
To check students' understanding of the book, ask the following:
✓ What word on page 4 has the /ou/ sound and is a tool that a farmer uses? (*plow*) Why do you think farmers used hand-held plows? (Answers may include: Farmers used hand-held plows because they did not have the technology we have today.)
✓ Look at page 6, and make an inference. What did people use before they had electric lights? (Answers may include: candles, lanterns, gas lamps)
✓ How are schools today different from schools long ago? (Answers may include: Students are divided into classes by grade level. We use computers and TVs in schools today. We ride on school buses.)

Reread to Develop Fluency
- Say: Today you will read the book to each other to practice reading with fluency. This means that you read the book as the author meant for it to be read aloud.
- Model reading fluently by reading the book aloud to students with ease.
- Have partners reread the book to each other. Suggest that they alternate reading one page at a time. Tell students to practice until they can read each page with ease. Students may struggle with decoding, comprehension, or vocabulary. For students who are struggling with decoding, say: I see that you're working on reading this word. Let's read it together and slowly sound out the letters. We did it! Now you try it on your own. Great! Can you try the whole sentence again?
- Send home a copy of *Life Now and Long Ago* for students to read to family members. Consider assessing a few students on fluency.

Connect to Written Language
↻ Review: Write the words *around, ground,* and *how* on the board. As a class, read the words together as you point to the letters. Then remove the beginning sound, and read the new words together.

✓ Dictate the following words for students to spell: *about, cow, down, found, house, look,* and *were*. When finished, write the words on the board. Have students self-correct their papers.

✓ Have students divide a sheet of paper in half. On one side, have them write "Now" at the top. Have them label the other side "Long Ago." Have students draw a picture of something that is used today and something that was used long ago. The items could be found in a school, house, city, or on a farm. Display the students' pictures around the school or in the school library to share with others.

Plant Parts

SKILLS

PHONICS SKILL INTRODUCED
- Variant Vowels /o͞o/ and /o͝o/

SIGHT WORDS
- *are, eat, grow, hold, many, some, these, water, you*

VOCABULARY WORDS–
Science Words
- *air, bloom, flowers, leaves, moves, plant(s), roots, seeds, soil, stem, sunlight, tree, trunk, water*

CURRICULUM LINK–
Science Focus
- Parts of a Plant

Plant Parts

BEFORE THE READING

Develop Phonemic Awareness and Phonics
Phonemic Manipulation: Deletion
- Say: Today we are going to remove one letter from some words and say their ending sounds.
- Write the words *shoot, boot,* and *food* on the board. Model removing the first sound in each word: shoot, oot; boot, oot; food, ood.
- Write *book, took, could,* and *would* on the board. Have students say each word without its beginning sound.

Introduce Phonics Skills
Variant Vowels /o͞o/ and /o͝o/
- Say: We just practiced saying some words with the /o͞o/ and /o͝o/ sounds. Now we are going to read some words with these sound-spellings.
- Write the words *soon, to, tube, true, truth,* and *group* on the board, and underline the vowels. Say: The letters *oo, o, u_e, ue, u,* and *ou* are the spellings for the /o͞o/ sound. Model reading the words, one sound at a time, while pointing to the letters: /s/ /o͞o/ /n/, /t/ /o͞o/, /t/ /o͞o/ /b/, /tr/ /o͞o/, /tr/ /o͞o/ /th/, /gr/ /o͞o/ /p/.
- Write the words *book, put,* and *could* on the board, and underline the vowels. Say: The letters *oo* and *u* can also stand for the /o͝o/ sound. The spelling *–ould* contains this sound too. Model reading the words, one sound at a time, while pointing to the letters: /b/ /o͝o/ /k/, /p/ /o͝o/ /t/, /k/ /o͝o/ /d/.
- Write the words *bloom, do, cube, blue, soup, cook,* and *would* on the board. Have students read the words as a class. Say: Slowly sound out each letter.
- Have students try reading the words *look, food,* and *should* independently, following the routine above. Walk around to support students. Students who are struggling may need extra modeling, practice, and feedback, such as: Let's look at the word *should.* When two consonants appear together in a word, the sound of each consonant is blended together. For example, the letters *sh* in *should* stand for the /sh/ sound. Let's slowly say the sounds of this word together as I point to each letter. Now you do it.

Introduce Sight Words
- Say: You are going to see some words today that you may not know, so you will need to keep them in your memory.
- Write the words *are, eat,* and *grow* on the board. Read them to students as you point to each letter.
- Write the words *hold, many,* and *some* on the board. Read the words, and have students echo read each word.
- Write the words *these, water,* and *you* on the board. Ask a volunteer to read them aloud, and have the rest of the class follow suit. Place the words on a sight-word bulletin board.
- The book also contains science words. Follow the steps above with these words, but this time provide a simple definition for words that may cause confusion: *air, bloom, flowers, leaves, moves, plant(s), roots, seeds, soil, stem, sunlight, tree, trunk,* and *water.* For example: A stem is the main part of a plant from which the leaves and flowers grow. Show students a picture of a stem from the book.

Build Oral Language
- Say: Today we will be reading a book about the parts of a plant. Before I read, I often think about the topic and try to recall what I already know about it.
- Select a student and discuss what you know about plant parts. Name some different parts of plants and describe how some of them look. Consider adding vocabulary to your discussion, such as *roots, soil, seed, stem, leaves, blossom,* and *buds.* Then have the student tell you what he or she knows about the parts of a plant.

- Say: Interview a partner about what he or she knows about the parts of a plant. Ask your partner to describe a plant he or she is familiar with and name its different parts.
- Pick five pairs of students, and encourage one student from each pair to share what they learned during the interviews. Recognize when students use previously taught key vocabulary.

DURING THE READING

Preview the Book
- Read the title of the book on the cover, and point to the picture. Turn to page 2 and read the sentences, pointing to each word as you read. Also point out the labels and read those words as well. Have students follow along in their books.
- Say: Do you know what the book will be about based on the title and the first page that I read? How do you know what it will be about?
- As needed, point out the words that have the /o͞o/ and /o͝o/ sounds: *roots, look.*

Read the Book
- Read the book to students as they follow along. Point out words that contain the sound-spellings taught. Tell students the different parts of plants if they don't know them: *flower, leaves, stem, roots.*
- Have students silently read the book. Ask a few students to whisper read the book to you, and help them sound out new words. When observing students, focus on the new words: *bloom, food, root(s), to, too, look, could.*
- **Science Connections:** Say: Many vegetables, such as carrots, are edible plant roots. For example, beets, potatoes, turnips, sweet potatoes, yams, parsnips, and onions are all roots that people eat.

AFTER THE READING

Check Comprehension
To check students' understanding of the book, ask the following:
- ✓ How does the picture on page 4 help you understand what you read? How does the text help you understand the picture? (Answers may include: The picture helps me understand what carrot roots look like underground. The text helps me understand the picture by explaining that carrots are part of a carrot plant's roots.)
- ✓ Explain the ways a stem helps a plant. (A stem helps a plant by holding it up. Stems also carry water to a plant's leaves.)
- ✓ What word on page 7 has the /o͞o/ sound and describes what flowers do? (*bloom*)

Reread to Develop Fluency
- Say: Today you will read the book to each other to practice reading with fluency. This means that you read the book as the author meant for it to be read aloud.
- Model reading fluently by reading the book aloud to students. Focus on pausing briefly whenever there is a comma.
- Have partners reread the book to each other. Suggest that they pause when they see a comma. Students may struggle with decoding, comprehension, or vocabulary. For students who are struggling with comprehension, say: I noticed that you seem unsure how to read this sentence. What are some clues we can use to help us understand what we read? Now that we understand the sentence a little better, let's try reading it again with proper expression.
- Send home a copy of *Plant Parts* for students to read to family members. Consider assessing a few students on fluency.

Connect to Written Language

↻ Review: Write the words *cloud, growl,* and *pouch* on the board. As a class, read the words together as you point to the letters. Then remove the beginning sound, and read the new words together.

✓ Dictate the following words for students to spell: *look, book, food, good, blooming, are,* and *you.* When finished, write the words on the board. Have students self-correct their papers.

✓ Say: Some words are pronounced the same way but have different meanings and spellings. These are called homophones. Write on the board: *The roots take in water too.* Read the sentence as a class and say: The word *too* in this sentence means "also." Write on the board: *Water moves up the stem to the leaves.* Read the sentence as a class and say: The word *to* in this sentence means "toward or in the direction of." Write on the board: *We have two plants at home.* Read the sentence as a class and say: The word *two* in this sentence "means the number 2." Encourage students to write additional sentences using the homophones *to, too,* and *two.* You may wish to use the following sentence frames about plants: *Plants have stems. Plants have leaves ____. Rain falls from the sky ____ a plant's roots. Carrots and sweet potatoes are ____ kinds of plant roots that we can eat.*

Up in the Sky

SKILLS

PHONICS SKILL INTRODUCED
- Variant Vowels /o͞o/ and /o͝o/

SIGHT WORDS
- *because, fit, inside, much, see, than*

VOCABULARY WORDS—
Science Words
- *circle, clouds, daytime, different, Earth, moon, nighttime, sky, stars, sun, warms*

CURRICULUM LINK—
Science Focus
- The Sky

Up in the Sky

BEFORE THE READING

Develop Phonemic Awareness and Phonics
Oral Blending
- Say: Today we are going to be blending sounds. Blending means putting sounds together to make words. We will listen for the /o͞o/ and /o͝o/ sounds.
- Write the words *foot* and *moon* on the board, and model blending the sounds as you point to each sound-spelling: /f/ /o͝o/ /t/, foot; /m/ /o͞o/ /n/, moon. Hold up one finger at a time as you say each sound.
- Write *hook* and *shoot* on the board. Say these sounds while pointing to the sound-spellings. Have students echo you as you blend the sounds and say the words: /h/ /o͝o/ /k/, hook; /sh/ /o͞o/ /t/, shoot.
- Write *spoon* and *took* on the board. Have students try blending the sounds out loud but independently. Walk around to support students. If a student is struggling with blending, model holding up one finger for each sound so students visually see how the sounds blend together. Have the student follow suit as he or she says the sounds.

Introduce Phonics Skills
Variant Vowels /o͞o/, /o͝o/
- Say: We just practiced blending the sounds in some words. Now we are going to read some words with these sound-spellings.
- Write the words *noon* and *look* on the board, and underline the *oo*. Say: The *oo* can stand for the /o͞o/ sound, as in *noon*, or the /o͝o/ sound, as in *look*. Model reading the words, one sound at a time, while pointing to the letters: /n/ /o͞o/ /n/, noon; /l/ /o͝o/ /k/, look.
- Write the words *hood* and *room* on the board. Have students read the words as a class. Say: Slowly sound out each letter, and notice the different sounds for each *oo* spelling.
- Have students try reading the words *wood, brook, pool,* and *zoom* independently, following the routine above. Walk around to support students. Students who are struggling may need extra modeling and practice, such as: Let's look at the word *brook*. Remember the letters *br* are blended together to make the /br/ sound. Let's say each of the sounds together as we point to the letters.
- Repeat the steps using these exemplars:
  1) oo, /o͞o/; 2) moon; 3) shoot, spoon, food; 4) loop, tool
  1) oo, /o͝o/; 2) foot; 3) look, good, wool; 4) hoof, stood

Introduce Sight Words
- Say: You are going to see some words today that you may not know, so you will need to keep them in your memory.
- Write *because* and *fit* on the board. Read them to students as you point to each letter.
- Write *inside* and *much* on the board. Read the words, and have students echo read each word.
- Write *see* and *than* on the board. Ask a volunteer to read them aloud, and have the rest of the class follow suit. Place the words on a sight-word bulletin board.
- The book also contains science words. Follow the steps above with these words, but this time provide a simple definition for words that may cause confusion: *circle, clouds, daytime, different, Earth, moon, nighttime, sky, stars, sun,* and *warms*. For example: The word *warms* describes how something grows hotter because of the sun's heat. Show students the picture of the sun on page 7, and discuss how it looks small to us, but it is actually very large.

Build Oral Language
- Say: Today we will be reading a book about the moon, stars, and the sun. These are different things we see in the sky. The moon and stars are things we see at night, and the sun is out during the day. Let's see if this book shows other things in the sky.

- Select a student and discuss the difference between the moon and the sun. Explain how the sun is too bright to look at directly, but it is safe to look at the moon. Then describe some other things you might see in the sky, like clouds or birds. Consider adding vocabulary to your discussion, such as *cloud, sun, nighttime, brightest, light, heat, million,* or *stars.* Then have the student describe the sun and the moon.
- Say: With a partner, discuss how the sun and moon are similar and how they are different. Write your ideas on sticky notes and post them on the board.
- Pick five pairs of students, and encourage each pair to share their ideas. Recognize when students use previously taught key vocabulary.

DURING THE READING

Preview the Book
- Read the title of the book on the cover, and point to the picture. Turn to page 2 and read the sentences, pointing to each word as you read. Have students follow along in their books.
- Say: This book is about things you can see in the sky. The cover shows a picture of the moon and stars. That's what you see at night. What would I see in the sky during the day? I wonder what this book will tell me about the sky.
- As needed, point out the words that have the variant vowels /o͞o/ and /o͝o/: *too.*

Read the Book
- Read the book to students as they follow along. Point out words that contain the sound-spellings taught. Explain the terminology as needed: *clouds, nighttime, curved, new moon, give off light, warms, one million Earths.*
- Have students silently read the book. Ask a few students to whisper read the book to you, and help them sound out new words. When observing students, focus on the new words: *look(s), moon, too.*
- **Science Connections:** Say: The moon is bright in the night sky, but it does not give off its own light like the sun. The moon's light is actually a reflection of the sun's light, shining on it across the universe. Think about how the sun shines on a watch you're wearing, creating a light that bounces onto a wall or the floor.

AFTER THE READING

Check Comprehension
To check students' understanding of the book, ask the following:
✓ Look at page 4. What is the shape of the moon when it is full? (Answers may include: It is the shape of a circle.) What does the moon look like when it is new? (Answers may include: You cannot see the new moon. It is just a sliver.)
✓ Why do stars look small to us? (Answers may include: Stars look small because they are far away.) Which star is close to us? (the sun)
✓ Look at the picture on page 7. How can you tell the sun is hot? (Answers may include: It is the color of fire.)

Reread to Develop Fluency
- Say: Today you will read the book to each other to practice reading with fluency. This means that you read the book as the author meant for it to be read aloud.
- Model reading fluently by reading the book aloud to students. Focus on pausing slightly when you come to a comma and paying attention to compound words.
- Have partners reread the book to each other. Suggest that they pause when they come to a comma within a sentence. Students may struggle with decoding, comprehension, or vocabulary. For students who are struggling with vocabulary, say: I noticed that you are not sure what that word means. That makes it hard to understand the text. Let's see if there are clues in the other words or in the picture that can help us understand. Now that we understand the word, let's try reading the page again fluently.
- Send home a copy of *Up in the Sky* for students to read to family members. Consider assessing a few students on fluency.

Connect to Written Language
↻ **Review:** Write the words *bloom, food,* and *roots* on the board. As a class, read the words together as you point to the letters. Then practice listening for the /o͞o/ sound in each word. Have students write a paragraph using all three words, and underline the *oo* in each word. Have them choose a title for the paragraph.

✓ Dictate the following words for students to spell: *hood, noon, room, looks, moon, because,* and *inside.* When finished, write the words on the board. Have students self-correct their papers.

✓ Say: Sometimes words sound the same, but are spelled differently and have different meanings. These are called homophones. For example, *two* and *too* sound the same, but they are spelled differently and have different meanings. The word *two* means "the number 2," and the word *too* means "also." Write on the board: *Where is the dress I will wear?* The word *where* is asking for a location, and the word *wear* means "putting on an item of clothing." Encourage students to brainstorm homophones, and then write a sentence using two homophones. Ask them to underline the homophones and explain what each word means.

Our Heroes

SKILLS

PHONICS SKILL INTRODUCED
- Variant Vowel /ô/ (*a, au, aw*)

SIGHT WORDS
- *after, better, came, good, open, people, ride, there, through, went*

VOCABULARY WORDS–
Social Studies Words
- *Dr. Martin Luther King Jr., fair(ly), George Washington, Mary McLeod Bethune, Puerto Rico, Roberto Clemente, Sacagawea, Sally Ride, Shoshone Indian, woman*

CURRICULUM LINK–
Social Studies Focus
- American Heroes

Our Heroes

BEFORE THE READING

Develop Phonemic Awareness and Phonics
Oral Segmentation

- Say: Today we are going to be listening to sounds and segmenting them to make words. Segmenting means pulling words apart by their sounds.
- Write the words *ball, cause,* and *walk* on the board. Model segmenting the sounds of the words as you point to each sound-spelling: /b/ /ô/ /l/, ball; /k/ /ô/ /z/, cause; /w/ /ô/ /l/ /k/, walk.
- Write *salt* and *paw* on the board. Say these sounds, while pointing to the sound-spellings, and have students echo you: /s/ /ô/ /l/ /t/, salt; /p/ /ô/, paw.
- Write *sauce* and *lawn* on the board. Have students try segmenting the words out loud but independently. Walk around to support students. If a student is struggling to segment the discrete sounds, model clapping once for each sound while saying it aloud, and have the student follow suit.

Introduce Phonics Skills
Variant Vowel /ô/ (*a, au, aw*)

- Say: We just practiced segmenting some words with the /ô/ sound. Now we are going to read some words with this sound-spelling.
- Write the words *talk, Paul,* and *claw* on the board, and underline the letters *a, au,* or *aw* in each word. Say: The letters *a, au,* and *aw* make the /ô/ sound. Model reading the words, one sound at a time, while pointing to the letters: /t/ ô/ /l/ /k/, talk; /p/ /ô/ /l/, Paul; /k/ /l/ /ô/, claw.
- Write the words *also, always,* and *law* on the board. Have students read the words as a class. Say: Slowly sound out each letter.
- Have students try reading the words *astronaut, baseball,* and *because* independently, following the routine above. Walk around to support students. Students who are struggling may need extra modeling, practice, and feedback, such as: Let's look at the word *astronaut.* Remember that words can be divided into syllables. Let's divide this word into syllables first: as-tro-naut. Now let's slowly say the sounds of this word together as I point to each letter. Now you do it.

Introduce Sight Words

- Say: You are going to see some words today that you may not know, so you will need to keep them in your memory.
- Write the words *after, better,* and *through* on the board. Read them to students as you point to each letter.
- Write the words *good, people, ride,* and *there* on the board. Read the words, and have students echo read each word.
- Write the words *open* and *went* on the board. Ask a volunteer to read them aloud, and have the class follow suit. Place the words on a sight-word bulletin board.
- The book also contains social studies words. Follow the steps above with these words, but this time provide a simple definition for words that may cause confusion: *Dr. Martin Luther King Jr., fair(ly), George Washington, Mary McLeod Bethune, Puerto Rico, Roberto Clemente, Sacagawea, Sally Ride, Shoshone Indian,* and *woman.* For example: A Shoshone Indian is a member of an American Indian group originally from California, Idaho, Nevada, Utah, and Wyoming.

Build Oral Language

- Say: Today we will be reading a book about American heroes. Before I read, I often think about the topic and try to recall what I already know about it.
- Select a student and discuss what you know about heroes. Consider adding vocabulary to your discussion, such as *Abraham Lincoln, admire, brave, famous, important, Dr. Martin Luther King Jr.* Then have the student tell you what he or

she thinks makes someone a hero. Ask the student about someone that he or she considers a hero.

- Say: With a partner, discuss what you think makes someone a hero. Who are some of your heroes? What did those people do to become heroes?
- Pick five pairs of students, and encourage one student from each pair to share in the discussion. Recognize when students use previously taught key vocabulary.

DURING THE READING

Preview the Book

- Read the title of the book on the cover, and point to the picture. Turn to pages 2 and 3 and read the sentences, pointing to each word as you read. Also point out the caption and read those words as well. Have students follow along in their books.
- Say: Do you know what the book will be about based on the title and the two pages that I read? How do you know what it will be about?
- As needed, point out the words that have the /ô/ sounds: *also, laws, Washington.*

Read the Book

- Read the book to students as they follow along. Point out words that contain the sound-spellings taught.
- Have students silently read the book. Ask a few students to whisper read the book to you, and help them sound out new words. When observing students, focus on the new words: *all, also, always, astronaut, baseball, because, laws, walked, Washington.*
- **Social Studies Connections:** Say: We honor American heroes in many ways. For example, George Washington has a state and our nation's capital, Washington, D.C., named after him. His picture is on the $1 bill, and his birthday is a holiday.

AFTER THE READING

Check Comprehension

To check students' understanding of the book, ask the following:

✓Which word on page 3 has the /ô/ sound and means "rules." (*laws*) Why is George Washington important? (He made laws and the United States a good place to live. He was the first president of the United States.)

✓Which two people in the book explored new places? What places did they explore? (Sacagawea and Sally Ride. Sacagawea explored the American West. Sally Ride explored space.)

✓Which American hero from the book do you admire the most? Why? (Answers will vary. Accept all reasonable responses.)

Reread to Develop Fluency

- Say: Today you will read the book to each other to practice reading with fluency. This means that you read the book as the author meant for it to be read aloud.
- Model reading fluently by reading the book aloud to students. Be sure to read at a consistent pace with the appropriate intonation. Read the book a second time, this time reading at an inconsistent pace and an inappropriate intonation. Ask students what was wrong with how you read the book the second time.
- Have partners reread the book to each other. Remind students to read at a consistent pace with the appropriate intonation. Students may struggle with decoding, comprehension, or vocabulary. For students who are struggling with decoding, say: I see that you're having some trouble reading this word. Let's read it together and slowly sound out the letters. We did it! Now you try it on your own. Great! Can you try the whole sentence again?
- Send home a copy of *Our Heroes* for students to read to family members. Consider assessing a few students on fluency.

Connect to Written Language

↻Review: Write the words *look, brook,* and *moon* on the board. As a class, read the words together as you point to the letters. Then replace the first letter of each word with a different consonant, and read the new words together.

✓Dictate the following words for students to spell: *also, astronaut, baseball, because, laws, there,* and *through.* When finished, write the words on the board. Have students self-correct their papers.

✓Have students draw a stamp or coin to honor their favorite hero. Suggest that they write 3–4 sentences below the drawing to describe who is pictured and what that person did to make him or her a hero.

*Learn About
Dinosaurs*

SKILLS

PHONICS SKILL INTRODUCED
- Variant Vowel /ô/ (*a, au, aw*)

SIGHT WORDS
- *long, three, want, which*

VOCABULARY WORDS–
Science Words
- *Coelophysis, Dilophosaurus, dinosaur(s), footprints, fossils, millions, past, scientists*

CURRICULUM LINK–
Science Focus
- Dinosaurs

Learn About Dinosaurs

BEFORE THE READING

Develop Phonemic Awareness and Phonics
Oral Segmentation
- Say: Today we are segmenting the sounds in words. Segmenting means pulling words apart by their sounds. Today we are listening for the /ô/ sound.
- Write the words *ball, fault,* and *jaw* on the board. Model segmenting the words as you say each sound and point to each sound-spelling: /b/ /ô/ /l/, ball; /f/ /ô/ /l/ /t/, fault; /j/ /ô/, jaw.
- Write *fall, sauce,* and *yawn* on the board. Say these sounds while pointing to the sound-spellings. Have students echo you as you segment the words and say each sound: /f/ /ô/ /l/, fall; /s/ /ô/ /s/, sauce; /y/ /ô/ /n/, yawn.
- Write *halt, pause,* and *dawn* on the board. Have students try segmenting the sounds out loud but independently. Support students who are struggling with segmenting by modeling tossing a bean bag back and forth as you say each sound.

Introduce Phonics Skills
Variant Vowel /ô/ (*a, au, aw*)
- Say: We just practiced segmenting the sounds in some words. Now we are going to read some words with these sound-spellings.
- Write the words *tall, haunt,* and *draw* on the board, and underline the *a, au,* and *aw.* Say: These spellings can each stand for the /ô/ sound. Model reading the words, one sound at a time, while pointing to the letters: /t/ /ô/ /l/, tall; /h/ /ô/ /n/ /t/, haunt; /dr/ /ô/, draw.
- Write the words *salt, launch,* and *hawk* on the board. Have students read the words as a class. Say: Slowly sound out each letter, and notice the different spellings for the /ô/ sound.
- Have students try reading the words *bald* and *thaw* independently, following the routine above. Walk around to support students. Students who are struggling may need extra modeling and practice, such as: Let's look at the word *bald*. Say each letter's sound as I point to it. Let's say the sounds together.

Introduce Sight Words
- Say: You are going to see some words today that you may not know, so you will need to keep them in your memory.
- Write *long* on the board. Read it to students as you point to each letter.
- Write *three* and *us* on the board. Read the words, and have students echo read them.
- Write *want* and *which* on the board. Ask a volunteer to read them aloud, and have the rest of the class follow suit. Place the words on a sight-word bulletin board.
- The book also contains science words. Follow the steps above with these words, but this time provide a simple definition for words that may cause confusion: *Coelophysis, Dilophosaurus, dinosaur(s), footprints, fossils, millions, past,* and *scientists.* For example: The word *fossil* means "the parts or the hardened impressions of an animal that lived long ago." Show students the picture of the footprint on page 3 and discuss what it tells us about this dinosaur.

Build Oral Language
- Say: Today we will be reading a book about dinosaurs. Dinosaurs don't exist now, but we have clues about them because scientists have found fossils and bones. I have many questions about dinosaurs. Let's see what this book teaches us.
- Select a student and discuss the kinds of dinosaurs that once lived on Earth. Explain how some dinosaurs were large or tall, but others were small. Ask students what else

they know about dinosaurs. Consider adding vocabulary to your discussion, such as *fossils, tracks, scientists,* or *extinct.* Then have the student describe what dinosaurs might have looked like. Draw a KWL chart on the board.

- Say: This is a KWL chart. K stands for *know.* With a partner, discuss what you know about dinosaurs. W stands for *want to know.* List things you want to know.
- Pick five pairs of students, and encourage each pair to chart their ideas. Recognize when students use previously taught key vocabulary. Have students chart what they learned in the L column.

DURING THE READING

Preview the Book
- Read the title of the book on the cover, and point to the picture. Turn to page 2 and read the sentences, pointing to each word as you read. Have students follow along.
- Say: This book is about dinosaurs. The cover shows a dinosaur skeleton. The skeleton helps us imagine what the dinosaur really looked like. This book might show us some dinosaurs.
- As needed, point out the word that has the variant vowel /ô/ (*a, au, aw*): *saw.*

Read the Book
- Read the book to students as they follow along. Point out words that contain the sound-spellings taught. Explain the terms if students need help with the words: *amazed, Arizona, fossils, toes, footprint.*
- Have students silently read the book. Ask a few students to whisper read the book to you, and help them sound out new words. When observing students, focus on the new words: *all, called, claws, draw, saw, smaller, tall, walked.*
- **Science Connections:** Say: Scientists compare the footprints they find in different places to identify the dinosaurs that made them. They examine the skeletons to see if the footprints match the bones, so they can be fairly sure about which kind of dinosaur it was.

AFTER THE READING

Check Comprehension
To check students' understanding of the book, ask the following:
✓ What kind of fossil is shown on page 4? (a plant) How are plant fossils different from dinosaur fossils? (Answers may include: A plant fossil is a print of the plant, and dinosaur fossils can include bones.)
✓ Look at page 5. How do you know this dinosaur was large? (Answers may include: The footprint is larger than the man's hand.)
✓ Page 7 describes Coelophysis. What does the text say about the number of toes? (Answers may include: It had four toes in all.) Look at the picture. Which parts of the dinosaur were small, and which were large? (Answers may include: The arms were small, but the head looks large.)

Reread to Develop Fluency
- Say: Today you will read the book to each other to practice reading with fluency. This means that you read the book as the author meant for it to be read aloud.
- Model reading fluently by reading the book aloud to students. Focus on reading at a consistent pace with the proper intonation.
- Have partners reread the book to each other. Suggest that they use expression in their voices. Students may struggle with decoding, comprehension, or vocabulary. For students who are struggling with decoding, say: I noticed that some of these words are very long. Let's break them down and slowly sound out one letter at a time. Let's try it a few times until you can say the word comfortably.
- Send home a copy of *Learn About Dinosaurs* for students to read to family members. Consider assessing a few students on fluency.

Connect to Written Language
↻ Review: Write the words *always, baseball,* and *laws* on the board. As a class, read the words together as you point to the letters. Then circle the *a* sounds in each word, and practice identifying the different sounds each spelling represents. Have students fold a piece of paper into thirds, and write a sentence for each word in each panel. Have them circle the *a* sound in each word and draw a picture for each sentence.

- Dictate the following words for students to spell: *all, called, claws, draw, walked, want,* and *which.* When finished, write the words on the board. Have students self-correct their papers.

- Say: When two words combine to make a new word, it is called a compound word. For example, *back* and *yard* combine to make *backyard.* Write on the board: *My footprints helped me backtrack.* Which words in this sentence are compound words? What words were combined? Use picture cards to help students create compound words. Have students use the words they create in two sentences. Ask them to underline the compound words in each sentence.

Baskets of Native Americans

SKILLS

PHONICS SKILL INTRODUCED
- Diphthong /oi/ (*oi, oy*)

SIGHT WORDS
- *carry, close, keep, today, until*

VOCABULARY WORDS–
Social Studies Words
- *art, bark, basket(s), coil(s), cornhusk(s), grass, Hopi, leaves, materials, museums, Native Americans, sew(s)*

CURRICULUM LINK–
Social Studies Focus
- Native Americans

Baskets of Native Americans

BEFORE THE READING

Develop Phonemic Awareness and Phonics
Oral Blending
- Say: Today we are blending sounds to make words. Blending means putting sounds together to make words. Today we are listening for the /oi/ sound.
- Write the words *coil* and *joy* on the board. Model blending the sounds as you point to each sound-spelling: /k/ /oi/ /l/, coil; /j/ /oi/, joy. Lightly clap as you say each sound.
- Write *moist* and *toy* on the board. Blend the sounds while pointing to the sound-spellings. Have students echo you as you blend each sound to create a word: /m/ /oi/ /st/, moist; /t/ /oi/, toy.
- Write *point* and *boy* on the board. Have students try blending the sounds out loud but independently. Support students who are struggling with blending by clapping as you say each sound. Have the student follow suit as he or she blends the sounds.

Introduce Phonics Skills
Diphthong /oi/ (*oi, oy*)
- Say: We just practiced blending the sounds in some words. Now we are going to read some words with these sound-spellings.
- Write the words *soil* and *boy* on the board, and underline the *oi* and *oy*. Say: These spellings can each stand for the /oi/ sound. Model reading the words, one sound at a time, while pointing to the letters: /s/ /oi/ /l/, soil; /b/ /oi/, boy.
- Write the words *boil* and *soy* on the board. Have students read the words as a class. Say: Slowly sound out each letter, and notice the different spellings for the /oi/ sound.
- Have students try reading the words *broil* and *Troy* independently, following the routine above. Walk around to support students. Students who are struggling may need extra modeling and practice, such as: Let's look at the word *broil*. Say each letter sound as I point to it, and remember, the letters *b* and *r* combine to make one sound: /br/. Let's say the sounds together. Now you try it.

Introduce Sight Words
- Say: You are going to see some words today that you may not know, so you will need to keep them in your memory.
- Write the word *carry* on the board. Read it to students as you point to each letter.
- Write the words *close* and *keep* on the board. Read the words, and have students echo read each word.
- Write the words *today* and *until* on the board. Ask a volunteer to read them aloud, and have the class follow suit. Place the words on a sight-word bulletin board.
- The book also contains social studies words. Follow the steps above with these words, but this time provide a simple definition for words that may cause confusion: *art, bark, basket(s), coil(s), cornhusk(s), grass, Hopi, leaves, materials, museums, Native Americans,* and *sew(s).* For example: A cornhusk is the leafy covering over an ear of corn. Show students the picture of the cornhusk basket on page 3, and discuss how the husk was used to make the basket.

Build Oral Language
- Say: Today we will be reading a book about baskets made by Native Americans. I wonder what kinds of materials were used to make the baskets? I hope this book tells me about that.
- Select a student and discuss why Native Americans needed baskets. Ask the student how he or she carries things, like groceries, or holds things, like books. Explain

that the bags and boxes we use today were not available for the Native Americans, but they built their own baskets for storage and for decoration. Consider adding vocabulary to your discussion, such as *gather, materials, bark, cornhusk, yucca, strips, Seminole,* or *museum.* Then have the student describe what baskets might be used for.

- Say: With a partner, brainstorm some materials that could be used to make a basket. Write or draw some of your ideas on a chart.
- Pick five pairs of students, and encourage each pair to share their ideas. Recognize when students use previously taught key vocabulary.

DURING THE READING

Preview the Book
- Read the title of the book on the cover, and point to the picture. Turn to page 2 and read the sentences, pointing to each word as you read. Have students follow along in their books.
- Say: This book is about Native American baskets. The cover shows a woman building a basket. Can you predict what shape it will be? I wonder how long it takes to make a basket.

Read the Book
- Read the book to students as they follow along. Point out words that contain the sound-spellings taught. Explain the terms if students don't know them: *gather, serve, materials, bark, grass, cornhusks, yucca, strips, sews, museums.*
- Have students silently read the book. Ask a few students to whisper read the book to you, and help them sound out new words. When observing students, focus on the new words: *coils, coins, enjoy, moist, point.*
- **Social Studies Connections:** Say: Many Native American groups made baskets. The Hopi from Arizona and the Seminoles from Florida each made baskets. They are all different shapes, from round and deep to rectangular and flat. Some had elaborate decorations and are considered pieces of art.

AFTER THE READING

Check Comprehension
To check students' understanding of the book, ask the following:
- ✓How are the baskets on page 2 being used? (Answers may include: She is gathering with one basket and carrying or storing with the other.)
- ✓What do the captions on page 3 describe? (Answers may include: The captions describe the materials of each basket.)
- ✓Look at the baskets on page 7. How many baskets have pictures of animals? (three) Which word on the page describes the basket with the picture of a bird? (*wings*)

Reread to Develop Fluency
- Say: Today you will read the book to each other to practice reading with fluency. This means that you read the book as the author meant for it to be read aloud.
- Model reading fluently by reading the book aloud to students. Focus on reading at a consistent pace with the proper intonation.
- Have partners reread the book to each other. Suggest that they pause when they come to a comma and use expression in their voices. Students may struggle with decoding, comprehension, or vocabulary. For students who are struggling with decoding, say: I noticed that some of these words are very long. Let's break them down by syllables and slowly sound out one letter at a time. Then we can blend the syllables together. Let's try it a few times. You did it! Now reread the sentence at a steady pace.
- Send home a copy of *Baskets of Native Americans* for students to read to family members. Consider assessing a few students on fluency.

Connect to Written Language
↻Review: Write the words *claw, draw,* and *tall* on the board. As a class, read the words together as you point to the letters. Then circle the /ô/ sound in each word, and practice identifying the different spellings for the /ô/ sound. Have students look in magazines to find pictures of each word. Then have them cut out the pictures, paste them onto cardstock, and write the words below the pictures along with a description of the picture.

✓Dictate the following words for students to spell: *coils, coins, enjoy, moist, point, carry,* and *until.* When finished, write the words on the board. Have students self-correct their papers.

✓Say: When two words combine to make a new word, it is called a compound word. For example, *corn* and *husk* combine to make *cornhusk.* Write on the board: *I keep my basketball in a basket.* Which word is a compound word? What words were combined? Use picture cards to help students create compound words. Have them use the words they create in two sentences. Ask them to underline the compound words in each sentence.

SKILLS

PHONICS SKILL INTRODUCED
- Digraphs (*ch, gh, ph, sh, tch, th, wh*)

SIGHT WORDS
- *after, better, hurt, take, together*

VOCABULARY WORDS–
Science Words
- *bacteria, doctor, germs, microscope, viruses*

CURRICULUM LINK–
Science Focus
- Health

What Are Germs?

BEFORE THE READING

Develop Phonemic Awareness and Phonics
Phonemic Manipulation: Deletion
- Say: Today we are going to delete sounds. Deleting means taking a sound away.
- Write the words *reach, cash, than, why,* and *phone* on the board. Model saying each word as you point to each sound-spelling: /r/ /ē/ /ch/; /k/ /a/ /sh/; /th/ /a/ /n/; /wh/ /ī/; /ph/ /ō/ /n/. Practice saying each word without the initial onset sound.
- Write *throw* and *chat* on the board. Say these sounds while pointing to the sound-spellings. Have students echo you as you delete the initial onset sounds and say the words: /th/ /r/ /ō/, throw; /r/ /ō/, row; /ch/ /a/ /t/, chat; /a/ /t/, at.
- Write *brush* and *ditch* on the board. Have students try saying the words and deleting the initial onset sound out loud but independently. Walk around to support students. If a student is struggling, model pushing a colored chip forward for each sound, then cover the first chip as you delete the first sound. Have the student follow suit.

Introduce Phonics Skills
Digraphs (*ch, gh, ph, sh, tch, th, wh*)
- Say: We just practiced deleting the sounds in some words. Now we are going to read some words as we point out the beginning and ending sounds in each.
- Write the words *coach, rough, phone, shell, catch, thin,* and *whale* on the board, and underline the digraphs (*ch, gh, ph, sh, tch, th, wh*). Say: When two consonants appear together in a word, sometimes they stand for a new sound, for example the /ch/ sound, as in *coach,* the /f/ sound, as in *rough,* the /f/ sound, as in *phone,* the /sh/ sound, as in *shell,* the /th/ sound, as in *thin,* or the /w/ sound, as in *whale.* Model reading the words, one sound at a time, while pointing to the letters: /k/ /ō/ /ch/, coach; /r/ /u/ /f/, rough; /f/ /ō/ /n/, phone; /sh/ /e/ /l/, shell; /k/ /a/ /tch/, catch; /th/ /i/ /n/, thin; /w/ /ā/ /l/, whale.
- Write the words *chimp, laugh, graph, rash, ditch, them,* and *when* on the board. Have students read the words as a class. Say: Slowly sound out each sound-spelling, and notice how each digraph makes one sound.
- Have students try reading the words *chop, tough, gopher, shape, patch, this,* and *white* independently, following the routine above. Walk around to support students. Students who are struggling may need extra modeling and practice, such as: Let's look at the word *gopher.* Remember that the letters *ph* make one sound: /f/, and the letters *er* make one sound, the /er/ sound. Let's slowly say each of the sounds together as we point to the letters. Now you try it by yourself.

Introduce Sight Words
- Say: You are going to see some words today that you may not know, so you will need to keep them in your memory.
- Write *after* and *better* on the board. Read them as you point to each letter.
- Write *hurt* and *take* on the board. Read the words, and have students echo read each.
- Write *together* on the board. Ask a volunteer to read it aloud, and have the rest of the class follow suit. Place the words on a sight-word bulletin board.
- The book also contains science words. Follow the steps above with these words, but this time provide a simple definition for words that may cause confusion: *bacteria, doctor, germs, microscope,* and *viruses.* For example: A microscope is a tool that helps us see tiny particles. Discuss the picture of the microscope on page 7.

Build Oral Language
- Say: We will be reading a book about germs. I know germs can make us sick and that washing our hands helps get rid of germs. I wonder what else I'll learn.
- Select a student and discuss a time he or she was sick with a cold. How did he or she catch the cold? Was someone else in the student's house or class sick? Consider adding vocabulary to your discussion, such as *stomach, medicine, microscope, sneeze, cough, bacteria, virus, fever,* or *rash.* Then have the student describe how it feels to be sick.

- Say: With a partner, discuss some things you can do to take care of yourself so you don't get sick, and some ways to help yourself get better. Write your ideas on sticky notes and post them on the board.
- Pick five pairs of students, and encourage one student from each pair to share their ideas. Recognize when students use previously taught key vocabulary.

DURING THE READING

Preview the Book
- Read the title of the book on the cover, and point to the picture. Turn to the Table of Contents and page 2 and read the sentences, pointing to each word as you read. Have students follow along in their books.
- Say: This book is about germs. The cover shows a picture of someone who might be sick. The Table of Contents gives me clues about the different ideas that this book will discuss. Page 2 starts with the first idea: what it feels like to be sick. What are the other topics included in this book?
- As needed, point out the words that have the digraphs taught (*ch, gh, ph, sh, tch, th, wh*): *what, healthy, throat, why*.

Read the Book
- Read the book aloud as students follow along. Point out words that contain the sound-spellings taught. Point to the Table of Contents, diagrams, and captions, and explain the kind of information each text feature provides. Explain the terminology as needed: *doctor, medicine, germs, microscope, spread, cough, sneeze, bacteria, viruses, rods, chain, shell, breathe, itch, brushing, flossing*.
- Have students whisper read to each other. Help students sound out new words, such as: *anything, breathe, brush, checkup, healthful, rash, scratch, teeth, throat*.
- **Science Connections:** Say: When you sneeze or cough, the germs can fly out of your mouth and nose. That's why it is important to cover your mouth and nose when you sneeze or cough.

AFTER THE READING

Check Comprehension
To check students' understanding of the book, ask the following:
- ✓Why is the doctor checking the boy's mouth in the picture on page 3? (Answers may include: Germs live in the throat, which is why it gets sore. The doctor is checking for germs.)
- ✓The pictures on page 8 show examples of bacteria. Which picture is real, and which is a drawing? (The larger picture is a drawing.) What does the heading tell us? (Answers may include: The heading describes the picture.)
- ✓Page 12 describes several things to do to stay healthy. Which bullet point describes the picture on that page? (Drink lots of water.)

Reread to Develop Fluency
- Say: Today you will read the book to each other to practice reading with fluency. This means that you read the book as the author meant for it to be read aloud.
- Model reading fluently by reading the book aloud to students. Focus on reading words in a series, pausing slightly at each comma.
- Have partners reread the book to each other. Suggest that they pause when they come to a comma within the sentence. Students may struggle with decoding, comprehension, or vocabulary. For students who are struggling with comprehension, say: I noticed that you seem unsure about the meaning of this sentence. Are there clues in the other words or in the pictures that we can use to help us understand what we read? Now that we understand the sentence a little better, let's try reading it again with proper expression.
- Send home a copy of *What Are Germs?* for students to read to family members. Consider assessing a few students on fluency.

Connect to Written Language
↻**Review:** Write the words *coil, moist*, and *enjoy* on the board. As a class, read the words together as you point to the letters. Then practice listening for the /oi/ sound in each word. Have students write a poem, and try to think of rhymes for at least two of the words. Have them choose a title for their poems.

✓Dictate the following words for students to spell: *anything, checkup, healthy, rough, phone, together*, and *hurt*. When finished, write the words on the board. Have students self-correct their papers.

✓Say: You may see words that are put together to make compound words. Compound words are good describing words. For example, *everywhere* means "all around," and *sometimes* means "once in a while." Write the word *microscope* on the board: The word *micro* means "very tiny," and the word *scope* means "to look at or examine." Put together, they describe a tool for helping us see tiny things. Have students describe how to stay healthy. Instruct them to include some compound words in their descriptions.

A Visit to the Library

SKILLS

PHONICS SKILL INTRODUCED
- Closed Syllables

SIGHT WORDS
- *around, bring, good, just, make, read, show, take, work*

VOCABULARY WORDS–
Social Studies Words
- *bookmobile, computer, librarian, library, online catalog*

CURRICULUM LINK–
Social Studies Focus
- Books and Libraries

A Visit to the Library

BEFORE THE READING

Develop Phonemic Awareness and Phonics
Oral Segmentation
- Say: Today we are going to segment words so that we can say them sound by sound. Segment means to pull words apart by their sounds.
- Write the words *dog, pumpkin, basket,* and *dress* on the board. Model saying the words sound by sound: /d/ /ô/ /g/, dog; /p/ /u/ /m/ /p/ /k/ /i/ /n/, pumpkin; /b/ /a/ /s/ /k/ /e/ /t/, basket; /dr/ /e/ /s/, dress.
- Write *carrot, tree,* and *slide* on the board. Sound out each word, and have students follow suit chorally: /k/ /ā/ /r/ /ə/ /t/, carrot; /tr/ /ē/, tree; /sl/ /ī/ /d/, slide.
- Write *computer, picnic,* and *library* on the board. Have students segment the words out loud but independently. Walk around to support students. If a student is struggling to segment the sounds in each word, model saying each sound as you move a chip onto a line or sound box, and have the student follow suit.

Introduce Phonics Skills
Closed Syllables
- Say: Some of the words we just practiced segmenting are two-syllable words with the vowel-consonant-consonant-vowel (vccv) pattern. These words can usually be divided between the two consonants. Each syllable must have a vowel. Now we are going to read some words with the vccv pattern.
- Write the word *until* on the board, and point out the vccv pattern. Draw a line between the *n* and the *t*. Say: The letters *unti* have the vccv pattern. Model reading the word, saying each syllable as you point to it.
- Write the words *basket* and *picnic* on the board. Have students point out the vccv patterns then divide each word into syllables. Read the words as a class. Say: Slowly sound out each letter.
- Have students try reading the words *traffic, rabbit,* and *napkin* independently, following the routine above. Walk around to support students. Students who are struggling may need extra modeling, practice, and feedback, such as: Let's look at the word *traffic*. When a consonant is doubled, the sound is only pronounced once. Let's slowly say the sounds of this word together as I point to each letter: /tr/ /a/ /f/ /i/ /k/, traffic. Now you do it.

Introduce Sight Words
- Say: You are going to see some words today that you may not know, so you will need to keep them in your memory.
- Write the words *around, bring,* and *good* on the board. Read the words to students as you point to each letter.
- Write the words *just, make,* and *read* on the board. Read the words, and have students echo read each word.
- Write the words *show, take,* and *work* on the board. Ask a volunteer to read them aloud, and have the rest of the class follow suit. Place the words on a sight-word bulletin board.
- The book also contains social studies words. Follow the steps above with these words, but this time provide a simple definition for words that may cause confusion: *bookmobile, computer, librarian, library, online catalog*. For example: An online catalog is a computer program you use to find books and other materials at the library. Show students the pictures of an online catalog being used on pages 8 and 12 of the book.

Build Oral Language
- Say: Today we will be reading a book about going to the library. Before I read, I often think about the topic and try to recall what I already know about it.
- Select a student and discuss what you know about visiting a library. Describe some reasons why you've gone to the library. Add vocabulary to your discussion, such as

online catalog, librarian, and *computer.* Then have the student tell you what he or she knows about going to the library.

- Say: Make a KWL chart with a partner. Model making a KWL chart on the board. In the first column, write what you both know about libraries. In the second column, write what you both want to know about libraries. In the third column, write what you both learned about libraries.
- Pick five pairs of students, and encourage one student from each pair to share their charts. Recognize when students use previously taught key vocabulary.

DURING THE READING

Preview the Book

- Read the title of the book on the cover, and point to the picture. Turn to page 2 and read the text. Also point out all the labels and accompanying images in the book and discuss them as well. Have students follow along in their books.
- Say: Do you know what the book will be about based on the title, what I've read, and the labels and images? How do you know what it will be about?
- As needed, point out the words with the vccv pattern: *public, borrow(ed).*

Read the Book

- Read the book to students as they follow along. Point out words that contain the vccv pattern. Tell students the names of things found in a library if they don't know them: *librarian, online catalog, magazines, computers, films.*
- Have students silently read the book. Ask a few students to whisper read the book to you, and help them sound out new words. When observing students, focus on the new words: *biggest, borrow, fiction, letter, number, public, shopping, subject.*
- **Social Studies Connections:** Say: Many public libraries offer special activities for children, such as story hours, book clubs, and summer reading programs. Libraries may also offer special programs for teens and adults.

AFTER THE READING

Check Comprehension

To check students' understanding of the book, ask the following:

✓Look at page 6. How is a bookmobile different from a regular library? (A bookmobile is a library that can move from place to place because it is on wheels. A regular library can't move because it is a building, so it stays in one place.)

✓How does the picture on page 7 help you understand what you read? How does the text help you understand the picture? (Answers may include: The picture helps me understand what the outside and inside of the Library of Congress look like. The text helps me understand where the Library of Congress is located and that it is the biggest library in the world.)

✓Look at page 8. How does an online catalog help you find a book? (You type in a title, an author name, or a subject on a library computer. Then the computer shows where to find what you're looking for in the library.)

Reread to Develop Fluency

- Say: Today you will read the book to each other to practice reading with fluency. This means that you read the book as the author meant for it to be read aloud.
- Model reading fluently by reading the book aloud to students. Reread any sentences that contain difficult words.
- Have partners reread the book to each other. Tell students to reread sentences with difficult words. Students may struggle with decoding, comprehension, or vocabulary. For students struggling with decoding, say: I see that you're trying to read this word. Let's read it together, slowly sounding out the letters of each word. You've got it! Reread the sentence now that you know the word.
- Send home a copy of *A Visit to the Library* for students to read to family members. Consider assessing a few students on fluency.

Connect to Written Language

↻Review: Write the words *check, wash,* and *than* on the board. As a class, read the words together as you point to the letters. Replace the vowels with *i,* then have students write the new words, and read them together.

✓Dictate the following words for students to spell: *until, basket, picnic, follow, napkin, show,* and *work.* When finished, write the words on the board. Have students self-correct their papers.

✓Say: Some words are made up of two different words. When these words are put together, they make a new word with a new meaning. You can figure out this new meaning by thinking about the two different words. Write *bookstore* on the board. Do you see two different words? Draw a line under *book* and say *book.* Draw a line under *store* and say *store.* A book is something you read, such as a mystery or an adventure. A store is a place where you can buy things. So a bookstore is a store where you can buy books. Write *bookmobile, raincoat,* and *sunglasses* on the board. Read the words as a class and encourage group discussion about their meanings. Ask students to think of more compound words and write them on a piece of paper.

At a Factory

SKILLS

PHONICS SKILL INTRODUCED
- Final *e* (*a_e, i_e*)

SIGHT WORDS
- *been, buy, five, such, today*

VOCABULARY WORDS–
Social Studies Words
- *factory(ies), machine(s), raw materials, store(s), worker(s)*

CURRICULUM LINK–
Social Studies Focus
- Goods and Services

At a Factory

BEFORE THE READING

Develop Phonemic Awareness and Phonics
Phonemic Manipulation: Substitution
- Say: Today we are going to be substituting one sound in a word. Substituting means replacing one sound in a word to make new words.
- Write the words *tap, mad,* and *scrap* on the board. Model saying each word, one sound at a time, as you point to each sound-spelling. Practice substituting each vowel sound with the /ā/ sound: /t/ /a/ /p/, tap, /t/ /ā/ /p/, tape; /m/ /a/ /d/, mad; /m/ /ā/ /d/, made; /scr/ /a/ /p/, scrap; /scr/ /ā/ /p/, scrape.
- Write *rid, dim,* and *fin* on the board. Say these sounds while pointing to the sound-spellings. Have students echo you as you substitute the short *i* sound with /ī/, and say the words: /r/ /i/ /d/, rid; /r/ /ī/ /d/, ride; /d/ /i/ /m/, dim; /d/ /ī/ /m/, dime; /f/ /i/ /n/, fin; /f/ /ī/ /n/, fine.
- Write *plan, spin,* and *pin* on the board. Have students try saying the words out loud but independently. Then substitute the short vowel sound with the long vowel sound by adding a final *e*. Walk around to support students. If a student is struggling with substituting, model using a colored chip for each sound, then substitute a red chip for the long vowel sound as you change it. Have the student follow suit.

Introduce Phonics Skills
Final *e* (*a_e, i_e*)
- Say: We just practiced substituting the sounds in some words. Now we are going to read some words with long vowel sounds.
- Write the words *make* and *bike* on the board, and underline the final *e* spelling. Say: The letters *a_e* stand for the long *a* sound as in *make*. The letters *i_e* stand for the long *i* sound as in *bike.* Model reading the words, one sound at a time, while pointing to the letters: /m/ /ā/ /k/, make; /b/ /ī/ /k/, bike.
- Write the words *male, mile, taste, skate,* and *like* on the board. Have students read the words as a class. Say: Slowly sound out each letter.
- Have students try reading the words *came, lime, dive, gate,* and *pile* independently, following the routine above. Walk around to support students. Students who are struggling may need extra modeling and practice, such as: Look at the word *came*. The letters *a_e* make the long *a* sound. Let's slowly say each of the sounds.

Introduce Sight Words
- Say: You are going to see some words today that you may not know, so you will need to keep them in your memory.
- Write *been* and *buy* on the board. Read them to students as you point to each letter.
- Write *five* and *such* on the board. Read the words, and have students echo read them.
- Write *today* on the board. Ask a volunteer to read it aloud, and have the rest of the class follow suit. Place the words on a sight-word bulletin board.
- The book also contains science words. Follow the steps above with these words, but this time provide a simple definition for words that may cause confusion: *factory(ies), machine(s), raw materials, store(s),* and *worker(s)*. For example: A factory is a place where machines and people build things. Show students the picture of a factory on page 3, and discuss some of the things that come from factories.

Build Oral Language
- Say: Today we will be reading a book about factories. Lots of things come from factories. I have seen pictures of cars being built in factories. I wonder what else comes from factories. Let's find out.
- Select a student and discuss how factories are able to make large quantities of items at one time. Have they ever made a waffle for breakfast? They probably make one at a time, but a factory can make many. Consider adding vocabulary to your discussion, such as *machines, raw materials, stores, workers,* or *jobs*. Then have the student tell about something in the classroom that may have come from a factory.

- Say: With a partner, discuss some things that might come from a factory. Brainstorm a list, and sort your ideas into categories, such as food, toys, clothes, and so on.
- Pick five pairs of students, and encourage each pair to share their ideas. Recognize when students use previously taught key vocabulary.

DURING THE READING

Preview the Book
- Read the title of the book on the cover, and point to the picture. Turn to the Table of Contents and page 2 and read the sentences, pointing to each word as you read. Have students follow along in their books.
- Say: This book is about factories. The cover shows a picture of bottles being filled in a factory. The Table of Contents describes different characteristics of factories, such as what is made at factories and who works there. On page 2, the girl is riding a bike that was made in a factory. The title of page 2 is the first chapter listed in the Table of Contents.
- As needed, point out the words with the final e (a_e, i_e): *place, game, baseball, bike*.

Read the Book
- Read the book aloud as students follow along. Point out words that contain the sound-spellings taught. Point to the flowchart on pages 12 and 13, and explain that a flowchart shows steps in a process. The chart helps us visualize which steps come first, next, and last.
- Have students silently read the book while a few whisper read it to you. Help students sound out new words. Focus on the new words: *bike, crate, drive, five, game, grape, inside, made, make, place, shape, take, time, United States*.
- **Science Connections:** Say: Some factories use assembly lines. A line of workers and machines work together to build a product. Each person or machine completes one step in the process, then the product moves down the line. Assembly lines are fast and efficient ways to build many items quickly.

AFTER THE READING

Check Comprehension
To check students' understanding of the book, ask the following:
- ✓What do the pictures on page 4 show? (Answers may include: The pictures show raw materials that are made into other things.)
- ✓What are some of the jobs that machines can do as described on page 6? (Answers may include: Machines can put wheels on bikes or labels on bottles.)
- ✓What is the worker on page 11 doing? (He is adding color to the wax.) What happens before adding the color? (The wax is melted and put into vats.)

Reread to Develop Fluency
- Say: Today you will read the book to each other to practice reading with fluency. This means that you read the book as the author meant for it to be read aloud.
- Model reading fluently by reading the book aloud to students. Focus on raising your voice when you come to a question mark, and adding emphasis when you come to an exclamation point.
- Have partners reread the book to each other. Remind them to adjust their voices at question marks and exclamation points. Students may struggle with decoding, comprehension, or vocabulary. For students who are struggling with comprehension, say: I noticed that you seem unsure about the meaning of this sentence. Are there clues in the other words or in the pictures that we can use to help us understand what we read? Now that we understand the sentence a little better, let's try reading it again with proper expression.
- Send home a copy of *At a Factory* for students to read to family members. Consider assessing a few students on fluency.

Connect to Written Language
- ↻ Review: Write the words *biggest, borrow,* and *shopping* on the board. As a class, read the words together as you point to the letters. Point out the double consonants, and discuss how adding an ending sometimes means doubling the final consonant. Then have students create a timeline outlining their day or their week with labels and explanations, and highlight any words with double consonants.

- ✓ Dictate the following words for students to spell: *bike, crate, inside, take, lime, such,* and *today*. When finished, write the words on the board. Have students self-correct their papers.

- ✓ Say: You may notice that sentences can be rearranged in a variety of ways. Some sentences are simple, and others combine ideas. Write on the board: *The store is crowded. There is a crowd at the store. At the store, a crowd is shopping.* Each of these sentences is similar, but the second sentence is rearranged, and the third sentence uses a comma to separate some of the ideas. Have students write one simple sentence, and then rewrite it in two different ways. Have them write a complete paragraph using a variety of sentence structures.

Healthy You!

SKILLS

PHONICS SKILL INTRODUCED
- Final *e* (*o_e, u_e*)

SIGHT WORDS
- *don't, down, grow, never, pull, three, try, very*

VOCABULARY WORDS–
Science Words
- *exercise, fitness, muscles, physical condition, vitamins*

CURRICULUM LINK–
Science Focus
- Health and Daily Living

Healthy You!

BEFORE THE READING

Develop Phonemic Awareness and Phonics
Oral Segmentation
- Say: Today we are going to be listening to sounds and segmenting them to make words. Segmenting means pulling words apart by their sounds.
- Write the words *code, dome,* and *mute* on the board. Model segmenting the sounds of the words as you point to each sound-spelling: /k/ /ō/ /d/, code; /d/ /ō/ /m/, dome; /m/ /ū/ /t/, mute.
- Write *hose* and *fume* on the board. Say these sounds, while pointing to the sound-spellings, and have students echo you: /h/ /ō/ /z/, hose; /f/ /ū/ /m/, fume.
- Write *mule* and *tone* on the board. Have students try segmenting the words out loud but independently. Walk around to support students. If a student is struggling to segment the discrete sounds, model clapping once for each sound while saying it aloud, and have the student follow suit.

Introduce Phonics Skills
Final *e* (*o_e, u_e*)
- Say: We just practiced segmenting some words with the final *e*. Now we are going to read some words with these sound-spellings.
- Write the word *hope* on the board, and underline the *o_e*. Say: The letters *o_e* stand for the /ō/ sound. Model reading the word, one sound at a time, while pointing to the letters: /h/ /ō/ /p/. Ask students to name other words that have the long *o* sound spelled *o_e*. List these words on the board, and have students circle the final *e* spelling in each word.
- Write the words *cube, note,* and *woke* on the board. Have students read the words as a class. Say: Slowly sound out each letter.
- Have students try reading the words *drove, pole,* and *use* independently, following the routine above. Walk around to support students. Students who are struggling may need extra modeling and practice, such as: Let's look at the word *use*. Remember that the *u_e* means we use the /ū/ sound. Let's just say the sounds, /ū/ /z/. Now, let's slowly say the sounds of the word together as I point to each letter. Now you do it.

Introduce Sight Words
- Say: You are going to see some words today that you may not know, so you will need to keep them in your memory.
- Write the words *grow* and *try* on the board. Read them to students as you point to each letter.
- Write the words *don't, never, pull,* and *very* on the board. Read the words, and have students echo read each word.
- Write the words *down* and *three* on the board. Ask a volunteer to read them aloud, and have the class follow suit. Place the words on a sight-word bulletin board.
- The book also contains science words. Follow the steps above with these words, but this time provide a simple definition for words that may cause confusion: *exercise, fitness, muscles, physical condition,* and *vitamins*. For example: Vitamins are substances found in the foods we eat that help keep us healthy.

Build Oral Language
- Say: Today we will be reading a book about keeping fit and staying healthy.
- Select a student and discuss what you know about keeping fit, exercise, and staying healthy. Consider adding vocabulary to your discussion, such as *exercise, fitness, muscles, physical condition,* and *vitamins*. Then have the student tell you about some things he or she does to exercise, keep fit, and stay healthy.

- Say: With a partner, discuss some ways to keep fit and stay healthy. What forms of exercise do you like?
- Pick five pairs of students, and encourage one student from each pair to share in the discussion. Recognize when students use previously taught key vocabulary.

DURING THE READING

Preview the Book
- Read the title of the book on the cover, and point to the picture. Turn to page 2 and read the sentences, pointing to each word as you read. Have students follow along in their books.
- Say: Do you know what the book will be about based on the title and the page that I read? How do you know what it will be about?
- Have students turn to the diagram on pages 6 and 7. Explain that a diagram shows information in a way that is easy to read and understand. Point out these features:
  - **Visual Organization:** Divides the diagram into sections by topic.
  - **Labels:** Tell which topic each section discusses.
  - **Sections:** Give pictures and details about each topic.
- Model for students how to read the diagram. Ask volunteers to show how they can get information from the diagram.

Read the Book
- Read the book to students as they follow along. Point out words that contain the sound-spellings taught.
- Have students silently read the book. Ask a few students to whisper read the book to you, and help them sound out new words. When observing students, focus on the new words: *alone, bones, cone, home, rope, use, whole.*
- **Science Connections:** Say: Along with eating healthful foods, it is important to drink plenty of fluids each day. Although fruit juice is good for people, the healthiest drink of all is plain, fresh water.

AFTER THE READING

Check Comprehension
To check students' understanding of the book, ask the following:
✓ Why is it important to eat well and exercise? What might happen to someone who doesn't eat well and exercise? (Answers may include: To stay healthy. The person might get sick or be unhealthy.)
✓ Use the diagram on pages 6 and 7 to describe what you can do during one week to stay fit. (Answers may include: play kickball, play soccer, dance, go for a walk, jump rope, ride a bike, take the dog for a walk, and so on.)
✓ Which long *o* word on page 14 names body parts that should be kept strong? (*bones*)

Reread to Develop Fluency
- Say: Today you will read the book to each other to practice reading with fluency. This means that you read the book as the author meant for it to be read aloud.
- Model reading fluently by reading the book aloud to students. Remind students that words in quotation marks are words that people say aloud to each other. Model reading the quotation on page 8.
- Have partners reread the book to each other. Students may struggle with decoding, comprehension, or vocabulary. For students struggling with vocabulary, say: I notice that you're not quite sure about the meaning of this word. Let's look for clues in the picture or other words around it to help us. We may have to look up the definition. Now that you know the word, reread the sentence, and use expression in your voice to show you understand the meaning.
- Send home a copy of *Healthy You!* for students to read to family members. Consider assessing a few students on fluency.

Connect to Written Language
↻ Review: Write the words *crate, drive,* and *grape* on the board. As a class, read the words together as you point to the letters. Then replace the beginning sound of each word with a new sound, and read the new words together.

✓ Dictate the following words for students to spell: *alone, phone, hope, mute, use, three,* and *very.* When finished, write the words on the board. Have students self-correct their papers.

✓ Have students draw a diagram of ways to stay healthy and fit. In a center circle, have the students draw a picture of themselves and label it "Healthy Me!" Have the students draw four circles orbiting the center circle and connect the outer circles to the inner circle with straight lines. In two of the outside circles, have students draw their favorite activities for getting exercise and keeping fit. In the other two outside circles, have them draw two of their favorite healthful foods. Help them label their drawings using the following sentence stems: *I like to ____. I like to eat ____.* Consider displaying the diagrams around the school in the cafeteria or gymnasium.

Matter All Around

SKILLS

PHONICS SKILL INTRODUCED
- Long *e* (*e, ea, ee, ey, y*)

SIGHT WORDS
- *around, could, its, just, read, water, would, your*

VOCABULARY WORDS–
Science Words
- *gas(es), liquid(s), matter, solid(s), water cycle, water vapor*

CURRICULUM LINK–
Science Focus
- Solids, Liquids, and Gases

Matter All Around

BEFORE THE READING

Develop Phonemic Awareness and Phonics
Oral Segmentation
- Say: Today we are segmenting words into individual sounds. Segmenting means pulling words apart by their sounds. Today we are listening for the /ē/ sound.
- Write the words *me, eat, keep, key,* and *lady* on the board. Model segmenting the words as you point to each sound-spelling: /m/ /ē/, me; /ē/ /t/, eat; /k/ /ē/ /p/, keep; /k/ /ē/, key; /l/ /ā/ /d/ /ē/, lady.
- Write *she, leaf, free,* and *funny* on the board. Segment the sounds while pointing to the sound-spellings. Have students echo you as you pull apart the sounds in each word: /sh/ /ē/, she; /l/ /ē/ /f/, leaf; /fr/ /ē/, free; /f/ /u/ /n/ /ē/, funny.
- Write *he, easy, tree, money,* and *muddy* on the board. Have students try segmenting the sounds out loud but independently. Support students who are struggling with segmenting by modeling snapping your fingers as you say each sound. Have the student follow suit as he or she slowly pulls apart the sounds.

Introduce Phonics Skills
Long *e* (*e, ea, ee, ey, y*)
- Say: We just practiced segmenting the sounds in some words. Now we are going to read some words with these sound-spellings.
- Write the words *be, heat, cheese, monkey,* and *bunny* on the board, and underline the long *e* spellings (*e, ea, ee, ey, y*). Say: Each of these spellings stand for the /ē/ sound. Model reading the words, one sound at a time, while pointing to the letters: /b/ /ē/; /h/ /ē/ /t/; /ch/ /ē/ /z/; /m/ /u/ /n/ /k/ /ē/; /b/ /u/ /n/ /ē/.
- Write the words *we, beam, feed, honey,* and *penny* on the board. Have students read the words as a class. Say: Slowly sound out each letter, and notice the different spellings for the /ē/ sound.
- Have students try reading the words *east, gooey,* and *party* independently, following the routine above. Walk around to support students. Students who are struggling may need extra modeling and practice, such as: Let's look at the word *gooey*. Say each letter sound as I point to it.

Introduce Sight Words
- Say: You are going to see some words today that you may not know, so you will need to keep them in your memory.
- Write *around* and *could* on the board. Read them aloud as you point to each letter.
- Write *its, just,* and *read* on the board. Read the words, and have students echo read each word.
- Write *water, would,* and *your* on the board. Ask a volunteer to read them aloud, and have the rest of the class follow suit. Place the words on a sight-word bulletin board.
- The book also contains science words. Follow the steps above with these words, but this time provide a simple definition for words that may cause confusion: *gas(es), liquid(s), matter, solid(s), water cycle,* and *water vapor*. For example: The words *water vapor* refer to the process of water turning into a gas, like when it evaporates. Show the diagram of the water cycle on page 12, and discuss how the water changes.

Build Oral Language
- Say: We will be reading a book about different states of matter: solids, liquids, and gases. I wonder how these states of matter are the same and different.
- Select a student and discuss the differences between solids, liquids, and gases. Ask the student to give an example of each. Explain that even if matter changes its form, it is still made of the same elements. Consider adding vocabulary to your discussion, such as *breathe, form, shape, puddles, space, melt, heat, vapor, chill,* or *cloud*. Then have the student describe a liquid that turns into both a solid and a gas.
- Say: With a partner, brainstorm solids, liquids, and gases. Write examples in the K column of a KWL chart. Discuss things you want to know in the W column.

- Pick five pairs of students, and encourage each pair to share their ideas. Recognize when students use previously taught key vocabulary. Have them include what they learned in the L column.

DURING THE READING

Preview the Book

- Read the title of the book on the cover, and point to the picture. Turn to the Table of Contents and point out the chapter headings and page numbers. Turn to page 2 and read the sentences, pointing to each word as you read. Have students follow along.
- Say: This book is about matter. The cover shows three types of matter. Can you guess what they are? Point to the solid, the liquid, and the gas. Let's see how this book explains each type.
- As needed, point out the words with the long *e* sound (*e, ea, ee, ey, y*): *heat, see, read, breathe, everything, everywhere.* Point out the section headings and show how they match the Table of Contents and how they describe the information in each section.

Read the Book

- Read the book to students as they follow along. Point out words that contain the sound-spellings taught. Explain the terms as needed: *beach, bean, breathe, freeze, heat, key, muddy, peek, penny, seas, seashell, steel, streams, sunny, trees.*
- Have students silently read the book. Ask a few students to whisper read the book to you, and help them sound out new words. When observing students, focus on the new words: *gas(es), liquid(s), matter, solid(s), water cycle, water vapor.*
- **Science Connections:** Say: Solids don't usually change their form unless something else interacts with them. But liquids and gases need containers to determine their shapes. Even if a liquid's shape changes by going into a new container, like pouring milk from a carton into a glass, its size does not. But a gas can change its shape and its size when it is in a different container, such as air into a tire or a balloon.

AFTER THE READING

Check Comprehension

To check students' understanding of the book, ask the following:

✓What form of water is pictured on page 3? (liquid)

✓The heading on page 7 says, "Heat It!" What would be heated on the page? (Answers may include: The ice and snow could be heated.) What will happen after heating? (Answers may include: The solid ice will melt and turn into liquid water.)

✓Look at the picture on page 11. Where is the water vapor in the picture? (Answers may include: The drops on the outside of the glass show the cooling water vapor.) Why did the vapor turn into a liquid when it touched the glass? (Answers may include: Because the vapor cooled when it touched the glass.)

Reread to Develop Fluency

- Say: Today you will read the book to each other to practice reading with fluency. This means that you read the book as the author meant for it to be read aloud.
- Model reading fluently by reading the book aloud to students. Focus on reading with expression in a conversational tone.
- Have partners reread the book to each other. Suggest that they pause when they come to a comma and use expression in their voices. Students may struggle with decoding, comprehension, or vocabulary. For students who are struggling with vocabulary, say: I noticed that you don't recognize some of these words. That makes it hard to read the sentence. Are there clues on the page or in the pictures? Maybe we could look up the words in the dictionary. Now let's reread the sentence at a steady pace.
- Send home a copy of *Matter All Around* for students to read to family members. Consider assessing a few students on fluency.

Connect to Written Language

↻Review: Write the words *home, pose,* and *mule* on the board. As a class, read the words together as you point to the letters. Then circle the *o_e* and *u_e* spellings in each word, and practice identifying the final *e* sounds in each word. Have students think of a rhyme for each word, and write the rhyme into a sentence.

✓Dictate the following words for students to spell: *beach, freeze, muddy, key, we, around,* and *your.* When finished, write the words on the board. Have students self-correct their papers.

✓Say: Sometimes you may see an apostrophe in a word. The apostrophe is a way to join two words together. This is called a contraction. For example, *it + is = it's.* We read it as one word, but it stands for two words. Write on the board: *Ice doesn't melt when it is too cold.* Which word is the contraction? The word *doesn't* is a contraction for the words *does + not.* Are there words that you could turn into contractions? Use word cards to help students create contractions. Have students sort their contractions into categories (for example, contractions using *is* and contractions using *not*.) Ask them to write sentences using contractions.

Communication Past and Present

SKILLS

PHONICS SKILL INTRODUCED
- Open Syllables

SIGHT WORDS
- *away, before, came, draw, found, know, made, people, soon, through, write, you*

VOCABULARY WORDS–
Social Studies Words
- *communication, e-mail, information, Pony Express, printing press*

CURRICULUM LINK–
Social Studies Focus
- Communication

Communication Past and Present

BEFORE THE READING

Develop Phonemic Awareness and Phonics
Oral Segmentation
- Say: Today we are going to segment words so that we can say them sound by sound. Segment means to pull words apart by their sounds.
- Write the words *idea, silent,* and *baby* on the board. Model saying the words sound by sound: /ī / /d/ /ē/ /ə/, idea; /s/ /ī/ /l/ /ə/ /n/ /t/, silent; /b/ /ā/ /b/ /ē/, baby.
- Write *acorn, even,* and *tulip* on the board. Sound out each word, and have students follow suit chorally: /ā/ /k/ /or/ /n/, acorn; /ē/ /v/ /ə/ /n/, even; /t/ /o͞o/ /l/ /i/ /p/, tulip.
- Write *tiger, open, tuba,* and *lazy* on the board. Have students segment the words out loud but independently. Walk around to support students. If a student is struggling to segment the sounds in each word, model saying each sound as you move a chip onto a line or sound box, and have the student follow suit.

Introduce Phonics Skills
Open Syllables
- Say: We just practiced segmenting words with open syllables. In words with open syllables, the first syllable ends with a long vowel sound. Now we are going to read some words with open syllables.
- Write the word *later* on the board and underline the *a.* Say: The letter *a* is the spelling for the /ā/ sound. Model reading the word, one sound at a time, while pointing to the letters: /l/ /ā/ /t/ /ə/ /r/.
- Write the words *pony* and *music* on the board. Have students read the words as a class. Say: Slowly sound out each letter.
- Have students try reading the words *rider, bonus,* and *fever* independently, following the routine above. Walk around to support students. Students who are struggling may need extra modeling, practice, and feedback, such as: Let's look at the word *bonus.* This word has an open syllable, so its first syllable ends with a long vowel sound. This means the *o* makes an /ō/ sound. Let's slowly say the sounds of this word together as I point to each letter: /b/ /ō/ /n/ /ə/ /s/. Now you do it.

Introduce Sight Words
- Say: You are going to see some words today that you may not know, so you will need to keep them in your memory.
- Write the words *away, before, came,* and *draw* on the board. Read the words to students as you point to each letter.
- Write the words *found, know, made,* and *people* on the board. Read the words, and have students echo read each word.
- Write the words *soon, through, write,* and *you* on the board. Ask a volunteer to read them aloud, and have the rest of the class follow suit. Place the words on a sight-word bulletin board.
- The book also contains social studies words. Follow the steps above with these words, but this time provide a simple definition for words that may cause confusion: *communication, e-mail, information, Pony Express, printing press.* For example: The Pony Express was a fast mail service in which riders carried mail on horseback from Missouri to California from 1860 to 1861. Show students the picture of the Pony Express rider from the book.

Build Oral Language
- Say: Today we will be reading a book about communication in the past and the present. Before I read, I often try to recall what I already know about it.
- Select a student and discuss what you know about communication. Compare the forms of communication used in the past to what we use now.

Add vocabulary to your discussion, such as *cell phones, communication, information, radio.* Then have the student tell you what he or she knows about communication.

- Say: Talk with your partner about what you know about communication. Write what you both know on a sticky note. When you are done, add the sticky note information to chart paper.

- Pick five pairs of students, and encourage one student from each pair to share what they wrote. Recognize when students use previously taught key vocabulary.

DURING THE READING

Preview the Book

- Read the title of the book on the cover, and point to the picture. Turn to page 2 and read the text. Point to the image and discuss that as well. Have students follow along.

- Say: Do you know what the book will be about based on the title and the first page that I read? How do you know what it will be about?

- Have students turn to page 16, and point to the heading "Index." Explain that the index comes at the end of a book. Readers can use it to find specific topics or information in the book.

- Point out the features of an index: entry word, alphabetical order, page numbers.

- Model how to use the index. Then ask volunteers to model how to use the index.

Read the Book

- Read the book to students as they follow along. Point out words that contain open syllables. Tell students what a printing press is if they don't know.

- Have students silently read the book. Ask a few students to whisper read the book to you, and help them sound out new words. When observing students, focus on the new words: *became, before, began, chosen, easy, even, moments, music, paper, people, pony, radio, riders, saying, story, writing.*

- **Social Studies Connections:** Say: In 1775 Benjamin Franklin began working on a postal system to get mail from place to place. Ten years later there were 75 local post offices in America. There are more than 30,000 today.

AFTER THE READING

Check Comprehension

To check students' understanding of the book, ask the following:

✓ Look at pages 2–6. How is it possible to communicate without speaking? (You can use your hands to wave hello or good-bye, and you can point to give directions. You can also communicate by writing words or drawing pictures.)

✓ Look at pages 7–9. How do people communicate faster today than they did in the past? (In the past people had to wait for mail to be delivered to receive communication. Today communication is sent and received instantly through e-mail and text messages.)

✓ How does the illustration on page 10 help you understand what you read? How does the text help you understand the illustration? (Answers may include: The illustration helps me understand what Pony Express riders looked liked. The text helps me understand that the best riders and fastest horses got picked for the job.)

Reread to Develop Fluency

- Say: Today you will read the book to each other to practice reading with fluency. This means that you read the book as the author meant for it to be read aloud.

- Model reading fluently by reading the book aloud to students. Focus on reading sentences with periods, exclamation points, and question marks appropriately.

- Have partners reread the book to each other. Remind students how to read sentences with exclamation points, question marks, and periods. Students may struggle with decoding, comprehension, or vocabulary. For students who are struggling with vocabulary, say: I noticed that you're not sure what that word means, which makes it hard to read the sentence. Let's look up the definition of the word.

- Send home a copy of *Communication Past and Present* for students to read to family members. Consider assessing a few students on fluency.

Connect to Written Language

↻ Review: Write the words *bean, heat,* and *read* on the board. As a class, read the words together as you point to the letters. Then replace the *ea* in each word with *i*, have students write the new words, and read them together.

✓ Dictate the following words for students to spell: *later, music, open, robot, rider, soon,* and *write.* When finished, write the words on the board. Have students self-correct their papers.

✓ Say: Some words are pronounced the same way but have different meanings and spellings. These are called homophones. Write on the board: *People communicate in other ways too.* Read the sentence as a class and say: The word *too* in this sentence means "also." Write on the board: *These were two ways to send a message.* Read the sentence as a class and say: The word *two* in this sentence means "the number 2." Encourage students to write additional sentences using the homophones *too* and *two.* You may wish to use the following sentence frames about communication: *This letter needs _____ stamps. Cell phones can send written messages. They can send pictures _____.*

SKILLS

PHONICS SKILL INTRODUCED
- Consonant + –le syllables

SIGHT WORDS
- *always, fly, gave, only, pick, was, thank*

VOCABULARY WORDS–
Social Studies Words
- *experiments, invention(s), inventor, scientist, timeline*

CURRICULUM LINK–
Social Studies Focus
- Inventors and Scientists

Great Inventions

BEFORE THE READING

Develop Phonemic Awareness and Phonics
Oral Segmentation
- Say: Today we are segmenting words. Segmenting means pulling words apart by their sounds or syllables. We will listen for two- and three-syllable words.
- Write the words *table, riddle,* and *needle* on the board. Model segmenting each word into syllables while clapping each syllable: ta|ble; rid|dle; nee|dle.
- Write *juggle, maple,* and *bicycle* on the board. Segment the syllables. Have students echo you as you pull apart the syllables in each word: jug|gle; ma|ple; bi|cy|cle.
- Write *buckle, gentle, syllable,* and *example* on the board. Have students try segmenting the syllables out loud but independently. Support students who are struggling with segmenting by modeling holding your hand under your chin and noticing how your chin moves down as you say each syllable. Have the student follow suit as he or she slowly pulls apart the syllables.

Introduce Phonics Skills
Consonant + –le syllables
- Say: We just practiced segmenting the syllables in some words. Now we are going to read some words as we point out each syllable.
- Write the words *able, simple,* and *little* on the board, and underline the –le spellings. Draw a line before the consonant + –le spellings. Say: The letters *le* can stand for the /əl/ sound. Model reading the words, one syllable at a time, while pointing to the letters: a|ble; sim|ple; lit|tle.
- Write the words *handle, bicycle, middle, edible,* and *apple* on the board. Have students read the words as a class. Say: Underline the consonant + –le, then slowly say each syllable, and count how many syllables you hear.
- Have students try reading the words *single, whistle, particle,* and *spectacle* independently, following the routine above. Walk around to support students. Students who are struggling may need extra modeling and practice, such as: Let's look at the word *particle*. Say each syllable as I point to it. The first syllable is *par–*, then *ti–*, and finally, *–cle*. Let's say the syllables together. Now you try it.

Introduce Sight Words
- Say: You are going to see some words today that you may not know, so you will need to keep them in your memory.
- Write *always, fly,* and *gave* on the board. Read them as you point to each letter.
- Write *only* and *pick* on the board. Read the words, and have students echo you.
- Write *was* and *thank* on the board. Ask a volunteer to read them aloud, and have the rest of the class follow suit. Place the words on a sight-word bulletin board.
- The book also contains social studies words. Follow the steps above with these words, but this time provide a simple definition for words that may cause confusion: *experiments, invention(s), inventor, scientist,* and *timeline.* For example: An inventor is someone who has an idea for a new product and finds a way to create it. Show students the pictures of the inventions shown throughout the book.

Build Oral Language
- Say: Today we will be reading a book about inventions. Have you ever wondered who was first person to create some of the things we use every day?
- Select a student and discuss some of the things he or she uses every day, such as an alarm clock or a refrigerator. Ask the student how life would be different if these things didn't exist? How do these inventions help us? Consider adding vocabulary to your discussion, such as *invention, vacuum, dishwasher, lightbulb, phonograph, machine, glider,* or *wiper.* Have the student describe an invention he or she uses at home.
- Say: With a partner, discuss an invention you would like to create, such as a flying car or glasses to see in the dark. How would your invention help people? Describe your invention to your partner.

- Pick five pairs of students, and encourage each pair to share their ideas. Recognize when students use previously taught key vocabulary.

DURING THE READING

Preview the Book
- Read the title of the book on the cover, and point to the picture. Turn to the Table of Contents and point out the headings and page numbers. Turn to page 2 and read the sentences, pointing to each word as you read. Have students follow along.
- Say: This book is about inventions. The girl on the cover is holding a lightbulb. A lightbulb was a very important invention. We use the image of a lightbulb over our heads to signify a good idea because an idea is like a light turning on in our minds. The inventions in this book all started out as good ideas.
- As needed, point out words with the new syllabication pattern: *table, single, puzzle*.

Read the Book
- Read the book to students as they follow along. Point out words that contain the sound-spellings taught. Show students the timeline on pages 14 and 15. Explain the features of the timeline: Dates show the year in which each item was invented. Headings name the inventor and explain what he or she invented. A timeline shows the order in which things happened.
- Have students silently read the book. Ask a few students to whisper read the book to you, and help them sound out new words. When observing students, focus on the new words: *bicycles, handle, little, middle, people, puzzles, simple, single, teakettle, whistles*.
- **Social Studies Connections:** Say: Many inventors have lots of great inventions, while others just have one or two. For example, Thomas Edison invented over 1,000 items. Leonardo da Vinci lived over 500 years ago, and he had ideas that were ahead of his time. He drew pictures of ideas including helicopters, airplanes, and more, but these things were invented hundreds of years later.

AFTER THE READING

Check Comprehension
To check students' understanding of the book, ask the following:
✓Page 3 describes different inventions. Which inventions make things easier for people? (Answers may include: lights, vacuums, and dishwashers.) Which make us safer? (Answers may include: Lights and traffic signals make us safer.)
✓Page 10 describes the first traffic signals. What does the red light in the picture mean to drivers? (Answers may include: A red light tells drivers to stop.)
✓Look at the timeline on pages 14 and 15. Use the timeline to put these inventions in order from earliest to latest: peanut butter, the vacuum cleaner, and the dishwasher. (Answers may include: The dishwasher was invented first, then peanut butter, then the vacuum cleaner.)

Reread to Develop Fluency
- Say: Today you will read the book to each other to practice reading with fluency. This means that you read the book as the author meant for it to be read aloud.
- Model reading fluently by reading the book aloud to students. Focus on adapting your voice when you come to a period, a question mark, and an exclamation point.
- Have partners reread the book to each other. Suggest that they stop and pause for periods, let their voice go up for a question mark, and add emphasis for an exclamation point. Students may struggle with decoding, comprehension, or vocabulary. For students who are struggling with comprehension, say: It seems you aren't sure how to read this sentence. What are some clues that might help you understand the text? Let's talk about the pictures and the other words. Try reading it again with confidence about what it means.
- Send home a copy of *Great Inventions* for students to read to family members. Consider assessing a few students on fluency.

Connect to Written Language
↻Review: Write the words *later, actor,* and *hello* on the board. As a class, read the words together as you point to the letters. Have students write a short story using these words.

✓Dictate the following words for students to spell: *handle, middle, little, teakettle, whistle, always,* and *thank.* When finished, write the words on the board. Have students self-correct their papers.

✓Say: Usually, we add an *-ed* at the end of verbs to show that the action happened in the past. Some verbs have unusual spellings for their past tense. For example, the verb *take* becomes *took.* Write on the board: *We played a game and spent money on a snack.* Which words show that something happened in the past? Describe how these terms are different. Use a word wall to sort regular and irregular verb tenses. Have students write two sentences using the past tense. Ask them to underline regular verbs once and irregular verbs twice.

Amazing Meat-Eating Plants

SKILLS

PHONICS SKILL INTRODUCED
- Final *e* (*a_e, e_e, i_e, o_e*)

SIGHT WORDS
- *away, because, fly, grow, have, made, more, new, start, take, three, wash*

VOCABULARY WORDS–
Science Words
- *Australia, digest, dissolve, flypaper, minerals, oxygen, soil*

CURRICULUM LINK–
Science Focus
- Plant Life

Amazing Meat-Eating Plants

BEFORE THE READING

Develop Phonemic Awareness and Phonics
Oral Blending
- Say: Today we are going to be listening to sounds and blending them to make words. Blending means putting sounds together to make words.
- Write the words *remake, awoke,* and *provide* on the board. Model blending the sounds of the words as you point to each sound-spelling: /r/ /ē/ /m/ /ā/ /k/, remake; /ə/ /w/ /ō/ /k/, awoke; /pr/ /ō/ /v/ /ī/ /d/, provide.
- Write *inside, survive,* and *decide* on the board. Say these sounds while pointing to the sound-spellings, and have students echo you: /i/ /n/ /s/ / ī/ /d/, inside; /s/ /ur/ /v/ /ī/ /v/, survive; /d/ /ē/ /s/ /ī/ /d/, decide.
- Write *confuse, locate,* and *escape* on the board. Have students try blending the words out loud but independently. Walk around to support students. If a student is struggling to blend the discrete sounds, model putting up one finger for each sound while saying it aloud, and have the student follow suit.

Introduce Phonics Skills
Final *e* (*a_e, e_e, i_e, o_e*)
- Say: We just practiced blending some two-syllable words with final *e* syllables. When you see final *e* syllables in words with more than one syllable, the long vowel plus the silent *e* must stay together in the same syllable. Now we are going to read some two-syllable words with final *e* syllables.
- Write the word *include* on the board, and draw a line between the two word parts, in|clude. Draw a line under the *u* and the *e*. Say: The *u* and the silent *e* stay together in the second syllable. Model reading the word, one sound at a time, while pointing to the letters: /i/ /n/ /k/ /l/ /oo/ /d/.
- Write the words *amaze, behave,* and *explode* on the board. Have students read the words as a class. Say: Slowly sound out each letter.
- Have students try reading the words *relate* and *compete* independently, following the routine above. Walk around to support students. Students who are struggling may need extra modeling, practice, and feedback, such as: Let's look at the word *compete*. Remember that the long *e* and silent *e* stay together in the same syllable. Let's say the sounds of this word together. Now you do it.

Introduce Sight Words
- Say: You are going to see some words today that you may not know, so you will need to keep them in your memory.
- Write *away, because, fly,* and *grow* on the board. Read the words to students as you point to each letter.
- Write *have, made, more,* and *new* on the board. Read the words, and have students echo read each word.
- Write *start, take, three,* and *wash* on the board. Have a volunteer read them aloud, and have the class follow suit. Place the words on a sight-word bulletin board.
- The book also contains science words. Follow the steps above with these words, but this time provide a simple definition for words that may cause confusion: *Australia, digest, dissolve, flypaper, minerals, oxygen, soil.* For example: Soil is the top layer of the earth where plants grow. Show students the image of soil from the book.

Build Oral Language
- Say: Today we will be reading a book about plants that eat meat. Before I read, I often think about the topic and try to recall what I already know about it.
- Select a student and discuss what you know about meat-eating plants. Describe what meat-eating plants do and what they look like. Consider adding vocabulary to your

discussion, such as *digest, dissolve,* and *flytrap.* Then have the student tell you what he or she knows about meat-eating plants.

- Say: **Ask a partner if he or she has ever seen a meat-eating plant.**
- Pick five pairs of students, and encourage one student from each pair to share in the discussion. Recognize when students use previously taught key vocabulary.

DURING THE READING

Preview the Book

- Read the title of the book on the cover, and point to the picture. Turn to page 2, read the text, and discuss the picture. Have students follow along in their books.
- Say: **Do you know what the book will be about based on the title and the first page that I read? How do you know what it will be about?**
- Point out the words that have final *e* syllables: *live, provide, breathe, these.*
- Have students turn to the picture with the caption on page 5. Explain that captions describe pictures and relate them to the main text.
- Model how to read the caption on page 5 and how the information relates to the photo as well as the main text. Then ask a volunteer to read the caption.

Read the Book

- Read the book to students as they follow along. Point out words that contain final *e* syllables. Tell students the names of different kinds of meat-eating plants if they don't know them: *Venus flytrap, bladderwort plant, sundew plant, pitcher plant.*
- Have students silently read the book. Ask a few students to whisper read the book to you, and help them sound out new words. When observing students, focus on the new words: *besides, escape, provide, survive, these, white.*
- **Science Connections:** Say: **The word *carnivorous* means "meat-eating."** The things that a carnivorous plant eats are its prey. The flowers of some carnivorous plants have the color and smell of meat that is decayed, or rotting. This attracts the plant's prey, such as bugs.

AFTER THE READING

Check Comprehension

To check students' understanding of the book, ask the following:

✓ **Look at page 3. Why do some plants eat meat?** (Some plants live in soil that does not have enough minerals, which plants need to survive. They get these minerals by eating meat.)

✓ **Look at page 6. How does a Venus flytrap catch bugs?** (Its leaves smell like sweet juice, which attracts bugs. The bugs fly to the leaves, which have little hairs. When the bugs walk on the hairs, the leaves know it's time to close and trap the bugs.)

✓ **How does the picture on page 12 help you understand what you read? How does the text help you understand the picture?** (Answers may include: The picture helps me understand what it looks like when a bug gets crushed by a sundew plant. The text helps me understand that the plant's sticky goo is used to break apart the bug and eat it.)

Reread to Develop Fluency

- Say: **Today you will read the book to each other to practice reading with fluency. This means that you read the book as the author meant for it to be read aloud.**
- Model reading fluently by reading the book aloud to students. Focus on pausing briefly when there is a comma.
- Have partners reread the book to each other. Remind students how to read sentences with commas. Students may struggle with decoding, comprehension, or vocabulary. For students who are struggling with comprehension, say: **I noticed that you seem unsure how to read this sentence. What are some clues we can use to help us understand what we read? Now that we understand the sentence a little better, let's try reading it again with proper expression.**
- Send home a copy of *Amazing Meat-Eating Plants* for students to read to family members. Consider assessing a few students on fluency.

Connect to Written Language

↻ **Review:** Write the words *handle, little,* and *simple* on the board. As a class, read the words together as you point to the letters. Then replace the first vowel in *simple* with an *a,* Have students write the new word, and read it together.

✓ Dictate the following words for students to spell: *escape, provide, awoke, inside, include, made,* and *wash.* When finished, write the words on the board. Have students self-correct their papers.

✓ Say: **Some words are made up of two different words. When these words are put together, they make a new word with a new meaning. You can figure out this new meaning by thinking about the two different words.** Write *flypaper* on the board. **Do you see two different words?** Trace a line under *fly* and say *fly.* Trace a line under *paper* and say *paper.* A fly is an insect with two wings. Paper is thin sheets of material used for writing on or wrapping things. So flypaper is a sheet of paper used to catch flies. Write *shoebox, goldfish,* and *wheelchair* on the board. Read the words as a class, and encourage group discussion about their meanings. Ask students to think of more compound words and to write them on a piece of paper.

SKILLS

PHONICS SKILL INTRODUCED
- *r*-controlled Vowel Syllables

SIGHT WORDS
- *again, bring, cold, find, green, just, must, put, right, stop, up, where*

VOCABULARY WORDS–
Social Studies Words
- *bananas, consumers, export(ed, ing), harvest(ed, ing), South America, transport(ed, ing), workers*

CURRICULUM LINK–
Social Studies Focus
- Goods and Services

Where Bananas Come From

BEFORE THE READING

Develop Phonemic Awareness and Phonics
Oral Segmentation
- Say: Today we are going to segment words so that we can say them sound by sound. Segment means to pull words apart by their sounds.
- Write the words *market* and *corner* on the board. Model saying the words sound by sound: /m/ /ar/ /k/ /i/ /t/, market; /k/ /or/ /n/ /ə/ /r/, corner.
- Write *carpet* and *person* on the board. Sound out each word, and have students follow suit chorally: /k/ /ar/ /p/ /i/ /t/, carpet; /p/ /ur/ /s/ /ə/ /n/, person.
- Write *burden, garden,* and *export* on the board. Have students segment the words out loud but independently. Walk around to support students. If a student is struggling to segment the sounds in each word, model saying each sound as you move a chip onto a line or sound box, and have the student follow suit.

Introduce Phonics Skills
r-controlled Vowel Syllables
- Say: We just practiced segmenting words with the /ar/ sound, as in the first syllable of *market*; the /ur/ sound, as in the first syllable of *person*; and the /or/ sound, as in the first syllable of *corner*. Now we are going to read some words with these sound-spellings.
- Write the word *harness* on the board. Draw a line between the *r* and the *n* to divide the word into syllables. Underline the /ar/ spelling. Say: The letters *ar* are the spelling for the /ar/ sound. Model reading the word, one sound at a time, while pointing to the letters: /h/ /ar/ /n/ /i/ /s/. Repeat for the /ur/ sound using the word *perfect*, and the /or/ sound using the word *forest*.
- Write the words *army, turnip,* and *fortune* on the board. Have students read the words as a class. Say: Slowly sound out each letter.
- Have students try reading the words *farther, termite,* and *morsel* independently, following the routine above. Walk around to support students. Students who are struggling may need extra modeling, practice, and feedback, such as: Let's look at the word *farther*. Remember that when two consonants appear together in a word, they sometimes stand for one sound. For example, the letters *th* together stand for the /th/ sound. Let's slowly say the sounds of this word together as I point to each letter: /f/ /ar/ /th/ /ə/ /r/. Now you do it.

Introduce Sight Words
- Say: You are going to see some words today that you may not know, so you will need to keep them in your memory.
- Write *again, bring, cold,* and *find* on the board. Read the words to students as you point to each letter.
- Write *green, just, must,* and *put* on the board. Read the words, and have students echo read them.
- Write *right, stop, up,* and *where* on the board. Ask a volunteer to read them aloud, and have the class follow suit. Place the words on a sight-word bulletin board.
- The book also contains social studies words. Follow the steps above with these words, but this time provide a simple definition for words that may cause confusion: *bananas, consumers, export(ed, ing), harvest(ed, ing), South America, transport(ed, ing), workers*. For example: *Harvesting* means "gathering crops from a field." Show students the picture from the book of bananas being harvested.

Build Oral Language
- Say: Today we will read a book about where bananas come from. Before I read, I often think about the topic and try to recall what I already know about it.

- Select a student and discuss what you know about where bananas come from. Add vocabulary to your discussion, such as *South America* and *export*. Then have the student tell you what he or she knows about where bananas come from.
- Say: Talk with your partner about what you know about where bananas come from. Write what you both know on a sticky note. When you are done, add the sticky note information to chart paper.
- Pick five pairs of students, and encourage one student from each pair to share what they wrote. Recognize when students use previously taught key vocabulary.

DURING THE READING

Preview the Book
- Read the title of the book on the cover, and point to the picture. Turn to page 2 and read the text. Point to the image and discuss that as well. Have students follow along.
- Say: Do you know what the book will be about based on the title and the first page that I read? How do you know what it will be about?
- As needed, point out words with the /ur/ sound: *wonder, perhaps, peppers, dinner.*
- Have students turn to the flowchart on page 15. Explain that this flowchart shows readers the steps in the process of getting bananas from the farm to the consumer.
- Point out the features of the flowchart: title, boxed details, and arrows.
- Model for children how to read the flowchart. Then ask volunteers to model how they would get information from the flowchart.

Read the Book
- Read the book to students as they follow along. Point out words that contain *r*-controlled vowel syllables.
- Have students silently read the book. Ask a few students to whisper read the book to you, and help them sound out new words. When observing students, focus on the new words: *harvest, market, supermarket, consumer, dinner, drivers, farmers, other, peppers, perfect, perhaps, weather, wonder, workers, export, sorted, transport.*
- **Social Studies Connections:** Say: Bananas are one of the most popular fruits in the world. More bananas are exported than any other fruit. Bananas are very important to the countries that export them because the countries depend on the money they make selling bananas in other parts of the world.

AFTER THE READING

Check Comprehension
To check students' understanding of the book, ask the following:
✓Look at page 4. How are bananas protected on the farms where they grow? (They are covered with plastic bags, which protect them from bugs, birds, and wind.)
✓Look at pages 8–10. How do bananas get from farms to your local grocery store? (Bananas are transported by truck from farms to ports for shipping. From there, they are moved by ships to ports in this country. Then they are moved by truck again to local stores.)
✓Use the flowchart on page 15 to tell what happens after bananas have ripened. (After they have ripened, bananas are transported to stores and sold to consumers.)

Reread to Develop Fluency
- Say: Today you will read the book to each other to practice reading with fluency. This means that you read the book as the author meant for it to be read aloud.
- Model reading fluently by reading the book aloud to students. Focus on reading at a consistent pace.
- Have partners reread the book to each other. Remind children to read sentences at a consistent pace. Students may struggle with decoding, comprehension, or vocabulary. For students who are struggling with decoding, say: I see that you're working on reading this word. Let's read it together, sounding out the letters of each word slowly. You've got it! Now that you know the word, reread the sentence.
- Send home a copy of *Where Bananas Come From* for students to read to family members. Consider assessing a few students on fluency.

Connect to Written Language
↻Review: Write the words *even, amaze,* and *behave* on the board. As a class, read the words together as you point to the letters. Have students write the words in a sentence.

✓Dictate the following words for students to spell: *market, dinner, order, person, export, again,* and *where.* When finished, write the words on the board. Have students self-correct their papers.

✓Say: Some words are made up of two different words. When these words are put together, they make a new word with a new meaning. You can figure out this new meaning by thinking about the two different words. Write *supermarket* on the board. Do you see two different words? Draw a line under *super* and say *super.* Draw a line under *market* and say *market.* *Super* can mean "very large." A market is a store where people buy food and other items. So a supermarket is a very large store where you can buy things. Write *afternoon, cupcake,* and *doghouse* on the board. Read the words as a class and encourage group discussion about their meanings. Ask students to think of more compound words and then write them on a piece of paper.

Animals and Their Habitats

SKILLS

PHONICS SKILL INTRODUCED
- Variant Vowel /o͞o/ (*ew, oo, ough, ue*)

SIGHT WORDS
- *because, four, good, green, never, together, warm, water, white*

VOCABULARY WORDS–
Science Words
- *Arctic, habitats, rain forest, reef, woodland(s)*

CURRICULUM LINK–
Science Focus
- Animal Habitats

Animals and Their Habitats

BEFORE THE READING

Develop Phonemic Awareness and Phonics
Phonemic Manipulation
- Say: We are going to delete a sound, which means we're taking a sound away.
- Write the words *few* and *boo* on the board, and model removing the first sound in each word: few, ew; boo, oo.
- Write *clue* and *loose* on the board. Say these words while pointing to the sound-spellings. Have students echo you as you delete the initial onset sounds and say the words: clue, ue; loose, oose
- Write *chew, through, true,* and *zoom* on the board. Have students try saying the words and deleting the initial onset sound out loud but independently. Walk around to support students. If a student is struggling with deleting, model pushing a colored chip forward for each sound, then cover the first chip as you delete the first sound. Have the student follow suit.

Introduce Phonics Skills
Variant Vowel /o͞o/ (*ew, oo, ough, ue*)
- Say: We just practiced deleting the sounds in some words. Now we are going to read some words as we point out the beginning and ending sounds in each.
- Write the words *boot, flew, through,* and *true* on the board, and underline the /o͞o/. Say: The letters *oo, ew, ough,* and *ue* are all spellings for the /o͞o/ sound. Model reading the words, one sound at a time, while pointing to the letters: /b/ /o͞o/ /t/, /fl/ /o͞o/, /th/ /r/ /o͞o/, /tr/ /o͞o/.
- Write the words *blue, broom,* and *stew* on the board. Have students read the words as a class. Say: Slowly sound out each letter.
- Have students try reading the words *moose, shrew,* and *spoon* independently, following the routine above. Walk around to support students. Students who are struggling may need extra modeling, practice, and feedback, such as: Let's look at the word *spoon.* When two consonants appear together in a word, the sound of each consonant is blended together. For example, the letters *sp* in *spoon* stand for the /sp/ sound. Let's slowly say the sounds of this word together as I point to each letter. Now you do it.

Introduce Sight Words
- Say: You are going to see some words today that you may not know, so you will need to keep them in your memory.
- Write the words *never, warm,* and *water* on the board. Read them to students as you point to each letter.
- Write the words *because, four, together,* and *white* on the board. Read the words, and have students echo you.
- Write the words *good* and *green* on the board. Ask a volunteer to read them aloud, and have the class follow suit. Place the words on a sight-word bulletin board.
- The book also contains science words. Follow the steps above with these words, but this time provide a simple definition for words that may cause confusion: *Arctic, habitats, rain forest, reef,* and *woodlands.* For example: A rain forest is a thick forest or jungle where rain falls nearly every day. Show students the picture of the rain forest from the book.

Build Oral Language
- Say: Today we will be reading a book about animal habitats. Before I read, I often think about the topic and try to recall what I already know about it.
- Select a student and discuss a time you saw an animal in its natural habitat. Explain what it looked like and what the habitat looked like. Consider adding vocabulary to

your discussion, such as *grassland, mossy, pond, reef, swampy, tropical*. Then have the student tell you about a time he or she saw an animal in its natural habitat.

- Say: With a partner, discuss a time you saw an animal in its natural habitat. Discuss the animal you saw, what it looked like, and describe the habitat.
- Pick five pairs of students, and encourage one student from each pair to share in the discussion. Recognize when students use previously taught key vocabulary.

DURING THE READING

Preview the Book

- Read the title of the book on the cover, and point to the picture. Turn to pages 2 and 3 and read the text. Point to the image on page 3 and read the label as well. Have students follow along in their books.
- Say: Do you know what the book will be about based on the title and the first pages that I read? How do you know what it will be about?
- Have students turn to page 16, and point to the heading "Index." Explain that an index comes at the end of a book. Readers can use it to find specific topics or information in the book.
- Point out the features of an index: entry word, alphabetical order, page numbers.
- Model for children how to use the index. Then ask volunteers to model how to use the index.

Read the Book

- Read the book to students as they follow along. Point out words that contain the sound-spellings taught. Tell students the names of the animals in the book if they don't know them.
- Have students silently read the book. Ask a few students to whisper read the book to you, and help them sound out new words. When observing students, focus on the new words: *blue, chew, cool, food, moose, roof, room, shrew, spoons, through, too.*
- **Science Connections:** Say: In addition to the habitats discussed in this book, there are other habitats around the world. For example, animals such as lizards and rattlesnakes live in a desert habitat, which is very hot and dry. Many plant-eating animals, such as giraffes and zebras, live in a grasslands habitat in Africa. These grasslands are called savannas.

AFTER THE READING

Check Comprehension

To check students' understanding of the book, ask the following:
- ✓Which word on page 8 has the /o͞o/ sound and is the name of a large woodland animal? (*moose*)
- ✓How are a rain forest habitat and a woodland habitat similar? How are they different? (Answers may include: Both have a lot of trees, but it is hot and wet in the rain forest, and it is cool in a woodland habitat, even in the summer. The types of animals that live in each habitat are also different.)
- ✓Use the Index to help you figure out where you would find information about the canopy in this book. (pages 10 and 11)

Reread to Develop Fluency

- Say: Today you will read the book to each other to practice reading with fluency. This means that you read the book as the author meant for it to be read aloud.
- Model reading fluently by reading the book aloud to students. Focus on reading sentences with periods, exclamation points, and question marks appropriately.
- Have partners reread the book to each other. Remind students how to read sentences with exclamation points, question marks, and periods. Students may struggle with decoding, comprehension, or vocabulary. For students who are struggling with vocabulary, say: I noticed that you're not sure what that word means, which makes it hard to read the sentence. Let's look up the definition of the word.
- Send home a copy of *Animals and Their Habitats* for students to read to family members. Consider assessing a few students on fluency.

Connect to Written Language

↻Review: Write the words *person, corner,* and *army* on the board. As a class, read the words together as you point to the letters. Then remove the beginning sound, and read the ending sounds together.

✓Dictate the following words for students to spell: *cool, food, good, moose, roof, because,* and *water.* When finished, write the words on the board. Have students self-correct their papers.

✓Ask students to choose a habitat. Have them draw a picture of a habitat that includes some of the animals that live in that habitat. Then have students write a few words about the habitat they chose and the animals that live there. You may suggest that they use the following sentence stems: *This is a _____ habitat. Animals such as _____, _____, and _____ live in this type of habitat.* You may wish to divide the pictures up by habitat and display them in different parts of the classroom, library, or school.

Gravity

SKILLS

PHONICS SKILL INTRODUCED
- Variant Vowel /o͞o/ (oo)

SIGHT WORDS
- *drink, funny, jump, pull, two*

VOCABULARY WORDS–
Science Words
- *force, gravity, mass, pull(s), weight*

CURRICULUM LINK–
Science Focus
- Earth and Space

Gravity

BEFORE THE READING

Develop Phonemic Awareness and Phonics
Oral Segmentation
- Say: Today we are segmenting words into individual sounds. Segmenting means pulling words apart by their sounds. Today we are listening for the /o͞o/ sound.
- Write the words *foot, soot,* and *book* on the board. Model segmenting the words as you point to each sound-spelling: /f/ /o͞o/ /t/, foot; /s/ /o͞o/ /t/, soot; /b/ /o͞o/ /k/, book. Push a colored chip forward as you say each sound.
- Write *hood* and *crook* on the board. Segment the sounds while pointing to the sound-spellings. Have students echo you as you pull apart the sounds in each word: /h/ /o͞o/ /d/, hood; /kr/ /o͞o/ /k/, crook.
- Write *good, look,* and *shook* on the board. Have students try segmenting the sounds out loud but independently. Support students who are struggling with segmenting by modeling with colored chips. Use one color consistently for the /o͞o/ sound, and show how the sound stays the same despite the other sounds surrounding it. Have the student follow suit as he or she slowly pulls apart the sounds.

Introduce Phonics Skills
Variant Vowel /o͞o/ (oo)
- Say: We just practiced segmenting the sounds in some words. Now we are going to read some words as we point out each sound-spelling. Today we are noticing the /o͞o/ sound.
- Write the words *hook* and *good* on the board, and underline the *oo* spellings. Say: The *oo* spelling can stand for the /o͞o/ sound. Model reading the words, one sound at a time, while pointing to the letters: /h/ /o͞o/ /k/, hook; /g/ /o͞o/ /d/, good.
- Write the words *cook, foot,* and *stood* on the board. Have students read the words as a class. Say: Sound out each letter, and notice the /o͞o/ sound in each word.
- Have students try reading the words *hoof, wood,* and *brook* independently, following the routine above. Walk around to support students. Students who are struggling may need extra modeling and practice, such as: Let's look at the word *brook*. Say each letter sound as I point to it, and remember that the letters *b* and *r* blend to make the sound: /br/. Let's say the sounds together. Now you try it.

Introduce Sight Words
- Say: You are going to see some words today that you may not know, so you will need to keep them in your memory.
- Write *drink* and *funny* on the board. Read them to students as you point to each letter.
- Write *jump* and *pull* on the board. Read them, and have students echo you.
- Write *two* on the board. Ask a volunteer to read it aloud, and have the rest of the class follow suit. Place the words on a sight-word bulletin board.
- The book also contains science words. Follow the steps above with these words, but this time provide a simple definition for words that may cause confusion: *force, gravity, mass, pull(s),* and *weight*. For example: The word *gravity* refers to the force that attracts something toward the ground.

Build Oral Language
- Say: Today we will be reading a book about gravity. I'm wondering about how gravity works. What is it? I think this book will answer some of my questions.
- Select a student and discuss what happens when you drop something. Why does it fall? Ask the student to give an example of something heavy and something light that falls. Explain again that gravity is a force that brings all things down to the ground. Consider adding vocabulary to your discussion, such as *Earth, force, ground, mass, moon, orbit, space,* or *spacecraft*. Then have the student describe what happens when a liquid falls to Earth.

- Say: With a partner, look at a list of words that you will see in this text and give your best guess about what these words mean. As we read the book, listen for the words and see if you were correct.
- Pick five pairs of students, and encourage each pair to share their ideas. Recognize when students use previously taught key vocabulary.

DURING THE READING

Preview the Book
- Read the title of the book and show students the picture on the cover. Read the Table of Contents, then read page 2, pointing to each word as you read.
- Say: This book is about a force called gravity. The cover shows children jumping, and it looks like they are floating. But we know the children will come down. That's because of gravity. Let's see what we can learn about this force.
- Show students the picture on page 12, and explain that we can "read" a picture too. A picture can be a primary source, meaning we can see exactly what was really happening. What does this picture tell us?

Read the Book
- Read the book to students as they follow along. Point out words that contain the sound-spellings taught. Explain the terms if students need help with the words: *gravity, force, float, orbit, space, moon, mass, weight.*
- Have students silently read the book. Ask a few students to whisper read the book to you, and help them sound out new words. When observing students, focus on the new words: *book, cook, foot, good, look, stood, took.*
- **Science Connections:** Say: One of the first scientists to study gravity was Isaac Newton. He lived 300 years ago, and he was interested in making mechanical things, like windmills. His work included many important discoveries about gravity, plus much more about science and math.

AFTER THE READING

Check Comprehension
To check students' understanding of the book, ask the following:
✓Read the text on page 2, then define *gravity* in your own words. (Answers may include: Gravity is a force that pulls us to Earth.) How is the word *stick* used to explain gravity? (Answers may include: We "stick" because gravity keeps us down.)
✓Look at page 8. Which item has more mass? (the case) How do you know? (Answers may include: The boy is struggling to lift the heavy case.)
✓What does the caption tell us about the picture on page 13? (Answers may include: It describes what we are looking at.) Name two ways the moon is different than Earth. (Answers may include: The moon has less mass and less gravity than Earth.)

Reread to Develop Fluency
- Say: Today you will read the book to each other to practice reading with fluency. This means that you read the book as the author meant for it to be read aloud.
- Model reading fluently by reading the book aloud to students. Focus on showing excitement in your voice when you read a sentence with an exclamation point.
- Have partners reread the book to each other. Suggest that they add expression in their voices as they read to match the punctuation. Students may struggle with decoding, comprehension, or vocabulary. For students who are struggling with vocabulary, say: I noticed that some of these words are new to you. Do you know a word that sounds similar? Let's look up the definition in a dictionary. Now that we know the word, try reading the sentence again.
- Send home a copy of *Gravity* for students to read to family members. Consider assessing a few students on fluency.

Connect to Written Language
↻Review: Write the words *blue, cool,* and *through* on the board. As a class, read the words together as you point to the letters. Then circle the *ue, oo,* and *ough* spellings in each word, and practice identifying the /$\overline{oo}$/ sounds in each word. Have students think of a rhyme for each word, and write the rhyme into a sentence. Have them take turns sharing their rhyming sentences.

✓Dictate the following words for students to spell: *book, good, hood, brook, took, pull,* and *too.* When finished, write the words on the board. Have students self-correct their papers.

✓Say: When two words combine to make a new word, it is called a compound word. For example, *rain* and *drops* combine to make *raindrops.* Write on the board: *You could not go to space without a spacecraft.* Identify the compound words. What words were combined? Use word cards to help students create compound words. Have students use the words they create in three sentences. Ask them to underline the compound words in each sentence.

Making Laws

SKILLS

PHONICS SKILL INTRODUCED
- Variant Vowel *a(lk)*, *a(lt)*, *au*, *aw*

SIGHT WORDS
- *don't, eight, four, know, right, white*

VOCABULARY WORDS–
Social Studies Words
- *Congress, government, governor, legislature, president, vote, White House*

CURRICULUM LINK–
Social Studies Focus
- Levels of Government

Making Laws

BEFORE THE READING

Develop Phonemic Awareness and Phonics
Oral Segmentation
- Say: Today we are segmenting words into individual sounds. Segmenting means pulling words apart by their sounds. Today we are listening for the /ô/ sound.
- Write the words *cause, lawn,* and *salt* on the board. Model segmenting the words as you point to each sound-spelling: /c/ /ô/ /z/, cause; /l/ /ô/ /n/, lawn; /s/ /ô/ /l/ /t/, salt. Tap one finger at a time to your thumb as you say each sound.
- Write *malt, chalk, fault,* and *draw* on the board. Segment the sounds while pointing to the sound-spellings. Have students echo you as you pull apart the sounds in each word: /m/ /ô/ /l/ /t/, malt; /ch/ /ô/ /k/, chalk; /f/ /ô/ /l/ /t/, fault; /dr/ /ô/, draw.
- Write *halt, haunt,* and *dawn* on the board. Have students try segmenting the sounds out loud but independently. Support students who are struggling with segmenting by modeling tapping your finger to your thumb as you say each sound. Have the student follow suit as he or she slowly pulls apart the sounds.

Introduce Phonics Skills
Variant Vowel *a(lk)*, *a(lt)*, *au*, *aw*
- Say: We just practiced segmenting the sounds in some words. Now we are going to read some words as we point out each sound-spelling.
- Write the words *talk, salt, sauce,* and *thaw* on the board, and underline the *a(lk)*, *a(lt)*, *au*, *aw* spellings. Say: These spellings can each stand for the /ô/ sound. Model reading the words, one sound at a time, while pointing to the letters: /t/ /ô/ /k/; /s/ /ô/ /l/ /t/; /s/ /ô/ /s/; /th/ /ô/.
- Write the words *law, chalk, launch,* and *halt* on the board. Have students read the words as a class. Say: Slowly sound out each letter, and notice the different spellings for the /ô/ sound.
- Have students try reading the words *paw, walk, pause,* and *alter* independently, following the routine above. Walk around to support students. Students who are struggling may need extra modeling and practice, such as: Let's look at the word *pause*. Say each letter sound as I point to it, and remember that in this word the *s* makes the /z/ sound. Let's say the sounds together. Now you try it.

Introduce Sight Words
- Say: You are going to see some words today that you may not know, so you will need to keep them in your memory.
- Write *don't* and *eight* the board. Read them to students as you point to each letter.
- Write *four* and *know* on the board. Read them, and have students echo you.
- Write the words *right* and *white* on the board. Ask a volunteer to read them aloud, and have the class follow suit. Place the words on a sight-word bulletin board.
- The book also contains social studies words. Follow the steps above with these words, but this time provide a simple definition for words that may cause confusion: *Congress, government, governor, legislature, president, vote,* and *White House*. For example: The word *Congress* refers to a group of people elected by each state to help make laws in government. Show students the picture of the Constitution on page 3, and discuss how our government represents everyone in the nation.

Build Oral Language
- Say: Today we will be reading a book about how laws are made. I know laws are like rules. We need rules to keep us safe and to make sure things are fair. This book will explain how those laws are decided upon.
- Select a student and discuss why rules and laws are important. Ask the student to give an example of a rule for the classroom. Explain that rules need to be fair and should be agreed upon by lots of people. Consider adding vocabulary to your discussion, such as *protect, government, council, voters, mayor, city hall, veto, capital,* or *elected*. Then have the student describe a law or rule that keeps us safe.

- Say: With a partner, discuss our class rules. Are there any you would change? What might you add? Brainstorm some ideas and add your ideas to a two-column chart under either the "Change" or "Add" headings.
- Pick five pairs of students, and encourage each pair to share their ideas. Recognize when students use previously taught key vocabulary.

DURING THE READING

Preview the Book

- Read the title of the book on the cover, and point to the picture. Turn to the Table of Contents and show how each heading represents a different subtopic. Read the sentences on page 2, pointing to each word as you read. Have students follow along.
- Say: This book is about how laws are made. The cover shows the White House. The White House is where the president lives. It is a symbol of our government. This book explains how our government works.
- As needed, point out the words that have the variant vowel /ô/ (alk, alt, au, aw): walking, because, laws.

Read the Book

- Read the book to students as they follow along. Point out the captions, and explain how a caption gives a short description of a picture. Explain the terms in the index if students need help with the words: capitol, Congress, council, governor, mayor, voters, White House.
- Have students silently read the book. Ask a few students to whisper read the book to you, and help them sound out new words. When observing students, focus on the new words: alter, because, law(s), sidewalks, talk, walking.
- **Social Studies Connections:** Say: Congress contains two different groups of lawmakers. One is the Senate, which consists of two people from each state, called senators. The other is the House of Representatives, in which each elected person, or representative, represents a large number of that state's population. Each group usually meets separately but sometimes together in a joint session.

AFTER THE READING

Check Comprehension

To check students' understanding of the book, ask the following:

✓ What is one reason we have laws? (Answers may include: to keep us safe or protect us)

✓ Look at the text on page 6. Are a mayor and city council in charge of a state? (Answers may include: No, they are in charge of a city.)

✓ Read the caption on page 9. What does it tell you about the picture? (Answers may include: It explains that the picture shows the capitol building of Minnesota.) Who works in the capitol building? (Answers may include: the governor and other state workers)

Reread to Develop Fluency

- Say: Today you will read the book to each other to practice reading with fluency. This means that you read the book as the author meant for it to be read aloud.
- Model reading fluently by reading the book aloud to students. Focus on pausing slightly at each comma.
- Have partners reread the book to each other. Suggest that they pause when they come to a comma and use expression in their voices. Students may struggle with decoding, comprehension, or vocabulary. For students who are struggling with decoding, say: I noticed that some of these words are very long. Let's break them down and slowly sound out one letter at a time. Let's try it a few times until you can say the word comfortably. You did it! Now reread the sentence at a steady pace.
- Send home a copy of Making Laws for students to read to family members. Consider assessing a few students on fluency.

Connect to Written Language

↻ Review: Write the words foot, stood, and took on the board. As a class, read the words together as you point to the letters. Then circle the oo spellings in each word, and practice substituting the beginning and ending sounds in each word. Have students think of a riddle using one or more of the words.

✓ Dictate the following words for students to spell: alter, because, law, sidewalk, talk, four, and eight. When finished, write the words on the board. Have students self-correct their papers.

✓ Say: A noun identifies a person, place, or thing. Sometimes a noun identifies a group. This is called a collective noun. For example, a council is a group of people who meet to decide laws. Write on the board: The city was quiet after dark. Which word is a collective noun? What kind of group is the collective noun referencing? Use pictures from magazines to help students brainstorm more collective nouns. Have students use the words in a short story.

Extreme Weather

SKILLS

PHONICS SKILL INTRODUCED
- Variant Vowels (*au*, o͞o); Vowel Team Syllables (Long *a*: *ai*, *ay*; Long *e*: *ea*, *ee*, *ey*; Long *o*: *oa*, *ow*; Diphthongs: *oi*, *ou*)

SIGHT WORDS
- *around, know, people, pretty, six, today, which*

VOCABULARY WORDS–
Science Words
- *blizzard, hurricane, meteorologist, tornado, weather systems*

CURRICULUM LINK–
Science Focus
- Weather

Extreme Weather

BEFORE THE READING

Develop Phonemic Awareness and Phonics
Oral Blending
- Say: Today we are going to be listening to sounds and blending them to make words. Blending means putting sounds together to make words.
- Write the words *sleepy* and *railroad* on the board. Model blending the sounds of the words as you point to each sound-spelling: /sl/ /ē/ /p/ /ē/, sleepy; /r/ /ā/ /l/ /r/ /ō/ /d/, railroad.
- Write *pointed* and *cookbook* on the board. Say these sounds while pointing to the sound-spellings, and have students echo you: /p/ /oi/ /n/ /t/ /e/ /d/, pointed; /k/ /o͞o/ /k/ /b/ /o͞o/ /k/, cookbook.
- Write *cloudy* and *faucet* on the board. Have students try blending the words out loud but independently. Walk around to support students. If a student is struggling to blend the discrete sounds, model putting up one finger for each sound while saying it aloud, and have the student follow suit.

Introduce Phonics Skills
Variant Vowels *au*, o͞o; Vowel Team Syllables Long *a*: *ai*, *ay*;
Long *e*: *ea*, *ee*, *ey*; Long *o*: *oa*, *ow*; and Diphthongs: *oi*, *ou*
- Say: We just practiced blending some words with different vowel sounds. Now we are going to read some words with these sound-spellings.
- Write the words *sauce* and *football* on the board, and underline the *au* and o͞o. Say: These spellings stand for the /ô/ and /o͞o/ sounds. Model reading the words, one sound at a time, while pointing to the letters.
- Write the words *paint, reach,* and *steamboat* on the board. Have students read the words as a class. Say: Slowly sound out each letter.
- Have students try reading the words *alley, August, cloudy,* and *snowman* independently, following the routine above. Walk around to support students. Students who are struggling may need extra modeling, practice, and feedback, such as: Let's look at the word *alley*. Remember that when two *l*'s appear together, they represent one sound. What sound is that? That's right, it's the /l/ sound. Let's slowly say the sounds of this word together as I point to each letter. Now you do it.

Introduce Sight Words
- Say: You are going to see some words today that you may not know, so you will need to keep them in your memory.
- Write the words *around, six,* and *today* on the board. Read them to students as you point to each letter.
- Write the words *pretty* and *people* on the board. Read the words, and have students echo read them.
- Write the words *know* and *which* on the board. Ask a volunteer to read them aloud, and have the class follow suit. Place the words on a sight-word bulletin board.
- The book also contains science words. Follow the steps above with these words, but this time provide a definition for words that may cause confusion: *blizzard, hurricane, meteorologist, tornado,* and *weather systems*. For example: A hurricane is an extremely powerful storm in the western Atlantic Ocean. Show students the pictures of hurricanes from the book.

Build Oral Language
- Say: Today we will be reading a book about extreme weather. Before I read, I often think about the topic and try to recall what I already know about it.
- Select a student and discuss a time you experienced extreme weather. Explain how it looked outside and how you felt about the weather. Consider adding vocabulary to

your discussion, such as *cloudy, freezing, rainy, snowy,* and *whiteout.* Then have the student tell you about a time he or she experienced extreme weather.

- Show students the weather map on page 3. Say: Meteorologists use maps like these to show people the weather that's headed their way. Point out your state and discuss what the weather will be like there according to this map.
- Divide the students into four groups, and assign each group a region of the United States (north, south, east, west). Have the groups study the map, then ask one student from each group to discuss the weather in their assigned part of the country according to the map. Recognize when students use previously taught key vocabulary.

DURING THE READING

Preview the Book

- Read the title of the book on the cover, and point to the picture. Turn to page 2 and read the sentences. Have students follow along in their books.
- Say: Do you know what the book will be about based on the title and the first page that I read? How do you know what it will be about?

Read the Book

- Read the book to students as they follow along.
- Have students silently read the book. Ask a few students to whisper read the book to you, and help them sound out new words. When observing students, focus on the new words, such as: *alley, around, cloud, freezing, moisture, rain, reach,* and *snow.*
- **Science Connections:** Say: The center of a hurricane is called the eye. When a hurricane's eye passes over a location, the winds may appear calm. Many people think that the hurricane is over and it's safe to go outside. But that could be a mistake because once the eye passes over a place, sometimes the hurricane's most powerful winds follow.

AFTER THE READING

Check Comprehension

To check students' understanding of the book, ask the following:
✓ Look at pages 8 and 9. Which kind of storm is often called a "twister"? Why is that a good name for this type of storm? (A tornado is known as a twister because its winds twist around and around in a circle.)
✓ What word on page 9 has two vowel team syllables and names a kind of transportation? (*railroad*)
✓ If you could meet a meteorologist or weather expert, what questions would you like to ask him or her? (Accept all reasonable responses.)

Reread to Develop Fluency

- Say: Today you will read the book to each other to practice reading with fluency. This means that you read the book as the author meant for it to be read aloud.
- Model reading fluently by reading the book aloud to students. Focus on reading at an appropriate rate.
- Have partners reread the book to each other. Remind students that when they read, they should read at a rate that suits the text they are reading. Explain that they may speed up or slow down in places to show excitement or suspense, but most of their reading should be at an even pace. Students may struggle with decoding, comprehension, or vocabulary. For students who are struggling with decoding, say: I noticed that some of these words are very long. Let's break them down and sound out one letter at a time. Let's try it a few times until you can say the word comfortably. You did it! Now reread the sentence at a steady pace.
- Send home a copy of *Extreme Weather* for students to read to family members. Consider assessing a few students on fluency.

Connect to Written Language

↻ **Review:** Write the words *because, talk,* and *sidewalk* on the board. As a class, read the words together as you point to the letters. Then circle the *au* and *alk* spellings in each word, and practice identifying those sound-spellings. Have students write a short story using all three words. Ask them to draw a picture and think of a title for their story.

✓ Dictate the following words for students to spell: *alley, around, football, freezing, moisture, people,* and *thundercloud.* When finished, write the words on the board. Have students self-correct their papers.

✓ Give students a printout of a map of the United States. Ask each student to make a weather map by drawing and labeling types of weather appropriate for each area of the country. Ask for volunteers to pretend to be meteorologists and present their weather forecasts to the class.

The World of Maps

SKILLS

PHONICS SKILL INTRODUCED
- Words with *–ed* and *–ing* Spelling Changes

SIGHT WORDS
- *five, found, green, hot, seven*

VOCABULARY WORDS–
Social Studies & Science Words
- *compass rose, continent(s), countries, deserts, equator, globe, lakes, map, map key, mountains, oceans, rivers*

CURRICULUM LINK–
Social Studies & Science Focus
- Geography
- Earth Science

The World of Maps

BEFORE THE READING

Develop Phonemic Awareness and Phonics
Phonemic Manipulation
- Say: Today we will be isolating sounds. When you isolate a sound, you say one sound in a word all by itself. We will focus on the *–ed* and *–ing* word endings.
- Write the words *decided, raced,* and *smiling* on the board. Model isolating the word endings by saying the words, then saying them again without their beginning sounds: decided, –cided; raced, –aced; smiling, –iling.
- Write *noticed, played,* and *clapping* on the board. Have students echo you as you eliminate the first sound: noticed, –oticed, –o–ti–ced; played, –ayed, –ay–ed; clapping, –apping, –ap–ping.
- Write *kicked, landed, making,* and *mapping* on the board. Have students try segmenting the word parts out loud but independently. Support students who are struggling with segmenting by snapping your fingers as you say each sound. Have the student follow suit as he or she slowly pulls apart the sounds.

Introduce Phonics Skills
Words with *–ed* and *–ing* Spelling Changes
- Say: We just practiced segmenting the parts in some words. Now we are going to read some words as we point out some ending sounds.
- Write the words *play, played, playing, hope, hoped,* and *hoping* on the board, and underline the *–ed* and *–ing* spellings. Say: The ending *–ed* shows that an action happened in the past. When the ending *–ing* is added, the meaning is in the present tense. If a word ends in *e*, you drop the *e* before adding *–ing.* If the word is a short-vowel word and ends in a single consonant, you sometimes double the consonant before adding *–ing.* Model reading the words, one sound at a time, while pointing to the *–ed* and *–ing* endings.
- Write the words *jump, jumped, yell, yelled, wave, waving,* and *shop, shopping* on the board. Have students read the words as a class. Say: Slowly sound out each word part, and notice how the word spellings changed when the endings were added.
- Have students try reading the words *reach, beg,* and *bake* independently, then add *–ed* and *–ing* endings following the routine above. Walk around to support students. Students who are struggling may need extra modeling and practice, such as: Let's look at the word *bake.* Say each word part as I point to it. Adding *–ing* to this word means dropping the last *e.* Let's say the parts together. Now you try it.

Introduce Sight Words
- Say: You are going to see some words today that you may not know, so you will need to keep them in your memory.
- Write *five* and *found* the board. Read them to students as you point to each letter.
- Write *green* and *hot* on the board. Read them, and have students echo you.
- Write *seven* on the board. Ask a volunteer to read it aloud, and have the rest of the class follow suit. Place the words on a sight-word bulletin board.
- The book also contains social studies words. Follow the steps above with these words, but this time provide a simple definition for words that may cause confusion: *compass rose, continent(s), countries, deserts, equator, globe, lakes, map, map key, mountains, oceans, rivers.* For example: The word *continent* means "a large piece of land." There are seven continents on Earth. Show students the map on page 9.

Build Oral Language
- Say: Today we will be reading a book about maps. We use maps in many ways. We use them when we drive, or when we travel. This book will explain how maps tell us about the world.
- Select a student and discuss the parts of a globe. Ask the student to point to the areas that are land and the areas that are water. Explain that globes are round maps of the Earth. Consider adding vocabulary to your discussion, such as *continent, equator,*

globe, countries, map keys, oceans, or *symbols.* Then see if the student can show where they live on the globe.

- Say: With a partner, list things you know about maps. Write your ideas in the K column of a KWL chart. Add things you want to know in the W column.
- Pick five pairs of students, and encourage each pair to share their ideas. Recognize when students use previously taught key vocabulary. Encourage students to add what they learned to the L column.

DURING THE READING

Preview the Book

- Read the title of the book on the cover, and point to the picture. Turn to the Table of Contents and predict what each section will be about. Turn to page 2 and read the sentences, pointing to each word as you read. Have students follow along.
- Say: This book is about reading maps of the world. There is a globe on the cover. Maps of the world can be flat or round. This book will explain all the parts of a world map.
- Explain that a map is a kind of diagram that can add information about locations. Maps are used to offer more explanations about a place. As needed, point out the words that have the *-ed* and *-ing* spelling changes: *reading, filled, amazing.*

Read the Book

- Read the book to students as they follow along. Point out words that contain the sound-spellings taught. Explain the terms if students need help with the words: *Amazon River, Antarctica, continents, equator, Europe, Sahara Desert, symbols.*
- Have students silently read the book. Ask a few students to whisper read the book to you, and help them sound out new words. When observing students, focus on new words: *divided, located, shaped, united, amazing, exciting, mapping, spinning.*
- **Social Studies Connections:** Say: A person who makes a map is called a cartographer. Cartographers use images from space satellites and computers to make maps of large areas. How do you think people made maps in the past?

AFTER THE READING

Check Comprehension

To check students' understanding of the book, ask the following:

✓Why would someone want to look at a globe instead of a flat map? (Answers may include: A globe shows the world as it really is.)

✓Look at the map on page 5. What does the map key tell us about the green and blue areas? (Answers may include: The green areas represent land, and the blue areas represent water.)

✓Look at the picture on page 13. Why are six oceans labeled in the picture? (Answers may include: The Pacific Ocean is labeled twice because the Earth is round, so it continues to the other side.)

Reread to Develop Fluency

- Say: Today you will read the book to each other to practice reading with fluency. This means that you read the book as the author meant for it to be read aloud.
- Model reading fluently by reading the book aloud to students. Model recognizing and pronouncing the proper nouns and geographic locations.
- Have partners reread the book to each other. Suggest that they practice rereading the proper nouns until they can read them fluently. Students may struggle with decoding, comprehension, or vocabulary. For students who are struggling with decoding, say: I noticed that some of these words are very long. Let's break them down and slowly sound out one letter at a time. Let's try it a few times until you can say the words comfortably. You did it! Now reread the sentence at a steady pace.
- Send home a copy of *The World of Maps* for students to read to family members. Consider assessing a few students on fluency.

Connect to Written Language

↻Review: Write the words *August, follow,* and *moisture* on the board. As a class, read the words together as you point to the letters. Then circle the *au,* long *o* (*ow*), and diphthong *oi* spellings in each word, and practice identifying the sounds in each word. Have students write a paragraph using all three words.

✓Dictate the following words for students to spell: *divided, shaped, amazing, inviting, spinning, five,* and *found.* When finished, write the words on the board. Have students self-correct their papers.

✓Say: When we write the name of a specific place on the globe, like a country, city, river, or ocean, we capitalize that name. For example, we write *ocean* to describe any ocean, but we capitalize *Pacific Ocean* because it is the name of a specific ocean. Write on the board: *France is a country on the continent of Europe.* Which words are capitalized? Why do you think they are capitalized? Do a word sort with specific and general geographic names. Have students choose three words from each category and write three different sentences using both general and capitalized geographic names.

Let's Go to the Museum!

SKILLS

PHONICS SKILL INTRODUCED
- Prefixes *pre–, un–*

SIGHT WORDS
- *before, buy, full, keep, most, much, such, three, time, work*

VOCABULARY WORDS–
Social Studies Words
- *admission, artifact, caretaker, display, extinct, floor plan, fragile, museum*

CURRICULUM LINK–
Social Studies Focus
- Museums

Let's Go to the Museum!

BEFORE THE READING

Develop Phonemic Awareness and Phonics
Phonemic Manipulation: Deletion
- Say: Today we are going to remove some letters from words to make new words.
- Write the words *preheat* and *unwrap* on the board, and model removing the prefix from each word: preheat, heat; unwrap, wrap.
- Write *precook, preschool, preview, undone, unfold,* and *unhappy* on the board. Have students say each word without its beginning prefix.

Introduce Phonics Skills
Prefixes *pre–, un–*
- Say: We just practiced creating new words by removing the prefixes *pre–* and *un–*. A prefix is a word part added to the beginning of a word. Adding a prefix to a word changes its meaning.
- Write the words *cut, precut, kind,* and *unkind* on the board. Underline the prefixes *pre–* and *un–*. Explain that the prefix *pre–* means "before." The prefix *un–* means "not." Model reading the words, one sound at a time, while pointing to the letters: /pr/ /ē/ /k/ /u/ /t/, precut; /u/ /n/ /k/ /ī/ /n/ /d/, unkind.
- Write the words *preview* and *undo* on the board. Have students read the words as a class. Say: Slowly sound out each letter.
- Have students try reading the words *pregame, preorder, unclean,* and *unlucky* independently, following the routine above. Walk around to support students. Students who are struggling may need extra modeling, practice, and feedback, such as: Let's look at the word *unclean*. Remember that when the letters *ea* appear together in a word, they usually make the long *e* sound, as in the words *cheap, eager,* and *teach*. Let's slowly say the sounds of this word together as I point to each letter: /u/ /n/ /k/ /l/ /ē/ /n/. Now you do it.

Introduce Sight Words
- Say: You are going to see some words today that you may not know, so you will need to keep them in your memory.
- Write the words *buy, keep,* and *much* on the board. Read them to students as you point to each letter.
- Write the words *before, full, such, three,* and *work* on the board. Read the words, and have students echo read them.
- Write the words *most* and *time* on the board. Ask a volunteer to read them aloud, and have the rest of the class follow suit. Place the words on a sight-word bulletin board.
- The book also contains social studies words. Follow the steps above with these words, but this time provide a simple definition for words that may cause confusion: *admission, artifact, caretaker, display, extinct, floor plan, fragile, museum.* For example: A floor plan is a type of diagram that looks like the map of a building. A floor plan shows where things are located inside a building. Show students the picture of the floor plan on p. 4 of the book.

Build Oral Language
- Say: Today we will be reading a book about museums. Before I read, I often think about the topic and try to recall what I already know about it.
- Select a student and discuss a time you visited a museum. Explain what it looked like and what you saw there. Consider adding vocabulary to your discussion, such as *artifact, caretaker, display, floor plan,* or *fragile*. Then have the student tell you about a time he or she visited a museum.
- Say: Today we will also be learning about floor plans. To read a floor plan, imagine that you are looking down at the inside of the building from the ceiling.

Explain some of the features of a floor plan. Say: Lines outline the outside walls of the whole building and the inside walls of rooms. Labels name the displays and places where important items are located, such as the entrance, gift shop, and information desk. Symbols represent items, such as stairs and elevators.

- Have students model using the floor plan by asking them to point out certain items.

DURING THE READING

Preview the Book

- Read the title of the book on the cover, and point to the picture. Turn to page 2 and read the sentences. Have students follow along in their books.
- Say: Do you know what the book will be about based on the title and the first page that I read? How do you know what it will be about?

Read the Book

- Read the book to students as they follow along. Point out words that contain the prefixes taught. Tell students the names of items if they don't know them.
- Have students silently read the book. Ask a few students to whisper read the book to you, and help them sound out new words. When observing students, focus on the new words: *predate, prehistoric, preplan, uncover, unfamiliar, unknown, unsafe.*
- **Social Studies Connections:** Say: Sometimes when you visit a museum, you can take a tour with a group of people. A museum tour guide is someone who tells you all about what you see in the displays as you go through the building.

AFTER THE READING

Check Comprehension

To check students' understanding of the book, ask the following:

✓ Use the floor plan on page 4 to describe how a floor plan is similar to a map. (Answers may include: Both show where things are located. Both use lines, labels, and symbols.)

✓ Which two words on page 8 both begin with the same prefix and have similar meanings? (*unfamiliar* and *unknown*)

✓ Suppose your family or class is going to visit a museum. Why might it be helpful to preplan your visit? (Answers may include: so you don't have to wait in line to buy tickets; so a tour guide can tell you interesting facts about the displays; so you can print out a floor plan and decide where you want to go ahead of time)

Reread to Develop Fluency

- Say: Today you will read the book to each other to practice reading with fluency. This means that you read the book as the author meant for it to be read aloud.
- Model reading fluently by reading the book aloud to students. Focus on pausing slightly when you come to a comma.
- Have partners reread the book to each other. Remind students to pause briefly when they come to a comma. Students may struggle with decoding, comprehension, or vocabulary. For students who are struggling with vocabulary, say: I noticed that you don't recognize some of these words. That makes it hard to read the sentence. Are there clues on the page or in the pictures? Maybe we could look up the words in the dictionary. Now reread the sentence at a steady pace, making sure to take a short pause when you come to a comma.
- Send home a copy of *Let's Go to the Museum!* for students to read to family members. Consider assessing a few students on fluency.

Connect to Written Language

↻ Review: Write the words *jumped, yelling,* and *hopped* on the board. As a class, read the words together as you point to the *–ed* and *–ing* spellings. Have students use each one in a sentence.

✓ Dictate the following words for students to spell: *before, predate, preplan, three, uncover, unfamiliar,* and *unsafe.* When finished, write the words on the board. Have students self-correct their papers.

✓ Create word cards and put them in a bag or box. Have pairs of students draw six cards to create three nonsense compound words. Ask them to create a picture glossary to define each of their made-up compound words. You may wish to bind up the class' glossaries to create a nonsense dictionary of compound words.

Fantastic Flowers

SKILLS

PHONICS SKILL INTRODUCED
- Suffixes *–ful*, *–tion*

SIGHT WORDS
- *almost, bring, could, find, grow, long, more, new, pretty, some, then, work*

VOCABULARY WORDS–
Science Words
- *blossom, calyx, flowers, fruit, nectar, orchard, petals, pistil, plant, pollen, pollination, seeds, sepal, stamen, stem*

CURRICULUM LINK–
Science Focus
- Characteristics of Organisms

Fantastic Flowers

BEFORE THE READING

Develop Phonemic Awareness and Phonics
Oral Segmentation
- Say: Today we are going to segment words so that we can say them sound by sound. Segment means to pull words apart by their sounds.
- Write the words *vacation* and *cheerful* on the board, and model saying the words sound by sound: /v/ /ā/ /k/ /ā/ /sh/ /ə/ /n/, vacation; /ch/ /î/ /r/ /f/ /ə/ /l/, cheerful.
- Write *addition* and *joyful* on the board. Sound out each word, and have students follow suit chorally: /ə/ /d/ /i/ /sh/ /ə/ /n/, addition; /j/ /oi/ /f/ /ə/ /l/, joyful.
- Write *direction, motion,* and *useful* on the board. Have students segment the words out loud but independently. Walk around to support students. If a student is struggling to segment the sounds, model saying each sound as you move a chip onto a line or sound box, and have the student follow suit.

Introduce Phonics Skills
Suffixes *–ful, –tion*
- Say: We just practiced segmenting words with the suffixes *–ful* and *–tion*. A suffix is a word part added to the end of a word. Adding a suffix to a word changes its meaning.
- Write the words *care, careful, invent,* and *invention* on the board. Underline the suffixes *–ful* and *–tion*. Explain that the suffix *–ful* means "full of." The suffix *–tion* changes an action word (or verb) like *invent* to a naming word (or noun) like *invention.* Model reading the words, one sound at a time, while pointing to the letters: /k/ /âr/ /f/ /ə/ /l/, careful; /i/ /n/ /v/ /e/ /n/ /sh/ /ə/ /n/, invention.
- Write the words *helpful* and *subtraction* on the board. Have students read the words as a class. Say: Slowly sound out each letter.
- Have students try reading the words *thankful, wonderful, action,* and *education* independently, following the routine above. Walk around to support students. Students who are struggling may need extra modeling, practice, and feedback, such as: Let's look at the word *thankful.* Remember that when two consonants appear together in a word, they sometimes make one sound. For example, the letters *th* together make the /th/ sound. Let's slowly say the sounds of this word together as I point to each letter. Now you do it.

Introduce Sight Words
- Say: You are going to see some words today that you may not know, so you will need to keep them in your memory.
- Write the words *almost, bring, could,* and *find* on the board. Read the words to students as you point to each letter.
- Write the words *grow, long, more,* and *new* on the board. Read the words, and have students echo read each word.
- Write the words *pretty, some, then,* and *work* on the board. Ask a volunteer to read them aloud, and have the rest of the class follow suit. Place the words on a sight-word bulletin board.
- The book also contains science words. Follow the steps above with these words, but this time provide a simple definition for words that may cause confusion: *blossom, calyx, flowers, fruit, nectar, orchard, petals, pistil, plant, pollen, pollination, seeds, sepal, stamen,* and *stem.* For example: A blossom is a flower on a fruit tree or other plant. Show students pictures of blossoms from the book.

Build Oral Language
- Say: Today we will be reading a book about flowers. Before I read, I often think about the topic and try to recall what I already know about it.
- Select a student and discuss what you know about flowers. Consider adding vocabulary to your discussion, such as *petals, pollen, stem,* and *colorful.* Then have the student tell you what he or she knows about flowers.

- Say: Interview a partner about what he or she knows about flowers. Ask what your partner's favorite flower is and what it looks like. Then switch roles.
- Pick five pairs of students, and encourage each pair to share what they learned during the interviews. Recognize when they use previously taught key vocabulary.

DURING THE READING

Preview the Book
- Read the title of the book on the cover, and point to the picture. Turn to page 2 and read the text. Point to the image and discuss that as well. Have students follow along in their books.
- Say: Do you know what the book will be about based on the title and the first page that I read? How do you know what it will be about?
- As needed, point out the words that have the suffixes –ful and –tion: beautiful, colorful, creation.
- Have students turn to the diagram on page 5. Remind them that a diagram is a drawing or picture that explains something. Point out the features of the diagram: labels and arrows. Model how to read the diagram. Then ask volunteers to model how they get information from the diagram.

Read the Book
- Read the book to students as they follow along. Point out words that have the suffixes –ful and –tion.
- Have students silently read the book. Ask a few students to partner read the book to you, and help them sound out new words. When observing students, focus on the new words: beautiful, colorful, healthful, helpful, creation, pollination.
- **Science Connections:** Say: Although tomatoes and cucumbers are commonly called vegetables, they are considered to be fruits by some scientists. The reason for this is that both the tomato and the cucumber are the part of a flowering plant that contains its seeds.

AFTER THE READING

Check Comprehension
To check students' understanding of the book, ask the following:
✓Use the diagram on page 7 to name the two main parts inside a flower's petals. (stamen and pistil)
✓Explain why hummingbirds are important to plants. (Hummingbirds stick their beaks into flowers to drink nectar. Pollen sticks to the hummingbirds' beaks while they drink. When the birds fly from flower to flower, some of the pollen from one flower rubs off the birds and lands on the pistils of another flower of the same kind. This enables pollination to occur.)
✓Which word on page 12 ends with –ful and describes food that is good for us? (healthful)

Reread to Develop Fluency
- Say: Today you will read the book to each other to practice reading with fluency. This means that you read the book as the author meant for it to be read aloud.
- Model reading fluently by reading the book aloud to students. Focus on reading sentences with exclamation points with excitement.
- Have partners reread the book to each other. Remind children how to read sentences with exclamation points. Students may struggle with decoding, comprehension, or vocabulary. For students who are struggling with comprehension, say: I noticed that you seem unsure how to read this sentence. What are some clues we can use to help us understand what we read? Now that we understand the sentence a little better, let's try reading it again with proper expression.
- Send home a copy of Fantastic Flowers for students to read to family members. Consider assessing a few students on fluency.

Connect to Written Language
↻Review: Write the words preheat, unkind, and unclear on the board. As a class, read the words together as you point to the letters. Then have students write simple definitions for each word.

✓Dictate the following words for students to spell: helpful, action, useful, careful, invention, almost, and work. When finished, write the words on the board. Have students self-correct their papers.

✓Say: Some words are made up of two different words. When these words are put together, they make a new word with a new meaning. You can figure out this new meaning by thinking about the meanings of the two different words. Write honeybee on the board. Do you see two different words? Draw a line under honey and say honey. Draw a line under bee and say bee. Honey is a thick, sugary material. A bee is an insect that eats pollen. So a honeybee is a bee that makes honey. Write sailboat, snowman, and basketball on the board. Read the words as a class, and encourage group discussion about their meanings. Ask students to think of more compound words and write them on a piece of paper.

Immigration

SKILLS

PHONICS SKILL INTRODUCED
- Prefixes *re–, mis–*

SIGHT WORDS
- *after, ask, ate, been, first, know, little, new, start, those, try*

VOCABULARY WORDS–
Social Studies Words
- *customs, Ellis Island, Europe, history, immigrants, steamships*

CURRICULUM LINK–
Social Studies Focus
- Immigration

Immigration

BEFORE THE READING

Develop Phonemic Awareness and Phonics
Phonemic Manipulation: Deletion
- Say: We are going to remove some letters from words to make new words.
- Write the words *replay* and *misbehave* on the board. Model removing the prefix from each word: replay, play; misbehave, behave.
- Write *recount, reorder, rewrite, mismatch, misspell,* and *mistrust* on the board. Have students say each word without its beginning sound.

Introduce Phonics Skills
Prefixes *re–, mis–*
- Say: We just practiced creating new words by removing the prefixes *re–* and *mis–*. A prefix is a word part added to the beginning of a word. Adding a prefix to a word changes its meaning. Now we are going to read some words with prefixes.
- Write the words *play, replay, spell,* and *misspell* on the board. Underline the prefixes *re–* and *mis–*. Explain that the prefix *re–* means "again." The prefix *mis–* means "wrong or incorrectly." Model reading the words, one sound at a time, while pointing to the letters: /pl/ /ā/; /r/ /ē/ /pl/ /ā/; /s/ /p/ /e/ /l/; /m/ /i/ /s/ /p/ /e/ /l/.
- Write the words *retell* and *mislead* on the board. Have students read the words as a class. Say: Slowly sound out each letter.
- Have students try reading the words *reapply, recheck, mislead,* and *misprint* independently, following the routine above. Walk around to support students. Students who are struggling may need extra modeling, practice, and feedback, such as: Let's look at the word *reapply.* When a prefix ends with a vowel and comes before a word that starts with a vowel, the vowels do not blend. Instead, each vowel has its own separate sound. Let's slowly say the sounds of this word together as I point to each letter: /r/ /ē/ /ə/ /pl/ /ī/. Now you do it.

Introduce Sight Words
- Say: You are going to see some words today that you may not know, so you will need to keep them in your memory.
- Write *after, new,* and *try* on the board. Read them as you point to each letter.
- Write *ask, ate, been, first, know,* and *little* on the board. Read the words, and have students echo read them.
- Write *start* and *those* on the board. Ask a volunteer to read them aloud, and have the class follow suit. Place the words on a sight-word bulletin board.
- The book also contains social studies words. Follow the steps above with these words, but this time provide a simple definition for words that may cause confusion: *customs, Ellis Island, Europe, history, immigrants,* and *steamships.* For example: An immigrant is a person who moves from one country to live in another. Show students the pictures of immigrants in the book.

Build Oral Language
- Say: Today we will be reading a book about immigration. Before I read, I often think about the topic and try to recall what I already know about it.
- Select a student and discuss what you know about moving to a new place. Explain what it felt like to be in a new place and possibly a new school with people and surroundings that were unfamiliar to you. Then have the student tell you about an experience he or she had moving to a new home, town, or school. Say: With a partner, discuss a time you or someone you know moved to a new place.
- Pick five pairs of students, and encourage one student from each pair to share in the discussion. Recognize when students use previously taught key vocabulary.

DURING THE READING

Preview the Book

- Read the title of the book on the cover, and point to the picture. Turn to page 2 and read the two sentences, pointing to each word as you read. Also point out the caption and read that word as well. Have students follow along in their books.
- Say: Do you know what the book will be about based on the title and the first page that I read? How do you know what it will be about?
- As needed, point out the word that has the *re–* prefix: *rebuild*.
- Point out the pie chart on page 15, and explain that a pie chart is one way to display and compare information. Explain the parts of a pie chart: the title tells what the pie chart is about and the labels describe each piece of the pie. In this case, each piece of the pie shows the percentage of people who came through Ellis Island from specific countries between 1880 and 1920.

Read the Book

- Read the book to students as they follow along. Point out words that contain the sound-spellings taught. Tell students the names of items if they don't know them: *Ellis Island, ferry, immigrant, steamship.*
- Have students silently read the book. Ask a few students to whisper read the book to you, and help them sound out new words. When observing students, focus on the new words: *misspelled, mistakes, mistreated, rebuild, renamed, return.*
- **Social Studies Connections:** Say: Ellis Island is no longer used for receiving immigrants. Today it is a museum filled with photos, documents, and other historical items. Visitors can walk through rooms that were once used by the immigrants. People from all over the world visit the museum to learn about Ellis Island, the immigrants who passed through there, and this special time in American history.

AFTER THE READING

Check Comprehension

To check students' understanding of the book, ask the following:
- ✓ Which word on page 4 begins with the prefix *mis–* and means "to be treated badly"? (*mistreated*) Why did the immigrants come to the United States? (for food and land, to avoid war, and out of fear of mistreatment)
- ✓ Why do you think most immigrants could bring only a few of their belongings with them when they came to the United States? (Accept reasonable responses.)
- ✓ Review the pie chart on page 15 to answer the question: From which country did the fewest number of immigrants come between 1880 and 1920? (Poland)

Reread to Develop Fluency

- Say: Today you will read the book to each other to practice reading with fluency. This means that you read the book as the author meant for it to be read aloud.
- Model reading fluently by reading the book aloud to students. Focus on raising the inflection of your voice at the end of a question.
- Have partners reread the book to each other. Suggest that they raise their voices at the end of a question. Students may struggle with decoding, comprehension, or vocabulary. For students who are struggling with decoding, say: I noticed that you are working on reading this word. Let's read it together, breaking it down by syllables or even by sounds. We can always sound out the letters of a word we don't know. Once you've said it correctly, try to reread the sentence now that you know the word.
- Send home a copy of *Immigration* for students to read to family members. Consider assessing a few students on fluency.

Connect to Written Language

↻ Review: Write the words *elevation, hopeful,* and *population* on the board. As a class, read the words together as you point to the word parts. Then circle the *–ful* and *–tion* suffixes in each word, and practice identifying how each suffix affects the meaning of the word. Have students write three sentences that include words with suffixes.

✓ Dictate the following words for students to spell: *misspell, mistreat, new, rebuild, rename, return,* and *those.* When finished, write the words on the board. Have students self-correct their papers.

✓ Have students imagine that they are going to live in a new country, and they can only take a small suitcase or backpack. Have them write a paragraph about what they would take with them. Ask them to illustrate their paragraphs.

Celebrating Cultures

SKILLS

PHONICS SKILL INTRODUCED
- Suffixes *–er, –or, –ly*

SIGHT WORDS
- *again, best, here, much, old, part*

VOCABULARY WORDS–
Social Studies Words
- *art, celebrate, culture(s), customs, dancer, heritage, immigrants, literature, musicians, traditions*

CURRICULUM LINK–
Social Studies Focus
- U.S. Cultural Heritage

Celebrating Cultures

BEFORE THE READING

Develop Phonemic Awareness and Phonics
Oral Segmentation
- Say: We will be segmenting words. Segmenting means pulling words apart by their sounds or by their parts. We will listen for suffixes, or endings of words.
- Write the words *painter, inspector,* and *kindly* on the board. Model segmenting the words into parts as you point to each part: painter, paint-er; inspector, in-spec-tor; kindly, kind-ly. Clap your hands as you say each word part.
- Write *teacher, collector,* and *quickly* on the board. Segment the word parts while pointing to each one. Have students echo you as you pull apart the syllables in each word: teacher, teach-er; collector, co-llec-tor; quickly, quick-ly.
- Write *player, sailor,* and *correctly* on the board. Have students try segmenting the word parts out loud but independently. Support students who are struggling with segmenting by snapping your fingers or clapping as you say each syllable. Have the student follow suit as he or she slowly pulls apart the sounds.

Introduce Phonics Skills
Suffixes *–er, –or, –ly*
- Say: We just practiced segmenting the parts in some words. Now we are going to read some words as we point out each word part.
- Write the words *play, player, invent, inventor, loud,* and *loudly* on the board, and underline the suffixes (*–er, –or, –ly*). Say: The endings that were added to these words are called suffixes. Suffixes are word parts that change the meaning of a word. The suffixes *–er* and *–or* mean, "a person who." The suffix *–ly* means "like, or in that way." Model reading the words, one syllable at a time, while pointing to the word parts: play, player, play-er; invent, inventor, in-vent-or; loud, loudly, loud-ly.
- Write the words *painter, actor,* and *slowly* on the board. Have students read the words as a class. Say: Sound out each word part, and notice the different suffixes.
- Have students try reading the words *dance, dancer, pot, potter, sculpt, sculptor, visit, visitor,* and *fond, fondly* independently, following the routine above. Walk around to support students. Students who are struggling may need extra modeling and practice, such as: Let's look at the words *pot* and *potter*. Say each syllable as I point to it. Notice that we doubled the consonant when we added the suffix *–er*.

Introduce Sight Words
- Say: You are going to see some words today that you may not know, so you will need to keep them in your memory.
- Write *again* and *best* the board. Read them to students as you point to each letter.
- Write *here* and *much* on the board. Read the words, and have students echo you.
- Write *old* and *part* on the board. Ask a volunteer to read them aloud, and have the rest of the class follow suit. Place the words on a sight-word bulletin board.
- The book also contains social studies words. Follow the steps above with these words, but this time provide a simple definition for words that may cause confusion: *art, celebrate, culture(s), customs, dancer, heritage, immigrants, literature, musicians, traditions*. For example: The word *literature* refers to stories, poems, plays, and books. Show students the picture of the storyteller on page 14, and discuss stories you have read in class.

Build Oral Language
- Say: Today we will be reading a book about different cultures. When I think about culture, I think of traditions that groups of people share, such as holiday celebrations, art, and dance. I wonder what else *culture* might mean?
- Select a student and discuss some things about his or her culture at home or the culture of the school. Ask the student to give an example of a tradition or custom he or she knows. Explain that we can be part of several cultures, and we are all part of the American culture. Consider adding vocabulary to your discussion, such as

heritage, traditions, spirituals, story, literature, art, dance, immigrants. Then have the student describe a tradition in his or her family.

- Say: Interview a partner about his or her heritage. What are some of the traditions or customs? Then tell your partner something about your heritage.
- Pick five pairs of students, and encourage each pair to introduce their partners and describe the custom. Recognize when students use previously taught key vocabulary.

DURING THE READING

Preview the Book

- Read the title of the book on the cover, and point to the picture. Turn to the Table of Contents and point out the chapter headings and page numbers. Turn to page 2 and read the sentences, pointing to each word as you read. Have students follow along.
- Say: This book is about cultures. The cover shows a girl in a pretty dress. It looks like she is part of a celebration or parade. Can you predict what is happening? What clues helped you make your prediction?
- Point out the captions in the book, and explain how they describe or give information about the pictures.

Read the Book

- Read the book to students as they follow along. Point out words that contain the sound-spellings taught. Explain the terms if students don't know them: *embroidery, dances, hula, Navajo, Laos, jazz, trickster tales.*
- Have students whisper read the book to each other, and help them sound out new words. When observing students, focus on the new words: *actor, carefully, dancers, potter, sculptor, singers, visitors, weavers, writers.*
- **Social Studies Connections:** Say: One way to learn about other cultures is through their celebrations or festivals. Chinese New Year, Cinco de Mayo, and Saint Patrick's Day are a few holidays that lots of people celebrate, even if they don't belong to that culture.

AFTER THE READING

Check Comprehension

To check students' understanding of the book, ask the following:

✓What are some examples of art described on page 4? (Answers may include: Art includes paintings, drawings, sculpture, weaving, and pottery.)

✓Identify the words on page 10 that have suffixes *-er, -or,* or *-ly.* (*lively, slowly, dancer, actor*)

✓Look at the picture on page 15. What is an example of literature on this page? (the book) What is another example of this girl's culture? (Answers may include: She is wearing a special head covering, which is part of her culture.)

Reread to Develop Fluency

- Say: Today you will read the book to each other to practice reading with fluency. This means that you read the book as the author meant for it to be read aloud.
- Model reading fluently by reading the book aloud to students. Focus on reading with expression in a conversational tone.
- Have partners reread the book to each other. Suggest that they pause when they come to a comma and change their voices when they read a period, exclamation point, and question mark. Students may struggle with decoding, comprehension, or vocabulary. For students who are struggling with vocabulary, say: I noticed that you don't recognize some of these words. That makes it hard to read the sentence. Are there clues on the page or in the pictures? Maybe we could look up the words in the dictionary. Now let's reread the sentence at a steady pace.
- Send home a copy of *Celebrating Cultures* for students to read to family members. Consider assessing a few students on fluency.

Connect to Written Language

↻Review: Write the words *mistakes, rebuild,* and *return* on the board. As a class, read the words together as you point to the word parts. Then circle the *mis-* and *re–* prefixes in each word, and practice identifying how each prefix adds to the meaning. Have students write three sentences using each of these words.

✓Dictate the following words for students to spell: *actor, lively, singer, visitor, writer, old,* and *again.* When finished, write the words on the board. Have students self-correct their papers.

✓Say: You may see two words put together as a compound word. For example, the word *back* means "behind," and *ground* means "on the floor." When we put them together, *background* means "the scene behind a main object." Write on the board: *The folktale is from my homeland.* Which words are the compound words? Look at the words that were put together. What do you think these words mean? Have students choose three compound words they are familiar with and use each in a sentence.

Science Tools

SKILLS

PHONICS SKILL INTRODUCED
- Irregular Plurals; Plurals with Spelling Changes

SIGHT WORDS
- *around, hard, never, want*

VOCABULARY WORDS–
Science Words
- *bacteria, examine, germs, lab(s), lens, magnifying glass, microscope, microscopic, scientists, study, telescope, tools*

CURRICULUM LINK–
Science Focus
- Technology and Science

Science Tools

BEFORE THE READING

Develop Phonemic Awareness and Phonics
Oral Segmentation
- Say: Today we are segmenting words. This means pulling words apart by sounds or parts. We will listen for sounds that make a word plural, or more than one.
- Write *families* and *children* on the board. Model segmenting the words into parts as you point to each part: fam-i-lies, families; chil-dren, children.
- Write *rubies, women,* and *shelves* on the board. Segment the word parts while pointing to each part, and have students echo you.
- Write *pennies, footsteps,* and *backpacks* on the board. Have students try segmenting the word parts out loud but independently. Support students who are struggling with segmenting by modeling holding up a finger for each syllable.

Introduce Phonics Skills
Irregular Plurals; Plurals with Spelling Changes
- Say: We just practiced segmenting the parts of some words. Now we are going to make some words into plurals.
- Write the words *butterfly, butterflies, leaf, leaves, man,* and *men* on the board, and underline the plurals (–*ies,* –*ves, men*). Say: Most of the time, we make a noun plural by adding an –*s* or –*es* to the end of the word. For example, *bush* becomes *bushes.* But some nouns are irregular, which means they don't follow the rules. For example, one tooth becomes several teeth, and one life becomes many lives. Explain that when a word ends in –*ly,* we change the *y* to *i* before adding –*es.* For example, *butterfly, butterflies; penny, pennies.* When a word ends in *f,* we change the *f* to *v* before adding –*es.* For example, *leaf, leaves.*
- Model reading the following words, one syllable at a time, while pointing to the plural endings: body, bodies; scarf, scarves.
- Write the words *baby, babies, loaf, loaves, person,* and *people* on the board. Have students read the words as a class. Say: Slowly sound out each word part, and notice the different spellings of the plurals.
- Have students try reading the words *fry, fries, bunny, bunnies, hoof, hooves, woman,* and *women* independently, following the routine above. Walk around to support students. Students who are struggling may need extra modeling and practice, such as: Let's look at the words *hoof* and *hooves.* Say each sound as I point to it.

Introduce Sight Words
- Say: You are going to see some words today that you may not know, so you will need to keep them in your memory.
- Write *around* on the board. Read it to students as you point to each letter.
- Write *hard* on the board. Read the word, and have students echo read it.
- Write *never* and *want* on the board. Ask a volunteer to read the words aloud, and have the class follow suit. Place the words on a sight-word bulletin board.
- The book also contains science words. Follow the steps above with these words, but this time provide a simple definition for words that may cause confusion: *bacteria, examine, germs, lab(s), lens, magnifying glass, microscope, microscopic, scientists, study, telescope, tools.* For example: The word *microscope* contains the word part *scope,* which means "to look at or examine." *Micro* means "very tiny." Show students the picture of the microscope on page 10.

Build Oral Language
- Say: Today we will be reading a book about different tools that scientists use. Scientists perform experiments and look closely at things.
- Select a student and discuss some tools he or she uses at home. Ask the student how the tools help him or her. Explain that scientists need tools to help them examine things, to hold things, and to study things. Consider adding vocabulary to your discussion, such as *study, germs, lenses, examine, magnify,* and *powerful.*

- Say: With a partner, discuss some of the ways tools help scientists. Write your ideas on sticky notes and post them on the board.
- Pick five pairs of students, and encourage each pair to share their ideas. Recognize when students use previously taught key vocabulary.

DURING THE READING

Preview the Book
- Read the title of the book on the cover, and point to the picture. Turn to the Table of Contents, and point out the chapter headings and page numbers. Turn to page 2, and read the sentences, pointing to each word as you read. Have students follow along.
- Say: This book is about tools used by scientists. The woman on the cover is wearing a special coat, goggles, and gloves. These tools keep her safe. She uses other tools too. What tools do you think we might learn about in this book?
- As needed, point out the irregular plural words: *teeth, factories.*
- Point out the diagram on page 10, and show how the captions name all the parts of the microscope. Remind students that a diagram can explain how something works.

Read the Book
- Read the book to students as they follow along. Point out words that contain the sound-spellings taught. Explain the terms if students need help with the words: *scissors, lab, scientist, magnify, rays of light, viruses, sample, telescope, lenses.*
- Have students silently read the book. Ask a few students to choral read the book with you, and help them sound out new words. When observing students, focus on the new words: *bodies, butterflies, factories, flies, leaves, lives, people, teeth.*
- **Science Connections:** Say: An observatory is a place where powerful telescopes help scientists look at stars, planets, and other objects far out in the universe. There are observatories all over the world, so telescopes see many things throughout the universe.

AFTER THE READING

Check Comprehension
To check students' understanding of the book, ask the following:
✓ What are the names of some of the tools described on page 4? (Answers may include: magnifying glass, microscope, and telescope.) How do these tools help scientists? (Answers may include: They all help to see things up close.)
✓ Read the description of a microscope on page 9. The caption identifies something you could see through a microscope. Would you use a microscope or a magnifying glass to look at germs? Why? (Answers may include: You would need a microscope because germs are too small to see with a magnifying glass.)
✓ Look at the diagram on page 10. Why are there arrows in the diagram? (Answers may include: The arrows point to specific parts named in the diagram.)

Reread to Develop Fluency
- Say: Today you will read the book to each other to practice reading with fluency. This means that you read the book as the author meant for it to be read aloud.
- Model reading fluently by reading the book aloud to students. Focus on reading long sentences by pausing between the subject and the predicate.
- Have partners reread the book to each other. Suggest that they insert pauses when they read long sentences. Students may struggle with decoding, comprehension, or vocabulary. For students who are struggling with comprehension, say: I noticed that you seem unsure how to read these long sentences. Let's chunk them. Now let's reread the sentence at a steady pace.
- Send home a copy of *Science Tools* for students to read to family members. Consider assessing a few students on fluency.

Connect to Written Language
↻ Review: Write the words *singer, sculptor,* and *lovely* on the board. As a class, read the words together as you point to the word parts. Then circle the *–er, –or,* and *–ly* suffixes in each word, and practice identifying how each suffix affects the meaning of the word. Have students use each of these words in a sentence.

✓ Dictate the following words for students to spell: *bodies, factories, leaves, people, teeth, around,* and *hard.* When finished, write the words on the board. Have students self-correct their papers.

✓ Say: You may see two words that sound the same but are spelled differently and mean different things. These are called homophones. For example, the words *to, too,* and *two* all sound the same, but *to* means "in that direction," *too* means "also," and *two* means "the number 2." Create a homophone tree diagram, and challenge students to write homophones on paper leaves. Paste each leaf to the diagram.

Exploring Fossils

SKILLS

PHONICS SKILL INTRODUCED
- Compound Words

SIGHT WORDS
- *away, been, could, do, found, green, long, may, put, show, together, water*

VOCABULARY WORDS–
Science Words
- *amber, animal(s), bones, carbon, cast, decay, dinosaur, fossil(s), mammoth(s), minerals, paleontologists, plant(s), sediment, skeleton*

CURRICULUM LINK–
Science Focus
- Life Science

Exploring Fossils

BEFORE THE READING

Develop Phonemic Awareness and Phonics
Oral Segmentation
- Say: Today we are going to segment words so that we can say them sound by sound. Segment means to pull words apart by their sounds.
- Write the words *thunderstorm* and *starfish* on the board, and model saying the words sound by sound: /th/ /u/ /n/ /d/ /ə/ /r/ /st/ /or/ /m/, thunderstorm; /st/ /ar/ /f/ /i/ /sh/, starfish.
- Write *skateboard* and *sunglasses* on the board. Sound out each word, and have students follow suit chorally: /sk/ /ā/ /t/ /b/ /or/ /d/, skateboard; /s/ /u/ /n/ /gl/ /a/ /s/ /i/ /z/, sunglasses.
- Write *birthday, butterfly,* and *watermelon* on the board. Have students segment the words out loud but independently. Walk around to support students. If a student is struggling to segment the discrete sounds, model saying each sound as you move a chip onto a line or sound box, and have the student follow suit.

Introduce Phonics Skills
Compound Words
- Say: We just practiced segmenting compound words. Compound words are made up of two smaller words put together. Now we are going to read some compound words.
- Write the words *popcorn* and *footprint* on the board. Have students identify the two smaller words in each compound word. Draw a line between the two smaller words. Tell students that sometimes the meanings of the smaller words can help them figure out the meanings of the compound word. Model reading the words, one sound at a time, while pointing to the letters: /p/ /o/ /p/ /k/ /or/ /n/, popcorn; /f/ /ōo/ /t/ /pr/ /i/ /n/ /t/, footprint.
- Write the words *underground* and *outside* on the board. Have students read the words as a class. Say: Slowly sound out each letter.
- Have students try reading the words *football, wallpaper,* and *bookmark* independently, following the routine above. Walk around to support students. Students who are struggling may need extra modeling, practice, and feedback, such as: Let's look at the word *wallpaper*. When two *l*'s appear together, they represent one sound. What sound is that? That's right, the /l/ sound. Let's say the sounds of this word together as I point to each letter. Now you do it.

Introduce Sight Words
- Say: You are going to see some words today that you may not know, so you will need to keep them in your memory.
- Write the words *away, been, could,* and *do* on the board. Read the words to students as you point to each letter.
- Write the words *found, green, long,* and *may* on the board. Read the words, and have students echo read each word.
- Write the words *put, show, together,* and *water* on the board. Ask a volunteer to read them aloud, and have the rest of the class follow suit. Place the words on a sight-word bulletin board.
- The book also contains science words. Follow the steps above with these words, but this time provide a simple definition for words that may cause confusion: *amber, animal(s), bones, carbon, cast, decay, dinosaur, fossil(s), mammoth(s), minerals, paleontologists, plant(s), sediment, skeleton.* For example: A mammoth is a now-extinct animal that looked like a large elephant with shaggy hair. Show students the picture of a mammoth from the book.

Build Oral Language
- Say: Today we will be reading a book about fossils. Before I read, I often think about the topic and try to recall what I already know about it.

- Select a student and discuss what you know about fossils. Add vocabulary to your discussion, such as *bones, dinosaur,* and *skeleton.* Then have the student tell you what he or she knows about fossils.
- Say: Interview a partner about what he or she knows about fossils, then switch roles.
- Pick five pairs of students, and encourage them to share what they learned during the interviews. Recognize when students use previously taught key vocabulary.

DURING THE READING

Preview the Book
- Read the title of the book on the cover, and point to the picture. Turn to page 2, and read the text. Point to the image and discuss that as well. Have students follow along in their books.
- Say: Do you know what the book will be about based on the title and the first page that I read? How do you know what it will be about?
- Have students turn to page 16 and read the heading "Index." Remind students that an index helps readers find information in the book.
- Model how to use the index. Then ask volunteers to model using the index to get information from the book.

Read the Book
- Read the book to students as they follow along. Point out compound words.
- Have students silently read the book. Ask a few students to whisper read the book to you, and help them sound out new words. When observing students, focus on the new words: *footprint, forever, outlines, outside, something, sometimes, underground.*
- **Science Connections:** Say: Fossils can be found almost everywhere. The oldest fossils of animals with backbones (vertebrates) are about 500 million years old. These are fish fossils.

AFTER THE READING

Check Comprehension
To check students' understanding of the book, ask the following:
✓ Look at the picture on page 2. How does the picture help you understand what you read? How does the text help you understand the picture? (The picture helps me understand what Earth may have looked like millions of years ago. The text helps me understand that the plants and animals from millions of years ago looked different from the ones we have today.)
✓ Which word on page 12 is a compound word and means "below the surface of Earth"? (*underground*)
✓ What kind of information can paleontologists get from fossils? (Fossils can help paleontologists learn how plants, animals, and Earth have changed over time. Paleontologists can also tell how old rocks are by looking at the fossils inside them. Rocks with fossils of shells or sea animals can tell paleontologists that the land where the fossils were found may have once been an ocean.)

Reread to Develop Fluency
- Say: Today you will read the book to each other to practice reading with fluency. This means that you read the book as the author meant for it to be read aloud.
- Model reading fluently by reading the book aloud to students. Focus on adjusting your reading rate as you read a passage or page.
- Have partners reread the book to each other. Remind students to read slowly when reading text with new words. Students may struggle with decoding, comprehension, or vocabulary. For students who are struggling with vocabulary, say: I noticed that you're not quite sure what that word means, which makes it hard to read the sentence. Let's look up the definition of the word.
- Send home a copy of *Exploring Fossils* for students to read to family members. Consider assessing a few students on fluency.

Connect to Written Language
↻ **Review:** Write the words *woman, shelf,* and *penny* on the board. As a class, read the words together as you point to the letters. Then have students write the plural form for each word.

✓ Dictate the following words for students to spell: *inside, footprint, outlines, birthday, starfish, found* and *show.* When finished, write the words on the board. Have students self-correct their papers.

✓ Say: Some words are pronounced the same way but have different meanings and spellings. Write on the board: *You can search for fossils too.* Read the sentence as a class and say: The word *too* in this sentence means "also." Write on the board: *The study of rocks and fossils is also helpful to oil companies.* Read the sentence as a class and say: The word *to* in this sentence is used to show the receiver of an action. Encourage students to write additional sentences using the homophones *too* and *to.* You may wish to use the following sentence frames: *Fossils can be found in amber. They can be found in rocks ____. The paleontologist gave the fossils ____ the museum.*

Farming Then and Now

SKILLS

PHONICS SKILL INTRODUCED
- Consonant + *–le* syllables

SIGHT WORDS
- *before, cuts, keep, out, ran*

VOCABULARY WORDS–
Social Studies Words
- *cow, farmers, fuel, gas, horse, machine, plow, soil, steam, technology, tools, tractor*

CURRICULUM LINK–
Social Studies Focus
- Technology Over Time

Farming Then and Now

BEFORE THE READING

Develop Phonemic Awareness and Phonics
Oral Segmentation
- Say: Today we are segmenting words. Segmenting means pulling words apart by their sounds or by their parts. Today we are listening for the *–le* ending.
- Write *bubble* and *fiddle* on the board. Model segmenting the words into parts as you point to each part: bub|ble, bubble; fid|dle, fiddle.
- Write *jungle, table,* and *title* on the board. Segment the word parts while pointing to each part, and have students echo you as you pull apart the syllables in each word: jun|gle, jungle; ta|ble, table; ti|tle, title.
- Write *wiggle, little,* and *jingle* on the board. Have students try segmenting the word parts out loud but independently. Support students who are struggling with segmenting by modeling moving magnets or chips as you say each syllable. Have the student follow suit as he or she slowly pulls apart the sounds.

Introduce Phonics Skills
Consonant + *–le* syllables
- Say: We just practiced segmenting the parts in some words. Now we are going to read some words as we point out each word part.
- Write the words *people, single,* and *handle* on the board, and underline the consonant + *–le.* Say: Some words end with a consonant + *–le.* The consonant and *–le* ending usually form one syllable. Model reading the words while pointing to the word parts: peo|ple, people; sin|gle, single; han|dle, handle.
- Write the words *able, cattle,* and *settle* on the board. Have students read the words as a class. Say: Slowly sound out the word parts, and notice the consonant + *–le.*
- Have students try reading the words *stable, candle,* and *wrinkle* independently, following the routine above. Walk around to support students. Students who are struggling may need extra modeling and practice, such as: Let's look at the word *stable.* Say each syllable as I point to it.

Introduce Sight Words
- Say: You are going to see some words today that you may not know, so you will need to keep them in your memory.
- Write *before* on the board. Read it to students as you point to each syllable.
- Write *cuts* and *keep* on the board. Read each word, and have students echo you.
- Write *out* and *ran* on the board. Ask a volunteer to read them aloud, and have the rest of the class follow suit. Place the words on a sight-word bulletin board.
- The book also contains social studies words. Follow the steps above with these words, but this time provide a simple definition for words that may cause confusion: *farmers, fuel, gas, horse, machine, plow, soil, steam, technology, tools, tractor.* For example: The word *plow* is a tool that helps farmers break up clumps of hard dirt so that seeds can be planted easily. Show students the picture on page 3.

Build Oral Language
- Say: Today we will be reading a book about some of the ways farming has changed over time. My grandparents did not have many of the tools that I use today. I can do many things faster and easier. It's the same with farming.
- Select a student, and discuss some tools that may have changed over time. Ask the student to give an example of a tool they use that didn't exist for their parents or grandparents. Consider adding vocabulary to your discussion, such as *by hand, cattle, technology, machines, gas,* and *fuel.* Then have the student describe a way that technology helps them at home or in school.
- Say: Discuss with a partner what your life would be like without technology. How would you communicate? What would you do for entertainment?
- Pick five pairs of students, and encourage each pair to share their ideas. Recognize when students use previously taught key vocabulary.

DURING THE READING

Preview the Book

- Read the title of the book on the cover, and point to the pictures. Turn to the Table of Contents and point out the chapter headings and page numbers. Turn to page 2 and read the sentences, pointing to each word as you read. Have students follow along in their books.
- Say: Do you know what the book will be about based on the title and the first page that I read? How do you know what it will be about?
- As needed, point out the consonant + –le words: *table, cattle, tackle*. Show students the timelines on pages 5, 9, and 10, and describe the purpose of each feature, including the dates, the arrow showing the direction, the captions, and the pictures.

Read the Book

- Read the book to students as they follow along. Point out words that contain the sound-spellings taught. Explain the terms if students don't know them: *dairy, chore, technology, oxen, plow, reins, power, boiler, gas, tractor, 1800s, 1900s*.
- Have students silently read the book. Ask a few students to whisper read the book to each other, and help them sound out new words. When observing students, focus on the new words: *able, bridle, cattle, handle, people, settles, single, stable, tackle*.
- **Social Studies Connections:** Say: A long time ago, people made plows out of strong wood. But the wood would wear down over time because the dirt and the work were so hard. Now we make plows out of more durable iron, which is strong and sturdy, even when used all the time or in very hard soil. The sharp blades of these modern plows cut very even rows, called furrows, in the dirt.

AFTER THE READING

Check Comprehension

To check students' understanding of the book, ask the following:

- ✓ What does a plow do? (Answers may include: Plows cut up the hard dirt.) Why do farmers use plows? (Answers may include: Farmers need to loosen the soil so they can plant seeds.)
- ✓ The compound word *timeline* describes a picture that shows the order events happened. What are the two words you see in *timeline*? (*time* and *line*) Use the timeline on page 5 to determine the year when horses stopped pulling plows. (around 1860)
- ✓ The timeline on page 14 shows five different changes in the way cows were milked. Which change was the most recent? (Fast machines can milk many cows at once.) How did people milk cows before electricity? (Answers may include: by hand, by hand-pump, or by steam-pump)

Reread to Develop Fluency

- Say: Today you will read the book to each other to practice reading with fluency. This means that you read the book as the author meant for it to be read aloud.
- Model reading fluently by reading the book aloud to students. Explain how you don't need to read the timeline aloud, but you should look at it and see how it helps you understand what you read.
- Have partners reread the book to each other. Suggest that they pause and discuss something they notice in a picture or a timeline. Students may struggle with decoding, comprehension, or vocabulary. For students who are struggling with vocabulary, say: I noticed that you don't recognize some of these words. That makes it hard to read the sentence. Are there clues on the page or in the pictures? Maybe we could look up the words in the dictionary. Now let's reread the sentence at a steady pace.
- Send home a copy of *Farming Then and Now* for students to read to family members. Consider assessing a few students on fluency.

Connect to Written Language

↻ **Review:** Write the words *forever, outside*, and *underground* on the board. As a class, read the words together as you point to the word parts. Then draw a line between the two words in the compound, and practice identifying what each word means by itself and what it means as part of a compound. Have students write a sentence using compound words.

✓ Dictate the following words for students to spell: *able, bridle, single, stable, tackle, before*, and *out*. When finished, write the words on the board. Have students self-correct their papers.

✓ Say: Words that describe nouns are called adjectives. For example, in the phrase "big truck," the word *big* tells us the way the truck looks. Words that describe verbs tell how or where the action takes place. They are called adverbs. For example, in the sentence, "She ran fast," the word *fast* describes how she was running. Have students expand simple sentences by adding adjectives and adverbs.

Get Moving!

SKILLS

PHONICS SKILL INTRODUCED
- Final *e* syllables

SIGHT WORDS
- *any, both, does, write*

VOCABULARY WORDS–
Science Words
- *accelerate, balance, force, inertia, motion, speed, velocity*

CURRICULUM LINK–
Science Focus
- Motion

Get Moving!

BEFORE THE READING

Develop Phonemic Awareness and Phonics
Oral Segmentation
- Say: Today we are segmenting words. Segmenting means pulling words apart by their sounds or parts. Today we are noticing words that have a final *e* ending.
- Write the words *alike, compare,* and *concentrate* on the board. Model segmenting the words into syllables as you point to each syllable: a|like, alike; com|pare, compare; con|cen|trate, concentrate.
- Write *erase, inside,* and *volume* on the board. Have students echo you as you segment the syllables in each word: e|rase, erase; in|side, inside; vol|ume, volume.
- Write *complete, polite,* and *remote* on the board. Have students try segmenting the syllables out loud but independently. Support students who are struggling with segmenting by tossing a beanbag as you say each syllable. Have the student follow suit as he or she slowly pulls apart the syllables.

Introduce Phonics Skills
Final *e* syllables
- Say: We just practiced segmenting the syllables in some words. Now we are going to read some words as we point out each syllable.
- Write the words *alike* and *escape* on the board, and underline the syllable with the final *e*. Say: When the last syllable in a word ends with a vowel + consonant + final *e* spelling, the final *e* usually gives the vowel a long vowel sound, as in the words *alike* and *escape.* Model reading the words, one syllable at a time, while pointing to the word parts: a|like, alike; es|cape, escape.
- Write the words *outside, suppose,* and *female* on the board. Have students read the words as a class. Say: Sound out the syllables, noticing the syllable with the final *e.*
- Have students try reading the words *athlete, picture,* and *rotate* independently, following the routine above. Walk around to support students. Students who are struggling may need extra modeling and practice, such as: Let's look at the word *athlete.* Say each syllable as I point to it.

Introduce Sight Words
- Say: You are going to see some words today that you may not know, so you will need to keep them in your memory.
- Write *any* on the board. Read it to students as you point to each syllable.
- Write *both* on the board. Read the word, and have students echo you.
- Write *does* and *write* on the board. Ask a volunteer to read them aloud, and have the rest of the class follow suit. Place the words on a sight-word bulletin board.
- The book also contains science words. Follow the steps above with these words, but this time provide a simple definition for words that may cause confusion: *accelerate, balance, force, inertia, motion, speed, velocity.* For example: Inertia is the tendency of an object to stay still or keep moving unless affected by another object. Show students the picture of the golf ball on page 8, and point out how it is unable to move until something moves it.

Build Oral Language
- Say: Today we will be reading a book about motion. Can you make predictions about how something will move?
- Select a student, and discuss the ways they can move. Ask the student to give an example of a game they play. Explain that we can change the way we move to go faster or to hit a ball harder. Consider adding vocabulary to your discussion, such as *speed, increase, accelerate, ramp, rate, rotate, force, gravity, equal, balance.* Have the student describe something that moves fast and something that moves slowly.
- Say: Discuss with a partner how wheels help us move.
- Pick five pairs of students, and encourage each pair to share their ideas. Recognize when students use previously taught key vocabulary.

DURING THE READING

Preview the Book

- Read the title of the book on the cover, and point to the picture. Turn to the Table of Contents, and point out the chapter headings and page numbers. Turn to page 2 and read the sentences, pointing to each word as you read. Have students follow along in their books.

- Say: **This book is about motion. The cover shows two girls in motion. They are running. We can move in lots of ways. Think of some of the ways you can move. Let's see if the book mentions some of those ways.**

- As needed, point out the final *e* words: *compete, prepare,* and *increase*. Show students the diagram on page 6, and describe how the arrows are used to tell us how her arm is moving in the picture.

Read the Book

- Read the book to students as they follow along. Point out words that contain the sound-spellings taught. Explain the terms if students need help with them: *accelerate, ramp, zoom, discus, teeball, tee, gravity, hoop, swish, opposite.*

- Have students silently read the book. Ask a few students to whisper read the book to you, and help them sound out new words. When observing students, focus on the new words: *accelerate, athlete, compete, outside, prepare, rotates, skateboard, sometimes, suppose, teeball.*

- **Science Connections:** Say: **More than 300 years ago a scientist named Isaac Newton studied the laws of motion, meaning things that will always be true about motion. He wrote about three laws of motion: inertia, acceleration, and balance. There is a legend that he got his ideas when an apple fell from a tree he was sitting under. Newton's curiosity about why it fell led him to study and discover these laws.**

AFTER THE READING

Check Comprehension

To check students' understanding of the book, ask the following:

- ✓ Read the text on page 4. Can you think of two ways to explain speed? (Answers may include: Speed is your rate of movement; it tells your velocity or your acceleration.)

- ✓ Look at the picture on page 9. What does the word *thwack* mean? (Answers may include: It is the sound made when the club hits the ball.)

- Look at the diagram on page 14. Which word in the label describes the arrows? (*opposite*) How does the picture help you understand the term *equal force*? (Answers may include: The picture shows two players who are the same size pushing against each other.)

Reread to Develop Fluency

- Say: **Today you will read the book to each other to practice reading with fluency. This means that you read the book as the author meant for it to be read aloud.**

- Model reading fluently by reading the book aloud to students. Explain that it's OK if you say a word incorrectly, but you should listen to yourself and correct a word right away when you mispronounce it.

- Have partners reread the book to each other one sentence at a time. Suggest that they listen and support their partner on pronunciation. Have them self-correct the word and continue reading. Students may struggle with decoding, comprehension, or vocabulary. For students who are struggling with decoding, say: **I noticed that you are working on reading this word. Let's read it together, breaking it down by syllables or even by sounds. We can always sound out the letters of a word we don't know. Once you've said it correctly, try to reread the sentence now that you know the word.**

- Send home a copy of *Get Moving!* for students to read to family members. Consider assessing a few students on fluency.

Connect to Written Language

- ↻ **Review:** Write the words *able, handle,* and *single* on the board. As a class, read the words together as you point to the consonant + *–le*. Then draw a line between the syllables and practice identifying each consonant + *–le* syllable. Have students write a sentence for each of these words, and underline the final syllables.

- ✓ Dictate the following words for students to spell: *compete, picture, prepare, rotates, suppose, any,* and *write*. When finished, write the words on the board. Have students self-correct their papers.

- ✓ Say: **You may notice two words put together to form a compound word. For example, the words *basket* and *ball* create the compound word *basketball*.** Write on the board: *Please ride your skateboard outside.* Which words are the compound words? The words *skateboard* and *outside* each combine two words. Can you explain *skate*, then explain *board,* and then explain *skateboard*? Have students use word cards to create compound words. Have them write a paragraph using at least three compound words.

SKILLS

PHONICS SKILL INTRODUCED
- *r*-controlled vowels (*ar, er, or, ur*)

SIGHT WORDS
- *as, called, day, down, oil, our*

VOCABULARY WORDS–
Science Words
- *chemical energy, electricity, kinetic energy, mechanical energy, potential energy, solar energy*

CURRICULUM LINK–
Science Focus
- Energy

Energy Everywhere!

BEFORE THE READING

Develop Phonemic Awareness and Phonics
Oral Blending
- Say: Today we are blending. Blending means putting word parts together to make words. We will listen for syllables with *r*-controlled vowels.
- Write the words *apart* and *purple* on the board. Model blending the word parts together as you point to each part: a|part; pur|ple.
- Write *market, perfect,* and *surprise* on the board. Blend the word parts while pointing to each one. Have students echo you as you blend the *r*-controlled syllables in each word: mar|ket; per|fect; sur|prise.
- Write *garden, story,* and *burger* on the board. Have students try blending the word parts out loud but independently. Support students who are struggling with blending by modeling snapping your fingers or clapping as you say each syllable.

Introduce Phonics Skills
r-controlled vowels (*ar, er, or, ur*)
- Say: We just practiced blending the parts in some words. Now we are going to read some words as we point out each word part.
- Write the words *army, mermaid, fortune,* and *hurdle* on the board, and underline the *r*-controlled syllable (*ar, er, or, ur*). Say: Look at the vowels in these words that appear next to an *r*. When the letter *r* follows a vowel, it is called *r*-controlled, and the vowel + *r* appears in the same syllable. Model reading the words, one syllable at a time, while pointing to the *r*-controlled syllables.
- Write the words *large, person, forward,* and *curtain* on the board. Have students read the words as a class. Say: Slowly sound out each word part, and notice the different *r*-controlled vowel syllables.
- Have students try reading the words *carpenter, service, inspector,* and *sturdy* independently, following the routine above. Walk around to support students. Students who are struggling may need extra modeling and practice, such as: Let's look at the word *carpenter.* Say each syllable as I point to it.

Introduce Sight Words
- Say: You are going to see some words today that you may not know, so you will need to keep them in your memory.
- Write *as* and *called* the board. Read them to students as you point to each letter.
- Write *day* and *down* on the board. Read each word, and have students echo you.
- Write *oil* and *our* on the board. Ask a volunteer to read them aloud, and have the rest of the class follow suit. Place the words on a sight-word bulletin board.
- The book also contains science words. Follow the steps above with these words, but this time provide a simple definition for words that may cause confusion: *chemical energy, electricity, kinetic energy, mechanical energy, potential energy, solar energy.* For example: The word *electricity* refers to a special type of energy that powers many of our machines. Show students the picture of the remote-controlled car on page 12, and discuss how the car uses electric energy to move.

Build Oral Language
- Say: Today we will be reading a book about energy. When I think about energy, I think of fuel and motion. I know that food gives us fuel, which makes energy for us to move. I bet this book describes other types of energy.
- Select a student and discuss some things that need energy to move. Ask the student to give an example of a type of energy that he or she uses every day. Explain that energy powers machines, our bodies, and also plants and the Earth. Consider adding vocabulary to your discussion, such as *pull, power, fuel, burn, resources, conserve, wasting, recycling, muscle.* Have the student describe what energy feels like.

- Say: With a partner, invent a pantomime about energy. Without words, find a way to use your bodies to represent energy.
- Pick five pairs of students, and encourage each pair to model their pantomimes, while the other students try to explain their movements. Recognize when students use previously taught key vocabulary.

DURING THE READING

Preview the Book
- Read the title of the book on the cover, and point to the picture. Turn to the Table of Contents, and point out the chapter headings and page numbers. Turn to page 2 and read the sentences, pointing to each word as you read. Have students follow along.
- Say: This book is about energy. The cover shows a roller coaster. How much energy will it take to get the cars through the loop? I'm wondering how energy works, where it comes from, and what it can do.
- Point out the graph on page 9, and explain how a graph is one way to display and compare information. Explain the parts of a graph: the title tells what the graph is about, the labels describe each axis of the graph, and the bars represent the amounts.

Read the Book
- Read the book to students as they follow along. Point out words that contain the sound-spellings taught. Explain the terms if students don't know them: *battery, electricity, fuels, kinetic, motion, resources, recycling, solar energy*.
- Have students whisper read the book to each other, and help them sound out new words. When observing students, focus on the new words: *started, energy, park, turn, favorite, roller, coaster, bars, hurtles, powers*.
- **Science Connections:** Say: There are more forms of energy to learn about. Some animals use sound energy to find their way, which is how bats can fly in the dark. Using sound energy is called sonar. Submarines use sonar to find their way underwater, just like dolphins and whales.

AFTER THE READING

Check Comprehension
To check students' understanding of the book, ask the following:
- ✓What is the fuel described on page 4 that gives our bodies energy? (Answers may include: Food in the form of plants and meat gives us the fuel to use as energy.)
- ✓Page 7 describes why it is important to conserve energy. What does it mean to conserve energy? (Answers may include: To conserve energy means to save, or not waste, energy.)
- ✓Look at the graph on page 9. In which month did the school recycle the most? (August) How many pounds of trash were collected in October? (6 pounds per person) Why do you think recycling is a good idea? (Answers may include: Recycling conserves our resources and reduces the amount of trash.)

Reread to Develop Fluency
- Say: Today you will read the book to each other to practice reading with fluency. This means that you read the book as the author meant for it to be read aloud.
- Model reading fluently by reading the book aloud to students. Focus on reading with expression and adjusting your pacing according to the punctuation in the sentence.
- Have partners reread the book to each other. Suggest that they pause when they come to a comma and slow their pace if the sentence seems too long. Students may struggle with decoding, comprehension, or vocabulary. For students who are struggling with vocabulary, say: I noticed that you don't recognize some of these words. That makes it hard to read the sentence. Are there clues on the page or in the pictures?
- Send home a copy of *Energy Everywhere!* for students to read to family members. Consider assessing a few students on fluency.

Connect to Written Language
- ↻Review: Write the words *athlete, picture,* and *suppose* on the board. As a class, read the words together as you point to the word parts. Have students write a poem about an athlete who prepares before he competes.

- ✓Dictate the following words for students to spell: *barter, conserve, energy, solar, perhaps, oil,* and *called*. When finished, write the words on the board. Have students self-correct their papers.

- ✓Say: Some words are related, but have different shades of meaning. This means that one word may be a better fit than another. For example, the word *walk* is related to *skip* and also *trot,* but each has a different meaning about the speed and style of the movement. Authors choose the best words to express an exact meaning. Write on the board: *The small girl glided down carefully, but the older boy barreled down the slide.* Which words are related? The words *glided* and *barreled* both describe how the children went down the slide, but the first word is a slow, careful ride, while the second word suggests a rough, fast ride. Have students write sentences with these words or others that have shades of meaning.

Women of the Civil War

SKILLS

PHONICS SKILL INTRODUCED
- Vowel Team Syllables

SIGHT WORDS
- *always, black, could, hurt, right, sing, words, write*

VOCABULARY WORDS–
Social Studies Words
- *enslaved, Red Cross, republic, rights, slavery, system, Underground Railroad*

CURRICULUM LINK–
Social Studies Focus
- American History

Women of the Civil War

BEFORE THE READING

Develop Phonemic Awareness and Phonics
Oral Segmentation
- Say: Today we are segmenting words into smaller parts. Segmenting means pulling words apart by their sounds or by their parts. Today we are reviewing words that have vowel teams.
- Write the words *explain, joyful,* and *peanut* on the board. Model segmenting the words into syllables as you point to each syllable: ex|plain, explain; joy|ful, joyful; pea|nut, peanut.
- Write *fifteen, maybe,* and *oatmeal* on the board. Segment and point to each syllable, and have students echo you as you pull apart the syllables in each word: fif|teen, fifteen; may|be, maybe; oat|meal, oatmeal.
- Write *disappoint, outside,* and *reheat* on the board. Have students try segmenting the syllables out loud but independently.

Introduce Phonics Skills
Vowel Team Syllables
- Say: We just practiced segmenting the syllables in some words. Now we are going to read some words as we point out each syllable.
- Write the words *alike, prepare,* and *escape* on the board, and underline the vowel team syllables. Say: When two vowels come together, they often work together as one syllable as in the words *beagle, painted,* and *toasted.* Model reading the words, one syllable at a time, while pointing to the word parts: bea|gle, beagle; paint|ed, painted; toast|ed, toasted.
- Write the words *joined, looped,* and *steamer* on the board. Have students read the words as a class. Say: Slowly sound out the syllables, and notice that the vowel teams work as one syllable.
- Have students try reading the words *boating, cooking, needle,* and *throat* independently, following the routine above. Walk around to support students. Students who are struggling may need extra modeling and practice, such as: Let's look at the word *throat.* Say the word as I point to it, and remember that the *thr* blends to make the /thr/ sound.

Introduce Sight Words
- Say: You are going to see some words today that you may not know, so you will need to keep them in your memory.
- Write the words *always, black,* and *words* on the board. Read them to students as you point to each letter.
- Write the words *could, hurt,* and *sing* on the board. Read the words, and have students echo read them.
- Write the words *right* and *write* on the board. Ask a volunteer to read them aloud, and have the rest of the class follow suit. Place the words on a sight-word bulletin board. Point out that the two words sound the same but are spelled differently and have different meanings. Use this as an opportunity to review homophones.
- The book also contains social studies words. Follow the steps above with these words, but this time provide a simple definition for words that may cause confusion: *enslaved, Red Cross, republic, rights, slavery, system,* and *Underground Railroad.* For example: The Underground Railroad wasn't a real railroad. It was a system of places where slaves could hide on their way to freedom in the North.

Build Oral Language
- Say: Today we will be reading a book about courageous women who lived during the Civil War. Before I read, I try to recall what I already know about the topic.

- Select a student and discuss the Civil War. Ask the student why it was fought and who was involved. Consider adding vocabulary to your discussion, such as *Confederates, rights, slavery,* and *Union.*
- Say: With a partner, discuss what you know about the Civil War. Share when it took place, why it was fought, and who was involved.
- Pick five pairs of students, and encourage one student from each pair to share in the discussion. Recognize when students use previously taught key vocabulary.

DURING THE READING

Preview the Book
- Read the title of the book on the cover, and point to the picture. Turn to pages 2 and 3 and read the sentences. Point out the caption, and read those words as well. Have students follow along in their books.
- Say: Do you know what the book will be about based on the title and the pages that I read? How do you know what it will be about?
- As needed, point out the words that have vowel team syllables: *believed, continue, each, freedom, fought, reasons, stood, years.*

Read the Book
- Read the book to students as they follow along. Point out words that contain vowel team syllables. Also point out the captions, and explain how a caption gives a short description of a picture.
- Have students silently read the book. Ask a few students to whisper read the book to you, and help them sound out new words. When observing students, focus on the new words: *about, always, away, enjoy, feelings, freedom, railroad, reasons, speaker, teacher, today, underground.*
- **Social Studies Connections:** Say: Most slaves moved along the Underground Railroad at night so they wouldn't be seen. Railroad terms were often used as secret codes. Hiding places were called "stations," the slaves traveling along the railroad were "passengers," and people who helped them were "conductors."

AFTER THE READING

Check Comprehension
To check students' understanding of the book, ask the following:
✓Which word on page 13 has a vowel team in the first syllable and means "a person who helps others learn"? (*teacher*) Why was Clara Barton called the "Angel of the Battlefield"? (She helped men who were injured on the battlefield.)
✓What kind of primary source was used in this book? Why are they helpful? (historical photos; Answers may include: to help us see what life was like long ago.)
✓Why do you think each woman profiled in the book was a woman of courage? (Accept all reasonable responses.)

Reread to Develop Fluency
- Say: Today you will read the book to each other to practice reading with fluency. This means that you read the book as the author meant for it to be read aloud.
- Model reading fluently by reading the book aloud to students. Focus on reading at a consistent pace and using the correct intonation.
- Have partners reread the book to each other. Remind them to read at a consistent pace and use the correct intonation. Students may struggle with decoding, comprehension, or vocabulary. For students who are struggling with comprehension, say: I noticed that you seem unsure how to read these long sentences. What are some ways we can break apart the sentences to make them easier to understand? Let's chunk the sentences and look for clues in the pictures.
- Send home a copy of *Women of the Civil War* for students to read to family members. Consider assessing a few students on fluency.

Connect to Written Language
↻Review: Write the words *charm, further, password,* and *service* on the board. As a class, read the words together as you point to the letters. Have students write and illustrate a sentence for each word.

✓Dictate the following words for students to spell: *about, always, could, freedom, railroad, speaker,* and *underground.* When finished, write the words on the board. Have students self-correct their papers.

✓Ask students: Which of the women profiled in the book did you enjoy reading about the most? Have students use reference materials and online sources to write a brief biographical report on the woman they chose. Students should also explain why the life of the woman they chose was interesting to them.

Parent Letter

Dear Family,

Welcome to *Phonics Connections!* These informational books for young children concentrate on specific phonic sounds and words commonly found in reading materials for this level. As your child progresses from book to book, he or she will be building upon previously covered phonics skills. Each book also explores a single science or social studies concept. The eye-catching photos and engaging topics are sure to capture your child's interest.

From time to time, your child will bring home a copy of a book he or she has read in class. Home-school connections make reading and learning more meaningful. When you take time to read these books with your child, you will not only provide the necessary practice early readers need, but you will also be creating memorable experiences for you to share.

Each child acquires reading skills at a different pace. As you begin to read the Phonics Reader with your child, start by inviting him or her to read it aloud to you. If your child needs a bit of support while reading, run your hand under the words as the two of you read aloud together. Remember, this should be a relaxed and enjoyable experience. Allow time for your child to discuss the photos and information in the book. This is an excellent opportunity to introduce other new words related to the book's concept.

You'll find a list of words at the back of each book. Your child will take pride in demonstrating mastery of the phonics concepts, the multi-syllable words, and the content-related words.

Enjoy *Phonics Connections* and watch your child read and learn!

Sincerely,

Carta A Los Padres

Querida familia,

¡Bienvenidos al programa de lectura, *Phonics Connections!* Estos libros infomativos para los niños jóvenes se concentran en los sonidos fónicos específicos y palabras encontradas comúnmente en los materiales de la lectura para este nivel. Mientras su niño progresa del libro al libro, él o ella se aumentará las habilidades de fónicas previamente cubiertas. Cada libro tambien explora un concepto singular de las ciencias o los estudios sociales. Las fotos atractivas y los temas interesantes son seguros de capturar el interés de su niño.

De vez en cuando su niño traerá a casa una copia de un libro que él o ella ya ha leído en clase. Las conexiones entre el hogar y la escuela hacen la lectura y el aprender más significativos. Cuando usted toma el tiempo para leer estos libros con su niño, no sólo proveerá la práctica necesaria que necesitan los lectores jóvenes sino también creará las experencias memorables que puedan los dos compartir juntos.

Cada niño adquiere habilidades de la lectura a su ritmo. Como ud. comienza a leer el programa de lectura "Phonics Reader" con su niño, comience por invitarle a leer en voz alta a ud. Si su niño necesita un poco de ayuda mientras lea, subraya las palabras con el dedo mientras los dos las lean juntos en voz alta. Recuerde: esto debe ser una experiencia relajada y agradable. Deje el tiempo para su niño para discutir las fotos y la información en el libro. Esta es una portunidad excelente de introducir otras nuevas palabras relacionadas con el concepto del libro.

Ud. encontrará una lista de palabras en la parte posterior de cada libro. Su niño tomará orgullo en demostrar la maestría de los conceptos fónicos, de las palabras de multi-sílabas, y de las palabras relacionadas con el contendio.

¡Disfrute del programa de lectura *Phonics Connections* y observe a su niño leer y aprender!

Muy atentamente,

Matrix of Skills

Title	Content Area Focus	Phonics Focus
On the Job	Social Studies: Jobs	short *a*; consonants *f, m, t*
Hot or Not?	Science: Properties of Materials	short *o*; consonants *h, n, s*
At the Farm	Social Studies: Farm Life	short *o*; consonants *g, l, p*
Animal Babies	Social Studies: Animal Families	short *i*; consonants *c, d, w, y*
In the Past	Social Studies: Life in the Past	short *i*; consonants *b, k, q, r*
Animal Homes	Science: Animal Habitats	short *e*, consonants *j, v, x, z*
Finding Animals	Science: Camouflage	short *e*; *r*-blends
Fun at the Fair	Social Studies: Traditions	short *u*; *s*-blends
Weather	Science: Weather	short *u*; *l*-blends
At the Vet	Social Studies: Service Providers	short vowels; *s*-blends
At a Fire	Social Studies: Everyday Heroes	final *e* (*a_e, i_e, o_e, u_e*); *r*-blends
Amazing Magnets	Science: Magnets	final *e* (*i_e, o_e, u_e*); *l*-blends
The U.S. Flag	Social Studies: Symbols of America	final *e* (*a_e, e_e, i_e, o_e*); digraph *wh*
Homes	Social Studies: Communities	final *e* (*a_e, e_e, i_e, o_e, u_e*); digraph *th*
Safe at Play	Social Studies: Need for Rules	long *a* (*ai, ay*); digraph *sh*
Holidays	Social Studies: Holidays	long *a* (*ai, ay*); digraph *ch*
How Plants Grow	Science: Plant Life	final *e* (*e_e*); long *e* (*e, ea, ee*), plurals
Terrific Teeth	Science: Teeth	long *e* (*e, ea, ee*); *r-*, *l-*, and *s*-blends
Frogs	Science: Frog Life Cycle	long *o* (*o, oa, ow*); digraphs (*ch, sh, th, wh*)

Sight Words	Content-Area Words
a, am, do, help, I, play, what, who	farmer, firefighter, musician, teacher
are, hot, is, not, or, these, this, what	soft, wet
a, has, I, is, it, little, on, pretty, red, see, the, what	cat, cow, farm, frog, hen, hog, rabbit
a, and, big, but, can, fast, get, has, is, it, jump, not, read, what, will	animals, baby, bill
a, about, and, big, did, hot, is, it, make, not, on, see, take, the, we, went, what, will	horseshoe, quilt, wax
a, an, and, can, does, fly, has, he, him, his, in, it, its, on, one, red, well, who	bees, cliff, den, eagle, fox, hive, live(s), nest, pup
a, big, can, I, in, into, is, it, on, pretty, red, see, the, went, white, yes, you	bird, bug, crab, fish, grass, lizard, rabbit, shell, striped, tiger
a, and, around, at, big, blue, can, fast, first, for, get, go, has, his, is, it, jump, make, of, over, people, pull, red, run, see, she, some, stop, the, they, time, to, too, yellow, you	fair, proud, ribbon, year
and, back, big, can, drink, get, help(s), is, it, its, light, make(s), now, the, them, up, us, warm, water, what, with, yellow, you	clouds, hot, rain, sun, warm, weather, windy
a, and, are, black, can, get(s), give(s), had, has, help, in, is, it, keep(s), little, make, much, not, now, of, on, out, soon, stop, the, this, to, well, white, who, will, your	heal, healthy, paw, scale, shot, sick, well
a, and, can, from, go, he, help, is, look, no, on, out, the, their, they, to, up, use(s), water, who, will, with	engine, firefighters, heroes, ladder, smoke, water
a, and, are, be, big, can, it, is, made, not, of, on, or, up, the, they, too, use, what, will, you	iron, magnet, metal
also, an, and, blue, each, even, first, for, from, has, in, is, it, look, of, on, one, our, red, that, the, there, they, this, up, white	flagpole, free, July 4
a, an, and, are, at, big, can, for, in, is, it, has, have, help, her, his, like, live, look, many, of, on, people, play, ride, see, she, small, take, the, there, these, they, to, where, with, your	cabs, country, mules
a, all, and, are, be, but, can, do, far, get, go, how, in, like, look, may, not, of, or, out, play, ride, run, safe, take, the, these, they, to, walk, way, when, with, you, your	rules, stay safe, take your turn
a, about, and, can, clean, eat, first, good, help, hot, is, it, of, on, or, our, pick, say, thank, that, the, think, this, to, too, up, we, what, which, you	celebrate, holiday, thankful, Thanksgiving
a, and, are, as, be, but, can, do, each, eat, first, from, give, has, help, how, in, into, it, like, many, new, next, on, pretty, see, the, then, these, they, to, too, we, will	bloom, fruits, grow, soil
a, also, and, are, big, can, come, do, eat, help, her, how, in, into, long, look, made, many, need, open, our, out, see, she, the, them, these, they, this, to, us, use(s), very, we, what, which, why, you	bite(s), chew(s), eat, food, front, sharp, smile, teeth
a, about, an, and, as, back, can, comes, from, get, go, has, how, in, into, is, it, its, like, live, looks, not, now, on, out, tell, the, this, to, very, water, what, will, with	air, breathe, egg(s), frog, gills, grow(s), lungs, swim, tadpole(s), tail, water

Matrix of Skills (continued)

Title	Content Area Focus	Phonics Focus
Astronauts in Space	Social Studies: Space Explorers	long *o* (*o*, *oa*, *ow*); soft *c*
Animals of the Rain Forest	Science: Rain Forest Animals	long *i* (*i*, –*igh*, –*y*); soft *g*
All About Bats	Science: Bats	long *i* (*i*, –*igh*, –*y*)
Push and Pull	Science: Pushes and Pulls	long *u* (*u_e*, *ew*); inflectional ending –*ed*
Using Maps	Social Studies: Maps	review long *a*, *e*, *i*, *o*, *u*; inflectional ending –*ing*
Seasons	Science: Seasons	*r*-controlled vowels (*er*, *ir*, *ur*)
Bears	Science: Animals	*r*-controlled vowels (*er*, *ir*, *ur*)
People at Work	Social Studies: Community Workers	*r*-controlled vowel (*ar*)
Plants and Animals	Science: Plant and Animal Needs	*r*-controlled vowel (*ar*)
Peanuts to Peanut Butter	Social Studies: Buy and Sell	*r*-controlled vowels (*or*, *ore*, *our*)
All Kinds of Sounds	Science: Sound	diphthong /ou/ (*ou*, *ow*)
Life Now and Long Ago	Social Studies: Now/Long Ago	diphthong /ou/ (*ou*, *ow*)
Plant Parts	Science: Parts of a Plant	variant vowels /o͞o/, /o͝o/

Sight Words	Content-Area Words
a, an, and, away, be, but, can, cold, could, day(s), down, each, eat, fun, get, go, has, he, help(s), him, his, hot, in, is, it, like, not, of, on, one, out, see, small, some, takes, the, they, this, time, to, too, under, walk(s), while will, work(s), would, you	air pack, astronaut(s), backpack, Earth, float, helmet, move, rockets, space, spacecraft, space suit
a, about, and, are, as, at, big, do, down, eat, every, fall, find, go, green, grow, has, help, hot, in, is, kind, like, make, many, of, on, play, read, sleep, small, some, take, the, they, to, up, what	jaguar, orangutan, rain forest
a, are, all, as, at, away, be, big, can, down, eat, find, for, from, have, help, here, in, is, it, many, may, new, not, of, on, one, only, other(s), see, so, some, that, the, them, these, they, too, two, us, very, well, when, will, you	bat, caves, fingers, fly, fur, hour, mammal
a, an, and, away, can, down, from, get, her, if, is, it, just, make(s), may, of, on, or, play(s), pull(ed), she, the, this, to, use(s), what, when, will, with, you	away, fast, force, hard, move, presses, pull(ed), push(ed)(es), slowly, tugs
a, and, are, at, be, blue, but, can, day, drawing(s), find, from, get, give(s), has, have, help, how, in, is, it, just, little, many, of, on, one, or, red, some, the, this, to, us, use, we, what, where, will, with, you	city, compass rose, directions, east, Florida, key, map, Miami Beach, north, roads, south, state, streets, symbols, United States, west
a, all, and, be, best, can, cold, day, do, each, eat, every, fall, fly, four, from, get, grow, has, have, help, hot, I, in, is, it, light, like, make, many, may, of, one, or, sleep, some, the, time, to, up, very, what, which, why, you	early, season, weather
a, and, are, as, be, big, black, bring, by, cold, eat, for, get, gives, grow, help, her, in, into, is, it, keep, little, long, make, must, not, she, sleep, that, the, their, them, to, too, two, up, use, very, warm, will	berries, cubs, den, mother, stream, twigs
a, and, are, at, call, come, do, far, first, from, get, grows, has, have, he, help, her, here, his, home, in, is, leave, makes, many, may, must, near, not, of, on, or, others, owns, people, red, she, some, starts, stop, take(s), the, their, them, there, these, to, too, well, what, when, who, with, work	bus, community, drives, farm, fields, fixes, jobs, makes, market, nurse, people, school, sells, teacher, work(ers)
a, also, and, as, at, can, come(s), do, eat, food, for, four, from, get(s), grow, has, have, home, in, is, it, like, live, make, many, most, or, some, the, these, they, things, to, too, turn(s), up, what	air, animals, den, drinking, food, grass, grow, home, leaves, light, live, meat, nest, plants, soil, sun, sunlight, water
a, and, are, at, before, best, big, but, buy, can, do, each, eat, end, even, fall, first, for, four, from, grow, how, in, into, is, it, know, made, make, many, off, of, on, one, or, over, people, put, small, so, take(s), the, their, them, then, these, they, things, to, under, uses, what, when, where, with, you	crushed, factory, farmer, harvesting, jar, lids, machine(s), oil, peanuts, plants, roasted, salt, shells, soil, sugar
a, all, are, around, at, back, can, do, falling, has, how, in, is, it, laugh(ing), made, more, now, of, on, put, say, so, some, the, then, us, what, when, you, your	hear, high, loud, low, move, pitch, quiet, sounds, speak, throat, vibrate(s)
a, about, all, and, are, as, be, can, down, find, for, found, from, go, had, has, have, how, in, is, it, long, look, made, many, much, no, not, now, of, on, one, only, or, our, out, over, pull, run, that, the, their, then, they, this, time, to, today, up, use, was, we, were, work, your	coach(es), computers, electric
a, and, are, at, be, big, by, can, could, each, eat, food, for, goes, grow, has, have, help(s), hold, in, is, its, live, look, make, many, most, new, of, on, part(s), small, some, take, the, them, these, they, this, to, too, up, use, water, we, when, you	air, bloom, flowers, leaves, moves, plant(s), roots, seeds, soil, stem, sunlight, tree, trunk, water

Matrix of Skills (continued)

Title	Content Area Focus	Phonics Focus
Up in the Sky	Science: The Sky	variant vowels /ōō/, /o͝o/
Our Heroes	Social Studies: American Heroes	variant vowel /ô/ (*a, au, aw*)
Learn About Dinosaurs	Science: Dinosaurs	variant vowel /ô/ (*a, au, aw*)
Baskets of Native Americans	Social Studies: Native Americans	diphthong /oi/ (*oi, oy*)
What Are Germs?	Science: Health	digraphs (*ch, gh, ph, sh, tch, th, wh*)
A Visit to the Library	Social Studies: Books and Libraries	closed syllables
At a Factory	Science: Goods and Services	final *e* (*a_e, i_e*)
Healthy You!	Science: Health and Daily Living	final *e* (*o_e, u_e*)

Sight Words	Content-Area Words
a, all, also, are, at, away, because, big, but, can, could, did, do, fit, from, give, go, in, inside, it, its, know, like, look(s), make(s), many, more, most, much, of, off, on, other, see, some, than, the, they, time(s), too, up, very, what, you	circle, clouds, daytime, different, Earth, moon, nighttime, sky, stars, sun, warms
a, after, all, also, always, an, and, are, be, because, better, came, could, do, eat, find, first, for, found, from, go, good, in, into, he, help, her, his, little, live, made, make, many, of, open, our, out, people, ride, she, some, that, the, them, there, they, through, to, use, walk, want, was, way, we, went, were, what, when, with, work	Dr. Martin Luther King Jr., fair(ly), George Washington, Mary McLeod Bethune, Puerto Rico, Roberto Clemente, Sacagawea, Sally Ride, Shoshone Indian, woman
a, about, all, are, and, at, back, by, came, could, day, each, from, had, have, he, in, it, like, long, made, of, one, or, over, people, saw, see, some, tell, that, the, there, they, this, three, to, us, want, was, were, what, where, which, with	Coelophysis, Dilophosaurus, dinosaur(s), footprints, fossils, millions, past, scientists
a, all, an, and, around, be, by, can, carry, close, could, did, do, done, find, for, found, from, have, her, hold, into, is, it, keep, kind, light, long, made, make, many, not, of, on, or, people, pretty, same, see, she, so, some, that, the, them, they, this, to, today, together, until, use(s), way, were, will, with, you	art, bark, basket(s), coil(s), cornhusk(s), grass, Hopi, leaves, materials, museums, Native Americans, sew(s)
a, after, all, also, and, are, at, away, be, better, but, can, clean, could, cut, day, do, does, drink, each, eat, even, find, first, for, found, from, get, give, good, has, have, help, here, hot, how, hurt, if, in, into, is, it, jump, keep, kind, know, like, little, long, look, make, many, may, most, much, no, not, of, on, one, or, out, over, part, ride, round, run, see, she, small, so, some, soon, start, take, than, that, the, them, then, there, they, think, this, time, to, together, too, two, under, up, use, very, warm, wash, water, ways, what, when, why, will, with, work, you, your	bacteria, doctor, germs, microscope, viruses
a, about, all, also, and, are, around, at, back, be, big, bring, but, by, call, can, do, each, even, find, for, found, from, good, has, have, help, how, in, is, it, its, just, kind, like, look, many, make, may, more, most, not, of, on, or, other, our, out, own, part, people, put, read, say, see, show, small, some, stop, take, tell, that, the, them, there, these, this, time, to, too, up, us, use, want, we, what, when, which, who, will, with, word, work, you, your	bookmobile, computer, librarian, library, online catalog
a, about, all, also, and, are, as, at, away, be, been, big, buy, by, call, can, clean, come, day, do, each, even, far, first, five, for, from, have, he, help, hot, in, into, is, it, keep, look, made, make, many, may, more, most, now, of, on, one, or, other, out, over, people, put, run, she, some, such, take, ten, than, the, then, these, they, think, this, time, to, today, too, up, use, were, what, where, will, with, you, your	factory(ies), machine(s), raw materials, store(s), worker(s)
a, about, all, an, and, are, around, as, at, be, but, by, can, could, cut, day, do, don't, down, eat, even, every, for, from, get, give, good, grow, have, help, if, in, is, it, jump, just, keep, kind, make, many, more, much, never, not, now, of, on, one, or, out, own, part, people, play, pull, ride, right, run, say, sit, some, than, that, the, their, there, these, they, this, three, time, to, too, try, up, use, very, walk, want, way, well, what, when, who, will, with, you, your	exercise, fitness, muscles, physical condition, vitamins

Matrix of Skills (continued)

Title	Content Area Focus	Phonics Focus
Matter All Around	Science: Solids, Liquids, and Gases	long *e* (*e, ea, ee, ey, y*)
Communication Past and Present	Social Studies: Communication	open syllables
Great Inventions	Science: Inventors and Scientists	consonant + *–le* syllables
Amazing Meat-Eating Plants	Science: Plant Life (Adaptations)	final *e* (*a_e, e_e, i_e, o_e*)
Where Bananas Come From	Social Studies: Goods and Services	*r*-controlled vowel syllables
Animals and Their Habitats	Science: Animal Habitats	variant vowel /o͞o/ (*ew, oo, ough, ue*)
Gravity	Science: Earth and Space	variant vowel /o͞o/ (*oo*)

Sight Words	Content-Area Words
a, all, also, and, are, around, as, at, be, big, call, can, cold, could, day, do, down, each, from, get, go, has, have, here, hot, how, if, in, into, is, it, its, just, kind, like, look, made, make, most, much, of, on, one, or, other, out, own, part, read, say, see, small, some, start, take, that, the, them, then, they, this, to, together, too, up, use, want, water, we, what, when, why, will, with, work, would, you, your	gas(es), liquid(s), matter, solid(s), water cycle, water vapor
a, about, all, an, and, are, around, at, away, be, before, best, better, by, call, came, can, come, could, day, did, do, does, down, draw, each, even, far, first, for, found, from, get, got, had, has, he, help, how, in, is, kind, know, long, look, made, many, more, new, not, of, off, on, one, or, other, part, people, play, read, she, show, soon, tell, the, their, them, then, there, these, they, think, this, through, time, to, today, together, too, two, use, very, want, was, way, we, went, were, what, when, who, will, with, words, work, would, write, you, your	communication, e-mail, information, Pony Express, printing press
a, about, after, all, also, always, an, and, are, around, be, but, by, came, clean, could, day, did, do, each, even, every, far, fast, first, fly, for, found, from, gave, get, give, go, had, have, he, help, her, him, his, how, if, in, is, it, keep, light, like, little, live, long, made, make, many, more, new, not, of, oil, on, one, only, or, other, our, out, over, people, pick, play, put, read, saw, see, she, so, some, stop, take, tell, than, thank, that, the, their, them, then, these, they, think, this, time, to, today, up, us, use, walk, warm, was, wash, way, we, went, were, when, which, who, with, words, work, would, you	experiments, invention(s), inventor, scientist, timeline
a, about, after, also, an, and, are, around, as, at, away, be, because, been, best, big, but, by, call, can, does, don't, each, eat, even, fall, first, fly, for, found, from, get, grow, has, have, help, here, how, if, in, into, is, it, its, just, kind, know, like, live, look, made, many, more, new, no, not, now, of, on, one, only, open, or, other, out, part, red, see, small, some, soon, start, such, take, than, that, the, them, then, there, these, they, this, three, time, to, too, two, under, up, us, use, wash, water, way, we, what, when, white, why, will, with	Australia, digest, dissolve, flypaper, minerals, oxygen, soil
a, about, again, and, are, as, at, away, be, bring, by, came, cold, come, did, do, each, eat, find, for, from, green, have, help, hot, how, if, in, is, it, just, keep, look, made, may, must, not, now, of, one, or, our, out, own, put, right, so, some, stop, take, that, the, them, then, there, these, they, those, to, too, up, us, use, we, were, when, where, who, with, you, your	bananas, consumers, export(ed, ing), harvest(ed, ing), South America, transport(ed, ing), workers
a, all, and, are, as, be, because, big, blue, by, call, can, cold, day, down, eat, even, fall, far, fast, find, for, four, from, go, good, green, grow, has, have, help, hot, if, in, is, it, its, keep, kind, like, little, live, long, look, make, many, may, most, must, never, no, not, of, on, or, other, out, part, see, small, so, some, such, that, their, them, there, they, this, through, time, to, together, too, under, up, use, warm, water, were, what, when, where, white, why, will, you	Arctic, habitat(s), rain forest, reef, woodland(s)
a, about, all, are, around, as, away, be, because, better, bring(s), but, can, could, did, do, does, down, drink, fall, far, for, from, funny, get, go, good, has, have, help(s), hold, how, if, in, into, is, it, its, jump, keep, lets, light, like, little, long, look, made, make(s), many, more, much, no, not, of, off, on, only, our, people, play, pull, put, read, ride, see, show(s), small, so, some, take, than, that, the, there, they, think, this, time, to, together, try, two, up, us, water, way, we, what, when, where, who, with, would, you, your	force, gravity, mass, pull(s), weight

Matrix of Skills (continued)

Title	Content Area Focus	Phonics Focus
Making Laws	Social Studies: Levels of Government	variant vowel (*a(lk)*, *a(lt)*, *au*, *aw*)
Extreme Weather	Science: Weather	variant vowels (*au*, *o͞o*); vowel team syllables (long *a*: *ai*, *ay*; long *e*: *ea*, *ee*, *ey*; long *o*: *oa*, *ow*; diphthongs: *oi*, *ou*)
The World of Maps	Social Studies: Geography	words with *–ed* and *–ing* spelling changes
Let's Go to the Museum!	Social Studies: Museums	prefixes *pre–*, *un–*
Fantastic Flowers	Science: Characteristics of Organisms	suffixes *–ful*, *–tion*
Immigration	Social Studies: Immigration	prefixes *re–*, *mis–*
Celebrating Cultures	Social Studies: U. S. Cultural Heritage	suffixes *–er*, *–or*, *–ly*

Sight Words	Content-Area Words
a, about, after, all, also, and, any, are, as, at, be, because, best, both, but, by, called, can, clean, do, does, don't, each, eight, even, for, four, from, get, good, has, have, he, help, how, in, is, it, its, keep, kind, know, like, live, made, make, many, may, more, most, must, new, no, not, of, old, on, one, only, or, other, our, out, own, people, read, right, run, say, she, so, some, take, tell, that, the, their, there, these, they, think, this, to, together, up, us, walk, want, water, way, we, what, where, white, who, with, work, yes, you, your	Congress, government, governor, legislature, president, vote, White House
a, about, again, all, also, an, and, any, are, around, as, at, be, because, big, but, by, call, can, cold, day, did, do, don't, down, each, every, fall, find, first, for, from, get, give, go, going, have, help, hot, how, if, in, into, is, it, its, kind, know, let, like, live, may, more, most, much, no, not, of, off, on, one, or, other, out, over, part, people, pretty, pull, run, see, show, six, so, start, such, take, than, that, the, them, then, there, these, they, this, through, time, to, today, too, use, very, want, warm, way, we, what, when, where, which, will, with, you, your	blizzard, hurricane, meteorologist, tornado, weather systems
a, about, all, also, always, and, are, around, as, at, be, big, blue, by, can, does, every, find, five, for, found, four, go, green, has, have, help, hot, how, if, in, is, it, just, know, like, look, many, of, on, one, or, people, read, see, seven, show, small, so, some, than, that, the, there, these, this, to, us, very, water, way, we, were, what, where, will, with, would, you, your	compass rose, continent(s), countries, deserts, equator, globe, lakes, map, map key, mountains, oceans, rivers
a, about, all, also, an, are, as, at, be, because, before, big, but, buy, by, can, come, do, don't, even, find, for, from, full, get, go, has, have, help, how, if, in, into, is, it, just, keep, kind, like, live, long, look, made, many, may, more, most, much, new, not, of, old, on, one, or, other, our, out, over, people, play, put, say, see, show, small, so, some, such, take, tell, that, the, them, there, these, they, this, three, through, time, to, up, us, use, very, walk, want, was, way, what, when, where, who, with, work, you, your	admission, artifact, caretaker, display, extinct, floor plan, fragile, museum
a, all, almost, also, an, and, are, as, be, bring, but, by, can, could, do, does, each, eat, find, for, from, grow, has, have, help, how, in, is, it, its, just, kind, like, long, made, make, many, may, more, new, of, on, one, our, out, over, part, people, pretty, same, small, some, than, that, the, their, them, then, there, they, this, time, to, today, too, two, us, use, we, were, what, when, work, would, you	blossom, calyx, flowers, fruit, nectar, orchard, petals, pistil, plant, pollen, pollination, seeds, sepal, stamen, stem
a, about, after, all, also, and, are, as, ask, at, ate, be, because, been, before, but, by, call, came, come, could, did, find, first, for, from, go, had, have, help, here, if, in, is, it, know, little, live, long, look, made, make, many, more, most, new, no, not, of, on, or, other, our, out, people, ride, show, small, some, start, such, take, the, their, them, then, these, they, this, those, time, to, today, together, too, try, two, use, very, want, was, we, went, were, what, when, where, who, why, with, work, would, you	customs, Ellis Island, Europe, history, immigrants, steamships
a, about, again, all, an, and, are, as, be, been, best, bring, but, by, came, can, come, down, fast, for, from, has, have, help, here, how, in is, just, kind(s), like, long, made, make, many, may, much, new, of, old, on, one, or, other, over, own, part, people, play, show, some, tell, that, the, their, them, then, there, these, they think, this, time, to, today, together, too, try, up, us, use, way, we, well, what, which, who, with, work, would, you, your	art, celebrate, culture(s), customs, dancer, heritage, immigrants, literature, musicians, traditions

Matrix of Skills (continued)

Title	Content Area Focus	Phonics Focus
Science Tools	Science: Technology and Science	irregular plurals; plurals with spelling changes
Exploring Fossils	Science: Life Science	compound words
Farming Then and Now	Social Studies: Technology Over Time	consonant + –le syllables
Get Moving!	Science: Motion	final e syllables
Energy Everywhere!	Science: Energy	r-controlled vowels (ar, er, or, ur)
Women of the Civil War	Social Studies: American History	vowel team syllables

Sight Words	Content-Area Words
a, about, all, and, are, around, at, away, be, because, before, big, but, by, came, can, do, does, each, every, find, for, from, hard, has, have, how, if, in, is, it, just, long, look, make(s), many, may, more, much, never, now, of, on, only, open, or, other, our, out, part(s), right, see, small, so, take, that, the, their, then, there, us, use, very, want, we, what, will, you	bacteria, examine, germs, lab(s), lens, magnifying glass, microscope, microscopic, scientists, study, telescope, tools
a, about, ago, all, also, and, any, arc, around, at, away, back, be, because, been, big, but, by, can, could, did, different, do, enough, even, find, for, found, from, give, got, green, hard, has, have, help, how, if, in, into, is, it, know, land, learn, leave, left, life, like, live, long, look, made, many, may, might, most, near, next, not, now, of, often, old, on, once, or, other, part, people, plant, put, see, show, sits, small, so, some, sometimes, still, tell, that, the, them, then, there, these, thing, this, those, time, to, today, together, too, tree, try, up, us, use, very, was, water, way, we, were, what, when, where, who, with, year(s), you	amber, animal(s), bones, carbon, cast, decay, dinosaur, fossil(s), mammoth(s), minerals, paleontologists, plant(s), sediment, skeleton
a, and, are, around, as, away, be, before, better, big, bring, but, by, can, clean, could, cut(s), did, do, fast, first, for, from, get, got, had, has, have, help, hot, how, if, in, into, is, it, just, keep, like, long, made, many, may, more, must, now, of, on, one, only, or, other, out, over, people, pull, put(s), ran, right, run, small, so, start, stop, tell, than, that, the, their, them, there, these, they, this, three, time, to, today, up, use, very, walk, was, water, we, were, what, with, work, would	cow, farmers, fuel, gas, horse, machine, plow, soil, steam, technology, tools, tractor
a, about, all, and, any, are, around, as, at, be, because, both, but, can, come, do, does, down, fall, fast, find, from, go, has, have, help(s), her, how, in, is, its, keep, know, let(s), little, no, now, of, off, on, one, only, or, over, play, pull(s), put(s), right, say(s) see, she, some, start(s), take, that, the, then, there, think, this, to, try, two, up, usc, wc, what, when, why, will, with, work, would, write, you, your	accelerate, balance, force, inertia, motion, speed, velocity
a, about, also, always, an, and, are, around, as, at, be, because, both, by, called, can, come, day, do, does, don't, down, each, eat, even, every, fall, find, for, from, get, give, goes, green, grow, has, have, help, hold, how, if, in, into, is, it, jump, just, kind, light, like, live, look, make, many, may, much, new, no, not, now, of, off, oil, on, one, or, other, our, people, play, pull, put, ride, run, see, show, sleep, so, some, soon, stop, such, take, that, the, then, there, these, they, think, this, those, to, too, up, us, use, very, warm, water, way, we, what, when, why, will, with, work, you, your	chemical energy, electricity, kinetic energy, mechanical energy, potential energy, solar energy
a, about, after, all, also, always, an, and, any, around, as, at, away, black, but, could, did, each, even, first, for, four, from, get, had, have, he, help, her, him, his, how, hurt, in, into, is, it, just, like, look, made, make, many, more, much, new, not, now, of, on, one, open, or, other, out, own, people, ran, red, right, see, she, sing, some, soon, stop, such, than, that, the, them, there, they, this, time, to, today, too, up, use, very, want, was, we, went, were, what, when, where, who, with, words, work, write	enslaved, Red Cross, republic, rights, slavery, system, Underground Railroad

Text Features Highlighted

Book Title	Text Feature
What Are Germs?	infographics, diagrams
A Visit to the Library	photographs, labels
At a Factory	flowcharts
Healthy You!	diagrams
Matter All Around	headings, infographics
Communication Past and Present	index
Great Inventions	timelines
Amazing Meat-Eating Plants	captions
Where Bananas Come From	flowcharts
Animals and Their Habitats	index
Gravity	primary sources
Making Laws	captions
Extreme Weather	maps
The World of Maps	maps
Let's Go to the Museum!	infographics, maps, floor plans
Fantastic Flowers	diagrams
Immigration	pie charts, graphs
Celebrating Cultures	captions
Science Tools	diagrams
Exploring Fossils	index
Farming Then and Now	timelines
Get Moving!	diagrams
Energy Everywhere!	graphs
Women of the Civil War	captions

Notes

Notes